# Serverless Web Applications with AWS Amplify

## Build Full-Stack Serverless Applications Using Amazon Web Services

Akshat Paul
Mahesh Haldar

Apress®

*Serverless Web Applications with AWS Amplify: Build Full-Stack Serverless Applications Using Amazon Web Services*

Akshat Paul
Gurgaon, Haryana, India

Mahesh Haldar
Bahraich, Uttar Pradesh, India

ISBN-13 (pbk): 978-1-4842-8706-4
https://doi.org/10.1007/978-1-4842-8707-1

ISBN-13 (electronic): 978-1-4842-8707-1

Managing Director, Apress Media LLC: Welmoed Spahr
Acquisitions Editor: James Robinson-Prior
Development Editor: James Markham
Coordinating Editor: Jessica Vakili

Distributed to the book trade worldwide by Springer Science+Business Media New York, 233 Spring Street, 6th Floor, New York, NY 10013. Phone 1-800-SPRINGER, fax (201) 348-4505, e-mail orders-ny@springer-sbm.com, or visit www.springeronline.com. Apress Media, LLC is a California LLC and the sole member (owner) is Springer Science + Business Media Finance Inc (SSBM Finance Inc). SSBM Finance Inc is a **Delaware** corporation.

For information on translations, please e-mail booktranslations@springernature.com; for reprint, paperback, or audio rights, please e-mail bookpermissions@springernature.com.

Apress titles may be purchased in bulk for academic, corporate, or promotional use. eBook versions and licenses are also available for most titles. For more information, reference our Print and eBook Bulk Sales web page at http://www.apress.com/bulk-sales.

Any source code or other supplementary material referenced by the author in this book is available to readers on the Github repository: https://github.com/haldarmahesh/amplify-book. For more detailed information, please visit http://www.apress.com/source-code.

Printed on acid-free paper

# Table of Contents

# About the Authors

**Akshat Paul** is the Founder and CTO of Company360, a technology leader, author of four books on React Native, Ruby, and RubyMotion, and a former consultant at McKinsey & Company. With his extensive experience in mobile and web development, coupled with his strategic insights gained at McKinsey, he has delivered numerous enterprise and consumer applications over the years. As an influential voice in the tech industry, Akshat frequently speaks at conferences and meetups on various technologies. He has given talks at React Native EU, Cross-Platform Mobile Summit, Devops@scale Amsterdam, the DevTheory Conference India, RubyConfIndia, and #inspect-RubyMotion Conference Brussels and was a keynote speaker at technology leadership events in Bangkok and Kuala Lumpur. Besides technology Akshat spends time with his family, is an avid reader, and is obsessive about healthy eating.

**Mahesh Haldar** is a passionate software engineer and expert in building scalable systems. With extensive experience in designing robust architectures, Mahesh empowers the team to fully harness the potential of cloud-based solutions. As a sought-after speaker, Mahesh has presented at technical meetups and conferences in Bangalore, Johannesburg, and Singapore. His outstanding contributions have earned recognition, including features in Yourstory magazine and being listed among India's top 20 apps. Currently serving as a Principal Software Engineer at Carrefour, Mahesh leads a team of talented developers, delivering exceptional eCommerce experiences. His expertise has been pivotal in designing and implementing high-impact functionalities, effectively serving millions of daily customer requests. With a proven track record in developing complex large-scale systems for start-ups and renowned enterprises like Jago Bank and Mckinsey & Company, Mahesh brings a wealth of practical knowledge and expertise to the table.

# Acknowledgments

As the saying goes, "If I have seen further, it is by standing on the shoulders of giants." In the context of this book, those giants are the individuals who offered their unwavering support and invaluable guidance throughout my journey.

Firstly, I want to express my profound gratitude to my parents, **Shakuntala Paul** and **Anup Paul**. Your unwavering belief in my abilities and steadfast encouragement have always propelled me forward. The spirit of continuous learning that you fostered in me has not only been instrumental in my personal growth, but it has also profoundly influenced my professional trajectory as a technology leader, and your tireless cheerleading during my biggest victories has always been my motivation to keep moving forward.

I am eternally thankful for my wife, **Anu Sharma**. She has been my rock and my sanctuary throughout the process of writing this book. Her understanding, patience, and unconditional love were invaluable during those late-night writing sessions and bouts of writer's block. Her ability to uplift my spirits during challenging moments and celebrate with me during my triumphs has been a constant source of inspiration. This book is as much her accomplishment as it is mine.

I would also like to extend my heartfelt thanks to the Apress team: **Jessica Vakili, James Robinson-Prior, and James Markham**. Your collective expertise, support, and collaboration have played a vital role in the successful completion of this book. Your dedication to maintaining the quality and integrity of this work has not gone unnoticed, and I am deeply grateful for your tireless efforts. A special acknowledgment to **Louise Corrigan**, who was instrumental in the initial conceptualization of this book.

To each and every one of you, I express my sincerest appreciation. This book would not have been possible without your enduring support, faith, and encouragement. Thank you for being a part of my journey.

—Akshat Paul

## ACKNOWLEDGMENTS

I would like to express my heartfelt gratitude to the following individuals who have been instrumental in the creation and completion of this book.

My dearest friend and mentor, **Akshat Paul**, whose guidance, expertise, and unwavering support have been invaluable throughout this journey. Your wisdom and insights have shaped not only this book but also my growth as a technologist and as a writer. Thank you for believing in me.

To my late father, **Ram Ratan Haldar**, who always taught me to work hard and instilled in me the love for knowledge and learning. Though you are no longer with us, your presence and influence continue to inspire me every day.

To my mother, **Champa Rani Haldar**, whose unwavering love, encouragement, and sacrifices have been a constant source of strength and motivation. Your belief in my abilities and your unwavering support have been the driving force behind this accomplishment.

And finally, to my loving wife, **Prachita**, who sacrificed many late nights and weekends without me while I was working on this book. Thank you for your unwavering support, encouragement, and patience.

I must also extend my earnest appreciation to the team at Apress: **Jessica Vakili, James Robinson-Prior, and James Markham**. Your combined knowledge, unwavering support, and collaborative efforts were pivotal to the book's successful completion.

I am deeply grateful to each and every person who has played a role, big or small, in the creation of this book. Your contributions, encouragement, and belief in my abilities have made this book possible.

—**Mahesh Haldar**

# Introduction

As we progress further into the digital age, serverless architectures and web applications are continuously reshaping the technological landscape. As technology leaders, we often faced challenges when searching for thorough, hands-on resources on this topic. This motivated us to compose *Serverless Web Applications with AWS Amplify*, a book that represents the guide we wished existed when we first ventured into the field of serverless architecture.

*Serverless Web Applications with AWS Amplify* is intended for a broad audience – from newbies taking their first steps in cloud development to advanced developers aiming to broaden their understanding of modern web application technologies. While prior knowledge of cloud computing might be helpful, it is not a prerequisite. The aim is to assist all readers in scaling their web applications, reducing costs, enhancing scalability, or simply exploring the expansive domain of serverless web development with AWS Amplify.

The structure of this book is carefully designed, beginning with the fundamentals of cloud computing and serverless architectures, followed by an introduction to AWS Amplify. Subsequent chapters dive into topics such as authentication, authorization, REST APIs, GraphQL, and offline-first applications. As we progress, we delve into data and storage, analytics, continuous integration/continuous delivery (CI/CD), with AWS Amplify, and, eventually, the integration of AI and ML capabilities into your applications, by building interactive chatbots and building application to convert text to speech.

In addition to detailed explanations, this book includes practical examples, code snippets, and hands-on exercises to solidify your understanding of the concepts. To further support your learning journey, additional online resources are available.

Reflecting on our journey, we recall the intriguing challenge that programming initially posed for us. It was the transformative power of code, the ability to turn ideas into reality, that fueled our fascination. AWS Amplify, in particular, revolutionized our approach to web application development. This book is the culmination of our journey, experiences, and accumulated knowledge, which we are eager to share with all readers.

As the famous quote by Albert Einstein goes, "The measure of intelligence is the ability to change." By the end of *Serverless Web Applications with AWS Amplify*, our hope is to provide you with the knowledge and skills to adapt to the fast-paced world of serverless web applications, fostering your growth in this dynamic field.

# CHAPTER 1

# Introduction to Serverless

*In the world of cloud, scale is the game changer.*

—Akshat Paul

Cloud computing has transformed the way we store, process, and manage data. In this chapter, we will cover the basics of cloud computing, including its evolution from traditional IT, its key advantages, and the next generation of cloud technologies. We will explore serverless architectures, BaaS (Backend as a Service) and FaaS (Function as a Service), discussing their benefits and weaknesses. We will also introduce AWS Amplify, a platform for building web and mobile applications with AWS services, and guide you through setting it up locally and configuring the Amplify CLI with AWS.

Whether you're new to cloud computing or an experienced developer looking to learn about next-generation cloud technologies, this chapter will provide you with a solid foundation to build upon. So, let's dive into the world of cloud computing and explore the latest and greatest technologies that it has to offer.

## A Little Background

In 2017 at AWS re:Invent, I became intrigued by a new architecture for application development called serverless architecture. Initially, I had reservations about serverless applications, as it seemed like someone else would be running a server for me, which meant giving up control. As a developer, I was reluctant to relinquish control over my application. However, I soon discovered that serverless architecture offers much more. In this book, we will explore how this game-changing architecture can save developers a significant amount of time on repetitive tasks, allowing them to focus on tasks that have the maximum impact. But before we dive into that, let's take a brief look at the background and history of how we arrived at this point.

© Akshat Paul, Mahesh Haldar 2023
A. Paul and M. Haldar, *Serverless Web Applications with AWS Amplify*,
https://doi.org/10.1007/978-1-4842-8707-1_1

If we time travel back to almost 20 years and see how traditional IT used to work, life was not easy. There used to be a dedicated team to handle all the operations tasks of the server setup and maintenance, and once the servers were ready, the developers would be writing business logic and deploy the application on those servers.

The server operations team was responsible for setting up firewalls and compute servers, installing the operating system, and configuring database servers. Additionally, they were tasked with monitoring the temperature of the server rooms to prevent server failures caused by excessive heat. They also had to plan for potential damage caused by natural calamities such as heavy rainfall or other extreme weather events.

In the past, hosting an application required a significant amount of time and effort. Before writing the first line of business logic, one had to perform a series of operational tasks. This was akin to having to build a car from scratch before embarking on a family trip. It was an extremely painful and time-consuming process.

However, a revolutionizing change came in the form of cloud computing. Services such as AWS transformed the hosting model. Rather than building a car from scratch, users could now simply rent one and focus on itinerary planning and enjoying the trip.

With AWS, hosting applications in the cloud has become incredibly easy. There is no need to invest in physical space or worry about maintaining data centers. Compute, storage, and databases can be quickly provisioned on demand, without having to worry about setting up and maintaining hardware.

This approach saves companies from up-front investments in procuring hardware, paying rent for a data center, and paying the bills for electricity. In addition, it enables businesses to scale their infrastructure as per their requirements, without having to worry about infrastructure management. As a result, cloud computing has become an essential component of modern software architecture, and AWS is a leading provider of cloud computing services.

EC2 (Elastic Computing Cloud) from AWS (Amazon Web Services) was one of the early Infrastructure as a Service (IaaS) products. IaaS allows users and companies to buy computing capacity on rent rather than setting up and buying all those physical machines on their own. It allowed them to provision infrastructure just in time when required, which means the commissioning of machines to availability will happen in minutes, if not in seconds. This was revolutionary at that time to even think.

IaaS is a type of cloud service that offers required resources like compute engine, database, storage, artificial intelligence services, and networking configurations on demand; these are basically on the model of pay as you go. Over the years, companies realized there is a huge overhead just to commence a digital footprint on the World Wide Web or even spinning up simple internal apps, which involved physical infrastructure operations like electric power for machines, setting up data centers. All these resources can be provisioned quickly and easily with the advent of cloud.

# Rise of Cloud Computing

If we look closely, all the things involved in computing infrastructure are a bunch of repetitive tasks. There were inefficiencies and a high learning curve for any new company to set up its infrastructure. Cloud computing giants were able to find this opportunity and establish best practices in order to take away this stress from end consumers.

Further, they also have multiple options in these instances. They also have options like spot instance which can further help you lower the costs; these are a few examples, but the probability to play around with options is huge to bring down cost and improve efficiency.

The evolution of cloud computing led to the introduction of Platform as a Service (PaaS). Among the most popular and my personal favorite PaaS services is Heroku. PaaS builds on the foundation of Infrastructure as a Service (IaaS) and provides additional tools and resources to help you deploy your application quickly. With PaaS, you can leverage prebuilt services such as OS installation, language-specific environment setup, service discovery, and monitoring, which are completed up front.

PaaS enables developers to focus on the core business logic of their application, rather than worrying about the underlying infrastructure. This significantly reduces the time and effort required for deployment while also providing greater flexibility and scalability. By leveraging PaaS, businesses can rapidly deploy and iterate on their applications, reducing time to market and improving overall efficiency. Heroku is an excellent example of a PaaS service that offers a wide range of features and capabilities, making it a top choice for many developers and businesses.

Platform as a Service (PaaS) is a layer that sits on top of virtual machines (VMs), but we can also use containers to achieve the same. Containers, such as Docker, are a popular example that isolates application requirements from operating system dependencies. When containers run on top of virtual machines, it is called

Container as a Service (CaaS). Container orchestration is a sophisticated task that requires tools such as Kubernetes and Mesos, which can be run on both public and private clouds (we will discuss private cloud in more detail shortly).

So far, we have discussed the three main genres of cloud computing: Infrastructure as a Service (IaaS), PaaS, and CaaS. Together, they come under the umbrella of compute as a service. All three are closely associated with each other and are interdependent. Now, let's review some of the advantages of cloud environments.

## Key Advantages of Cloud Environments

By leveraging cloud computing services, businesses can focus on their core competencies and achieve greater operational efficiency.

The following are some key advantages:

- Cheaper cost: Before Infrastructure as a Service, you would need to set up data centers which in turn would require specialized skilled engineers who would work in these data centers to maintain apps and servers. Things from networking to installations, power, and physically fixing issues which means high cost of assets and team. With IaaS, all this cost is outsourced to cloud providers like AWS (in the case of EC2), and you can pay as you go.

- Less risk: Managing your own physical servers can expose you and your company to many unplanned incidents like hardware failure, downtime during high volume, or scaling up the servers due to unplanned surge in traffic. There is also a high risk that the servers you own are in a region which has become hostile. With IaaS spread across continents and backups available in multiple regions, you are secured in every manner. Downtime is managed since cloud providers have endless computing capacity, so risk is pretty much at bay.

- Scaling: Scaling has a cost attached to it, and it is significantly pulled down when we bring IaaS. With IaaS, there is flexibility in paying as you scale. You are no longer required to make up-front investment on servers which might never be used or could be used very quickly. There is also an option to start with the minimal configuration of infrastructure and move to high-power infrastructure as and when needed. You are also free from procurement and provisioning of servers every time you start a new proof of concept or a planned application. If you just want to try an idea for a short period of time with IaaS, you can go live in minutes instead of months. This is one of the main reasons of small start-ups experimenting ideas like any big corporation and scaling only when required.

- Increased efficiency: Cloud environments provide automated provisioning, orchestration, and management, which results in increased efficiency and reduced downtime.

- Improved agility: With cloud computing, developers can rapidly deploy and iterate on applications, reducing time to market and improving overall agility.

- Flexibility: Cloud environments provide the flexibility to run workloads on public, private, or hybrid clouds, as well as the ability to leverage multiple cloud providers for different services.

Now that we've discussed the advantages of cloud computing, let's dive into the next evolution in cloud development: serverless computing. With serverless, developers can take their applications to the next level, leveraging the power of the cloud without worrying about the underlying infrastructure.

# The Emergence of Serverless Computing: A Game-Changer for Cloud Development

After a decade of cloud computing, the technology industry started exploring new ideas for the next evolution of infrastructure outsourcing. The focus was to make the process more efficient and cost-effective for the end consumer. The concept of serverless emerged from this, but it does not mean that applications run without servers. Instead, serverless architecture allows applications to run without being tied to a specific server. Traditionally, an application would require a dedicated server even if it was only needed for a few hours a day. With serverless architecture, when a request is made, one of the available servers is assigned to execute the required business logic, and the function runs on that server. This means that the same function may not run on the same server if it is required at different times of the day. With serverless architecture, you only pay for the time the function consumes the computing engine, making it a more cost-effective solution.

Serverless architecture is a way of providing backend services on an as-needed basis. In this architecture, resources are not held in volatile memory. Computation is done in short bursts of requests, and the results are persisted. When the application is not in use, no computing resources are allocated. However, serverless architecture comes with a range of techniques and technologies that can be grouped into two categories: Backend as a Service (BaaS) and Function as a Service (FaaS). Let us take a closer look at these two categories.

# Backend As a Service (BaaS)

In the Backend as a Service (BaaS) model, developers can focus solely on building the client side of applications while outsourcing the backend activities as services through APIs (Application programming interfaces). This means the various essential functionalities such as authentication, database management, and push notifications, can be outsourced to third party service providers, and directly consumed in the applications, without managing it. To put it simply, it is similar to a fast-food restaurant where the waitstaff is responsible for serving clients and chef prepares the food in the back kitchen. The basic idea of BaaS is to reduce complex backend tasks that can be reused and enable the team to focus more on the frontend development.

BaaS can be seen as a variation of Software as a Service (SaaS), where business processes are consumed through tools and services such as GitHub, Salesforce, Dropbox, and Google apps. BaaS breaks down an application into smaller pieces, where the implementation can be entirely in-house, using external products, or a combination of both, with APIs and SDKs (software development kits) being the typical integration methods used. BaaS has become very popular ever since the advent of single-page web apps and mobile apps. Some common features which BaaS services easily provide are

1. Authentication

2. CDN (Content Delivery Network)

3. API integration

4. Database management

5. Geographical location

6. Cloud storage and backup

7. Email service and verification

8. Regulatory compliance

9. Social media integration

10. Push notifications

Popular BaaS service providers include

- Apache Usergrid

- Auth0

- Back4App

- Backendless

- 8Base

- Built.io Backend

- Couchbase

- Kii

- Kumulos

- Kuzzle

- MongoDB Stitch

- Parse

- Firebase

- Windows Azure Mobile Services

- AWS Amplify (one we will discuss in depth in this book)

Now let's move on to Function as a Service (FaaS), which is another type of serverless architecture that focuses on the backend code execution.

# Function As a Service/Serverless Computing

Function as a Service (FaaS) is another part of serverless computing where an environment is provided to customers to develop, execute, and manage application functionalities without setting up or maintaining complexity of building a full-blown server. By full-blown server here we mean instead of deploying server-side software, the deployment is limited to only functions and operations. The most popular form of FaaS implementation is Lambda from AWS. Figure 1-1 shows the evolution path of application infrastructure from a physical machine to serverless.

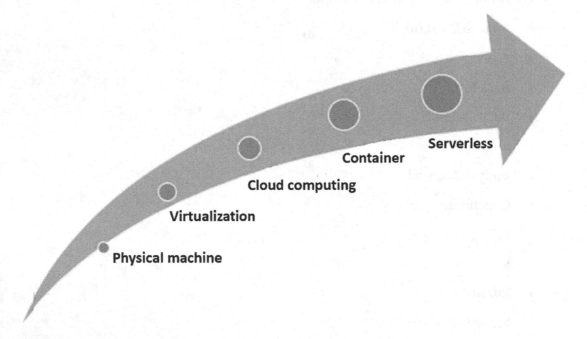

***Figure 1-1.***  *Evolution of IT infrastructure*

The evolution of serverless computing can be analogous to human evolution; with every passing step, the productivity and ease for end users increased manyfolds.

Traditionally, applications had to deploy their server-side software with a host instance, which used to be a virtual machine (VM) instance or container. The application contains functions that have the business logic to act based on user requirements. However, with the rise of Function as a Service (FaaS), developers can now focus only on writing these functions, while the service providers manage everything else. FaaS is at the top of the chain, offering developers a way to execute code on demand without the need to manage servers, operating systems, or infrastructure. The block diagram in Figure 1-2 explains parts of infrastructure managed by you and the provider in different strategies.

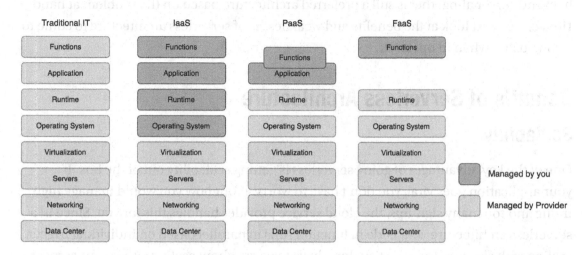

***Figure 1-2.*** *Infrastructure components managed under different infrastructure strategies*

As seen in Figure 1-2, with FaaS we strip away everything from the host instance to the application process from our model. Instead, we focus on just the individual operations or functions that express our application's logic. We upload those functions individually to a vendor-supplied FaaS platform.

The functions or operations are the basic and only unit in a FaaS system. They are not constantly active but sit idle until they need to be run. A FaaS platform is set up to listen for a specific event for each operation; basically, it works on an event-driven approach. When that event happens, the function is triggered.

AWS Lambda is a highly popular and stable FaaS option, which was launched in 2014 and has since become a go-to choice, especially for those using AWS services. Apart from AWS Lambda, other widely used FaaS offerings are provided by Google, Microsoft, IBM, and smaller players such as Auth0.

# Benefits and Weaknesses of a Serverless Architecture

While architecting an application, it is necessary to take the right decision; though we are focusing on serverless applications in this book, traditional architecture having a backend server altogether is still a preferred architecture based on the problem at hand. Hence, we must look at the benefits and weaknesses of serverless architecture to come to a conclusion when to opt for it.

# Benefits of Serverless Architecture

## Scalability

One of the key advantages of going serverless is getting scalability out of the box. If your application goes viral, you don't have to worry about how you would manage high traffic and too many sign-ups, the cloud service provider handles this for you. Since in a serverless architecture your code in function runs in parallel based on individual trigger, scaling with size is automatic. You don't have to worry about scaling either your server or databases.

## Less Code

Less code is not just a buzzword, it is actually the crux of serverless architecture. Since you are focused on writing the business logic, most of the repetitive and bootstrapping part is already managed by cloud providers. This also makes things simple for new team members to understand a simple architecture and corresponding functions. Though it's not guaranteed, usually less complexity means less bugs and it's easy to debug them. The tech team often plugs existing managed services to implement features, further reducing burden of building and maintaining code.

## Better Velocity

With fewer features to build and complex repetitive ones outsourced to other services, developer velocity increases drastically. Spinning up features like authentication, databases, APIs, etc., is super fast, and developers can focus on core business logic.

## Fail Fast

Most of the repetitive tasks are outsourced to other services; there is ample time to experiment new features with less risk. A focus is on to go live with business features that work and retire the features which are not making any impact is totally possible in such environment. This type of testing is called A/B testing where we can compare different versions of an application to conclude which one performs the best.

## Improved Reliability

Serverless architectures often include built-in fault tolerance and redundancy features, which can help ensure that your applications remain available and reliable even in the face of failures.

## Cost

The pricing of a serverless architecture is far different from traditional on-premises infrastructure and cloud-based hosting. In a traditional infrastructure, there are exuberant costs for data centers and day-to-day maintenance of the application, while cloud-based hosting also has many of the costs associated with maintaining an application. With serverless technologies, you basically pay for what you use. FaaS further drops your price arrangement to the number of requests your functions serve, reserved memory for each function, and time taken for the code to execute.

You are not paying anything when your app is sitting idle. Besides that, most of cloud providers have managed services to satisfy key complex requirements, and the cost is only based on usage. This significantly reduces overall costs and allows developers to spend time on the unique features of the application rather than implementing the same features again like authentication, etc. This also means reduced time to market, which is additional saving.

## Security and Stability

Since we are going to consume many services related to core functionalities, we are actually reusing time-tested software which comes with security and scalability. For example, authentication is a very complex piece of software in a serverless architecture; we will outsource it to a managed service, which means we don't need to worry about implementation but also day-to-day vulnerabilities which are managed by the respective owner.

11

Another advantage of using these managed services is that service owners make sure to avoid any kind of downtime possible. We basically outsource them, not just building but also deploying and maintaining these services, keeping them stable for day-to-day operations.

# Weaknesses of Serverless

## The Cold Start

A *cold start* happens when a function is invoked, but there is no running function available to execute; rather, a new function container will spin up; this will increase time for users to start interacting with the app. Developers avoid this situation by keeping functions warm, but this workaround kind of beats the purpose of going serverless at the first place.

This cold start issue is there but continues to have less impact with time. For example, AWS Lambda significantly improved its start-up time for cold starts by reinventing how it connects a function to a private network.

## VPC/Network Issues

If the application needs to operate within a private network, there may be limitations in a serverless architecture. Subnets with limited IP addresses have a constraint on the number of concurrent executions. Depending on your company's requirements, it is important to plan the capacity of private networks adequately to ensure they are large enough to accommodate the application. Additionally, it is advisable to avoid relying heavily on classic serverless architecture, where we can outsource many core features to cloud services.

## Application Size

We have discussed about cold start time earlier, and it becomes a serious problem if the application size is huge. The impact of this limitation is, you cannot pack a huge Java application or node application with huge dependencies to a serverless function; therefore, a choice of better technology that complements well with your serverless architecture could be an alternate strategy.

## Debugging

Chances of failure are inevitable, so a strategy of debugging has to be part of software development; however, when the runtime is dynamic, debugging at times becomes complicated. However, the savior here is, since core functionalities can be outsourced to managed services, we can pinpoint the issue if our architecture is set up correctly.

## Vendor Lock-In

Moving from one serverless platform to another may be challenging due to the proprietary nature of serverless architectures.

# AWS Amplify Introduction

AWS Amplify is a comprehensive suite of services and tools that empowers frontend and mobile developers to build highly scalable and secure full-stack applications by leveraging the robust features of AWS. Amplify offers an open source framework that provides libraries tailored to specific use cases and a robust toolchain to easily integrate cloud-based functionalities into your application. Additionally, Amplify includes a web hosting service that enables hassle-free deployment of static web applications.

Amplify boasts a plethora of services in its toolkit, which we will explore in detail in subsequent chapters. However, to provide a brief overview, Amplify offers the following services as part of its out-of-the-box offerings:

- Authentication: Enable sign-in, sign-up, and sign-out within minutes with prebuilt UI components and powerful authentication APIs

- Storage: A simple mechanism for managing user content in public, protected, or private storage

- GraphQL API: Easy and secure solution to access your backend data with support for real-time updates using GraphQL

- DataStore: Seamlessly synchronize and persist online and offline data to the cloud as well as across devices

- REST API: A straightforward and secure solution for making HTTP requests using REST APIs

- Analytics: Make informed decisions with drop-in analytics to track user sessions, custom user attributes, and in-app metrics

- Push notifications: Drive customer engagement using push notifications with campaign analytics and targeting

- XR (Extended Reality): Engage your customers in a different dimension with augmented reality (AR) and virtual reality (VR) content within your app

- PubSub: Provide best-in-class real-time experiences by connecting your application with a message-oriented middleware in the cloud

- Interactions: Automate customer workflows by enlisting the help of conversational chatbots powered by deep learning technologies

- AI/ML predictions: Design delightful experiences with the power of AI (artificial intelligence) and ML (machine learning) functionality such as computer vision, translation, transcription, and more

## Local Setup

In this book, we will be creating a web application which will use React as frontend technology.

For that purpose, let's use create-react-app npm package to create our hello world React application, using the following command:

```
npx create-react-app react-amplified
```

---

**Note**    Since we are creating our React application using create-react-app please install node and npm globally if you haven't. You might have to add sudo based on your system policy.

---

Next, let's set up the AWS Amplify CLI so that we can get started working with Amplify.

# Setting Up AWS Amplify CLI

The Amplify Command Line Interface (CLI) is a unified toolchain to create, integrate, and manage the AWS cloud services for your app. Basically, with React we build the frontend or client side of a web application, and Amplify helps us set up anything related to the backend.

The following are prerequisites for setting up the Amplify CLI:

1. Install Node.js and NPM if they are not already on your machine.

2. Verify that your Node.js version is at least 10.x and npm version 6.x or greater; this can be done by the following commands: `node -v` and `npm -v`.

3. You must have a valid AWS account. In order to create an AWS account, simply visit https://aws.amazon.com/ and sign up. There is no up-front cost for creating a new account with AWS; however, you would have to provide your credit card to get started.

Install the Amplify CLI using the following command:

```
npm install -g @aws-amplify/cli
```

---

**Note**    Since we are installing the CLI globally, you might have to add sudo based on your system policy.

---

While writing this book, I have used Amplify CLI version @aws-amplify/cli@4.45.2; please use the same version in order to run all the examples exactly how we implement throughout this book, avoiding any confusion. To specify the exact version, you can add it in the following way:

```
npm install -g @aws-amplify/cli@12.1.1
```

Before we start using the Amplify CLI, we would have to configure it with our AWS account; let's do that in this section.

## Configuring Amplify CLI with AWS

To set up our AWS account with the Amplify CLI, we would have to run the following command, which we would be using just one time to tie our AWS account with the Amplify CLI:

```
→ react-amplified git:(develop) amplify configure
Follow these steps to set up access to your AWS account:
```

```
→ react-amplified git:(develop) amplify configure
Follow these steps to set up access to your AWS account:
```

```
Sign in to your AWS administrator account:
https://console.aws.amazon.com/
Press Enter to continue
```

What happens now is that a browser page opens up, and we will be prompted to sign in into our AWS account. Enter your AWS account email and password. This is illustrated in Figure 1-3.

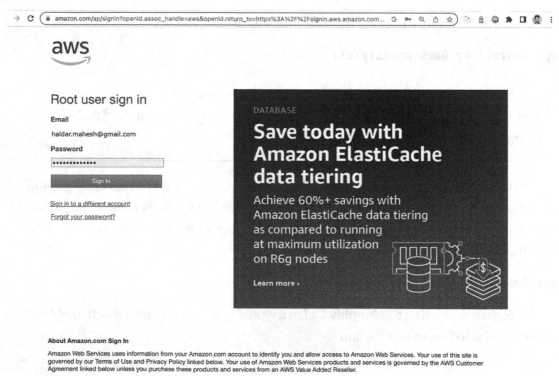

***Figure 1-3.*** *Amazon Web Services login*

Upon successful login, as shown in Figure 1-4, we will be taken to the home page of AWS Management Console.

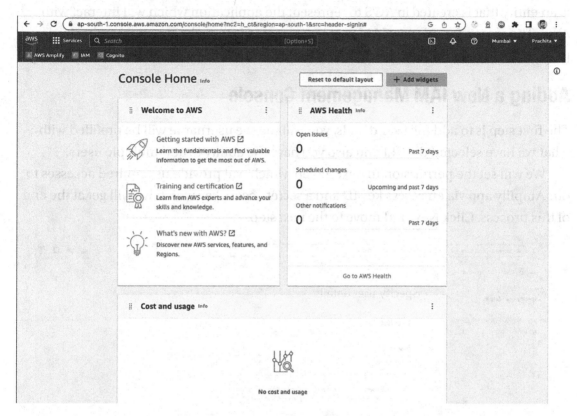

***Figure 1-4.***  *AWS Management Console*

We don't have to do anything here; simply switch back to your terminal. You will have to now select your AWS region. Select the closest one from all the provided options:

```
Specify the AWS Region
? region:
  ca-central-1
  me-south-1
  sa-east-1
> us-east-1
  us-east-2
  us-west-1
  us-west-2
(Move up and down to reveal more choices)
```

Next, you will be navigated to AWS console on browser to create a new user and you will be asked to name your new IAM (Identity and Access Management) user. This user is an entity that is created in AWS to represent the application which will interact with AWS. The reason for this new IAM user to be created is to make sure only authorized person can manage and modify different resources.

## Adding a New IAM Management Console

The first step is to add the user details, you will see the username will be prefilled with what we have selected the CLI and also you have the ability to add multiple users.

We will set the permission in next screen, which will provide us required accesses to our Amplify app via an access key ID and a secret access key which we will get at the end of this process. Click Next and move to the next step.

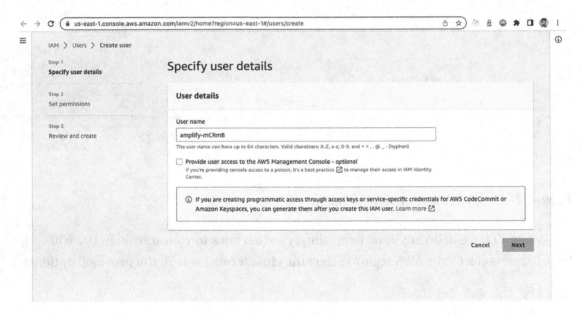

*Figure 1-5.* *IAM user addition and access*

In this setup, we will provide a policy for our user; click on `Attach policies directly` tab to attach the policy for this user. In our case, since we have one user and we want to provide it full access, let's select AdministratorAccess-Amplify, you can type in the filter input as illustrated in Figure 1-6. If you had created multiple users, we could add them in groups and select desired limited access with limited policies. Click Next to move forward.

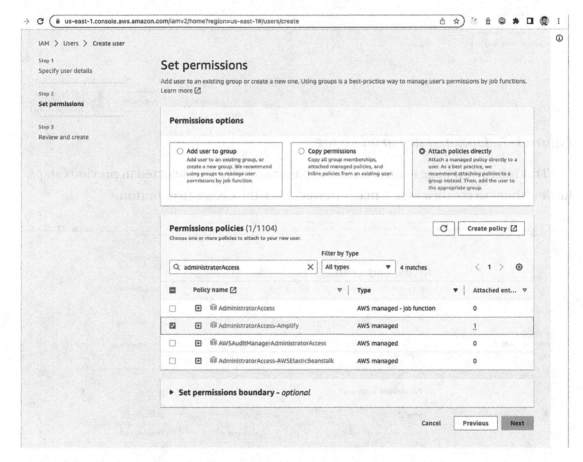

***Figure 1-6.***  *User policy*

In this section, we can provide certain tags to our user. This is an optional step; we will skip it and move to the next step, as shown in Figure 1-7.

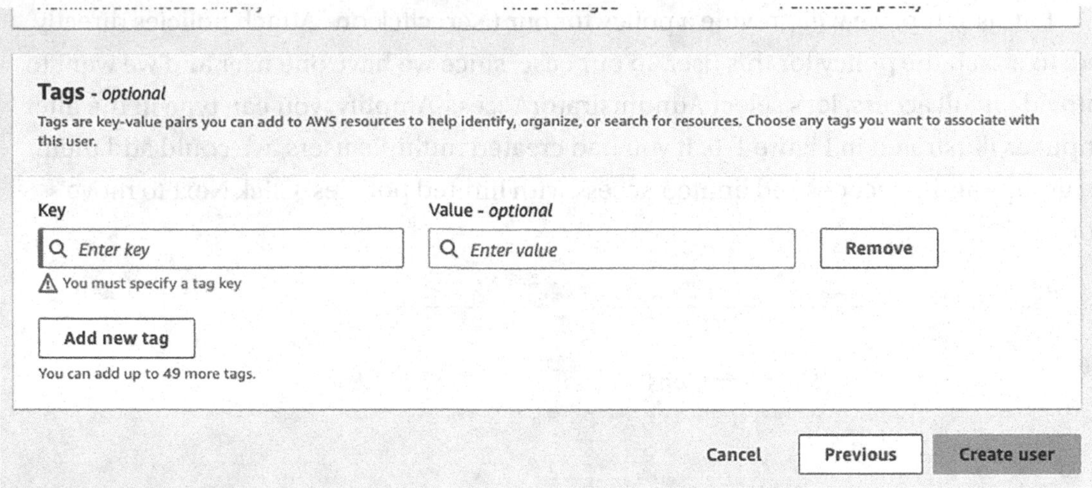
Tags - optional
Tags are key-value pairs you can add to AWS resources to help identify, organize, or search for resources. Choose any tags you want to associate with this user.
Key
Value - optional
Enter key
Enter value
Remove
You must specify a tag key
Add new tag
You can add up to 49 more tags.
Cancel
Previous
Create user

***Figure 1-7.*** *Optional step to add a tag*

This is a review page to review various parameters we had selected in previous steps. Review them to create a user. Once reviewed, click the Create user button.

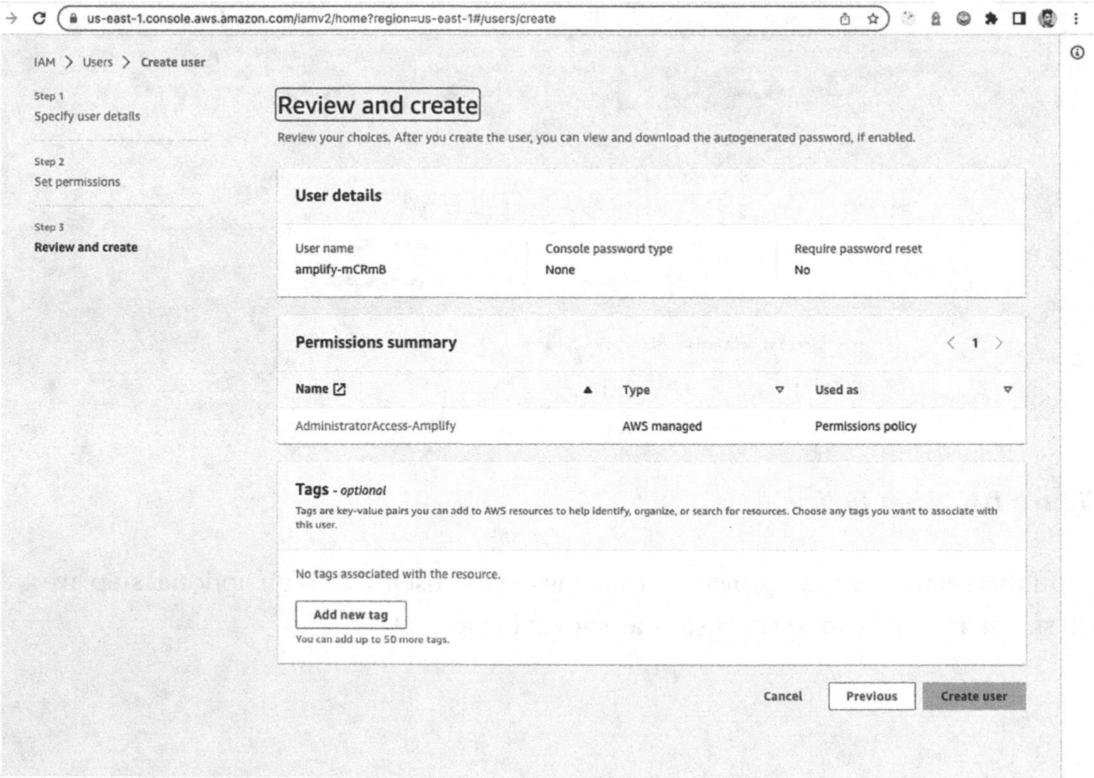
us-east-1.console.aws.amazon.com/iamv2/home?region=us-east-1#/users/create
IAM > Users > Create user
Step 1
Specify user details
Step 2
Set permissions
Step 3
Review and create
Review and create
Review your choices. After you create the user, you can view and download the autogenerated password, if enabled.
User details
User name
amplify-mCRmB
Console password type
None
Require password reset
No
Permissions summary
Name
Type
Used as
AdministratorAccess-Amplify
AWS managed
Permissions policy
Tags - optional
Tags are key-value pairs you can add to AWS resources to help identify, organize, or search for resources. Choose any tags you want to associate with this user.
No tags associated with the resource.
Add new tag
You can add up to 50 more tags.
Cancel
Previous
Create user

***Figure 1-8.*** *Create user review page*

This is the final step where our new user is created and we get a success message. We will require to generate this user's access key, as the terminal in next step will ask to enter the access key and secret, so that it can validate the user. From the success screen shown in Figure 1-9, select the user you just created, navigate to **Security credentials** tab, and under **Access keys** section click on the **Create access key** button. Next you will be asked to select the use case for the access keys, select Command Line Interface (CLI) option and click on confirm to create access key. It's important to note that we can only see these values once. The secret access key is hidden, but we can reveal it by clicking the Show button or download the .csv file to store it locally. Before you move forward, make sure you copy both values.

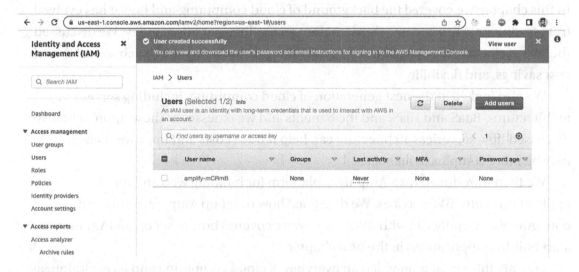

***Figure 1-9.*** *User creation page with keys*

Go back to the terminal and press enter to continue.

After pressing enter, we get an option to add accessKeyId and secretAccessKey – press enter. You get an option to add a profile name; you can skip it as default and hit enter again. With this step, you get successfully set up new user message, and we have configured AWS Amplify successfully before we start building our first app.

```
Enter the access key of the newly created user:
? accessKeyId: ********************
? secretAccessKey: ************************************
This would update/create the AWS Profile in your local machine
? Profile Name: default

Successfully set up the new user.
```

# Summary

In this chapter, we covered the background of cloud computing and how it has evolved from traditional IT to become the dominant technology paradigm today. We discussed the rise of cloud computing and the key advantages that it provides, such as scalability, cost savings, and flexibility.

We also looked at the next generation of cloud computing, including serverless architectures, BaaS and FaaS, and the benefits and weaknesses of these approaches. We discussed how serverless architecture can help reduce costs and improve scalability, but may be more complex to manage.

We then introduced AWS Amplify, a platform for building web and mobile applications with AWS services. We discussed how to set up Amplify locally and configure the Amplify CLI with AWS. Finally, we covered how to set up an IAM user to start building applications in the next chapter.

Overall, this chapter provided an overview of cloud computing and its evolution, as well as an introduction to AWS Amplify and the tools needed to build applications with it, which we will use in next chapter.

# CHAPTER 2

# UI Component and Authentication

*The essence of authentication is being able to prove the assertion you are making.*

—Akshat Paul

In this chapter, we will explore the concepts of authentication and authorization and how they are essential for secure application development. We will discuss different types of authentication and authorization mechanisms. Furthermore, we will dive into the AWS Cognito service, which is used for managing registered users and their access to the application. We will also demonstrate how to implement a login flow, sign-up flow, and basic password management in a React app using AWS Amplify.

Additionally, we will showcase how to implement social authentication, such as using a Google email ID and password.

## Authentication Basics

Can you watch a Netflix show without having a valid login credential or without paying with your credit card? Obviously not. Imagine if there was a security flaw in Netflix's security systems and users could watch the shows without subscribing, this may cost billions of dollars to the business, and if not fixed in time, it could lead to a significant loss, ultimately impacting the financials of the company. This is the business importance of the user login credential in the digital industry.

Similarly, the offices require employees to carry an access card to enter the office and access specific areas like meeting rooms and cafeterias. The repercussions of allowing

A. Paul and M. Haldar, *Serverless Web Applications with AWS Amplify*, https://doi.org/10.1007/978-1-4842-8707-1_2

unauthorized access could be severe, leading to potential losses for the company, in many aspects. Hence, it is essential to have a security check at the gateway to avoid any such losses.

In this chapter, we will discuss the importance of authentication and authorization in digital platforms and implement it in our app using AWS Amplify. We will discuss the various types of authentication, along with the AWS Cognito service, a fully managed service that provides basic user management, sign-up, sign-in, and access control, without having to rebuild the authentication and authorization system. We will also use the AWS Amplify to implement the login flow, sign-up flow, and basic password management in our React app. Additionally, we will also explore how to implement social login, like using Google email ID and password for logging in.

## What Is Authentication?

Authentication is a fundamental aspect of security and access control in the digital world. It involves verifying the identity and credibility of a user and granting access to the resources of a system. The authentication process typically requires the user to provide proof of their identity, such as a password, PIN, or biometric information.

In our daily lives, we interact with authentication systems frequently, often without realizing it. For example, we need to provide a PIN to withdraw cash from an ATM and valid login credentials to access our social media accounts. The importance of authentication becomes even more apparent in the business world, where a security flaw can lead to significant financial losses and damage to a company's reputation.

## How Can Users Prove Credibility?

To authenticate a user or incoming request, the request must meet the specific criteria:

1. **Proof of who the user is claiming to be.**

   The user should provide some proof to validate their identity such as login ID, password, or token.

2. **Proof should be understandable by the system.**

   The proof should be understandable by the system and should be present in the system records. If the proof is a user ID and password, then it should be registered already in the system.

If the proof is an access token or certificate, then it should be in line with the agreed format between the server and the client or should be generated by the system itself.

3. **Proof should be valid.**

   The proof provided by the user should be valid, such that the access token should not be expired or the password should be correct.

Once the process of authentication is successful, the next step is authorization.

# What Is Authorization?

Let us consider a scenario where you have booked a flight ticket from Tokyo to Berlin. Along with you, there are other passengers, air hostesses, and pilots who will be boarding the same flight. As long as you possess a valid ticket, you are authenticated to board the flight, along with the pilots and air hostesses.

However, if someone like Mr. Professor tries to board the same flight without a valid ticket, they will not be authenticated to board the flight. Once you, the pilots, and the air hostesses board the flight, each individual has a different level of access within the aircraft. For instance, you can only use the seats and washrooms, but cannot go to the cockpit or visit the pantry section of the aircraft to take food from the oven.

Similarly, air hostesses have different seats and cannot enter the cockpit to take control of the aircraft. This rule of different users having different levels of access to resources is what is known as authorization. The authentication and authorization flow can occur either between a server and users or between two servers. Regardless of the combination, the authorization server acts as the server, while the requester functions as the client. The client can be any web application, mobile application, or any program such as the CLI or backend server.

Figure 2-1 and the subsequent steps outline the flow of how the authentication occurs in a web application when a user logs in and subsequently accesses other resources.

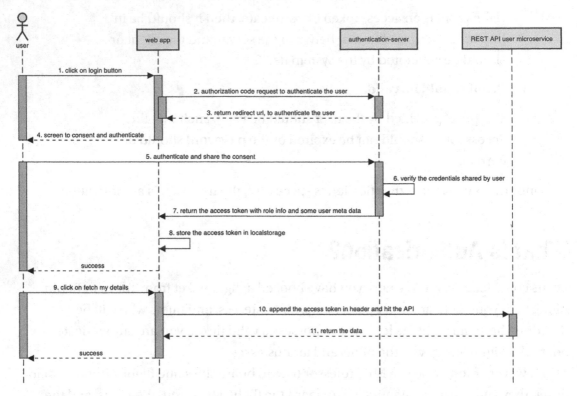

**Figure 2-1.** *The authentication flow between the application and the server*

1.  The user clicks the login button.

2.  This triggers the whole flow of the authentication process, and in return, the authentication server returns a redirect URL, where the user needs to add credentials and grant consent if required.

3.  The user is then presented with the screen on the browser, prompting them to enter their credentials. In the case of social login via Gmail, the Google sign-in screen will be displayed.

4.  The user enters their credentials and grants their consent by acknowledging the login.

5.  The authentication server verifies the provided credentials and returns a success response, if they are correct.

6.  Upon successful authentication, the authentication server appends metadata such as TTL (time to live), user role, and other useful information to the access token, which is then returned to the web app.

7. The web app can store the access token and use it until it expires, which is typically a few minutes to hours depending on the token's importance.

8. After a successful login, the user is inside the application and can access other resources such as their personal information. When a new API request is made with the access token, the server or API gateway checks if the user's token is valid and has a valid role. If it does, the server responds to the request successfully; otherwise, the request is rejected.

# Broken Authentication

The configuration of the authentication system in any digital system should be robust enough to prevent malicious users from gaining unauthorized access to resources or sensitive data. Broken authentication refers to vulnerabilities in the system that allow an attacker to log in and gain access to sensitive data that they should not be able to access. This can result in significant financial loss, loss of customers, and damage to a company's reputation. Broken authentication vulnerabilities can be caused by various factors such as poor session management, nonsecure protocols, nonsecure cookies, and poor password policies. A survey conducted by the National Cyber Security Centre (NCSC) in Great Britain revealed that a significant number of users, about 23.2 million, were using weak passwords such as "123456". Additionally, passwords such as "qwerty" and "password" were used by more than 3 million accounts.

Here are a couple of examples of real-world cases where broken authentication mechanisms were exploited:

- In 2014, Yahoo suffered a data breach that compromised billions of user accounts due to weak passwords and unencrypted communication. As a result, Yahoo suffered significant financial losses and damage to its reputation.

- Similarly, in 2018, hackers were able to access the Marriott hotel chain's system by exploiting compromised credentials, leading to exposure of personal information of up to 500 million guests.

These incidents highlight the importance of implementing strong authentication mechanisms to protect sensitive data and prevent unauthorized access. The improper authentication mechanism can result in various types of losses such as financial, theft, and compromising of confidential data. This further leads to losing customers. Therefore, organizations should implement strong security measures to ensure the confidentiality, integrity, and availability of their systems.

The following are ways to prevent broken authentication:

1.  Disallow infinite attempts of the wrong password, as this can prevent hackers from using automated programs to guess the password.

2.  Never store passwords in clear text and always encrypt them with additional salt for extra security, such that even if some malicious user gets access to the database, they should not be able to understand the passwords.

3.  Enforce the password complexity, for example, a combination of uppercase and lowercase letters as well as at least one special character to make guessing the password abstruse.

4.  Have an automated alert mechanism that sends notifications when multiple failed login attempts reach a certain threshold.

5.  HTTPS should be the default protocol for all communications.

6.  Implement the latest authentication protocols that have been thoroughly tested against most of the security vulnerabilities to ensure the highest level of security.

# Types of Authentication

- Basic authentication: This is the most basic type of authentication; in this method, a user's credentials (username and password) are encoded and sent in all the HTTP request header.

  This type of authentication is not secure as the credentials are to be saved on the device in order to send in every request. To mitigate this risk basic authentication, is recommended.

- Token authentication: This type of authentication is a widely used method for authentication in modern applications; in this method, the client (user or application) provides their credentials, username and password, once to the server. In return, the server generates a unique and encrypted token, which is then sent back to the client. The token contains metadata about the user or client, as well as information to validate its authenticity. This token serves as proof of authentication and is used for subsequent interactions with the server or for making API calls. The client includes this token in the request headers for each subsequent request, rather than sending the credentials (e.g., username and password) repeatedly.

  Token authentication offers several advantages. It reduces the risk of transmitting sensitive credentials with each request. It also enables better scalability and performance, as the server does not need to perform expensive authentication checks for every request but can validate the token quickly. Additionally, tokens can have expiration times, improving security by automatically invalidating them after a certain period. Overall, token authentication provides a more secure and efficient way to authenticate clients and protect sensitive data in web and mobile applications.

- Biometric authentication: Biometric authentication is a method of verifying a user's identity based on their unique physical characteristics. These characteristics, such as fingerprints, voice patterns, or facial features, are captured by sensors or cameras and compared with stored digital records for authentication purposes. Let us delve to discuss a few types of biometric authentication:

  - Fingerprint authentication is one of the most commonly used biometric authentication methods. It involves scanning and matching the unique patterns present in an individual's fingerprint. This method is widely used in smartphones and fingerprint-based laptops, where users can unlock their devices by simply placing their finger on a sensor.

- Face authentication is another popular biometric authentication method. It utilizes facial recognition technology to identify and authenticate users based on their facial features. Many mobile phone companies have implemented this method, allowing users to unlock their devices by scanning their registered face.

- Eye or iris authentication is a more advanced biometric method. It involves scanning the unique patterns of the iris for authentication purposes. By comparing the scanned iris pattern with the stored record, access to resources can be granted if there is a match.

- Certificate-based authentication is a robust method of authentication that involves the use of digital certificates to gain access to specific resources. These certificates employ various algorithms, ensuring their uniqueness and making them nearly impossible to predict or replicate. However, it is crucial to emphasize that the security of the certificate storage is of utmost importance, as the system relies on trusting any client or process that presents a valid certificate.

- Multifactor authentication (MFA) is a powerful authentication approach that enhances the security of a system by requiring users to provide multiple proofs of their identity. This additional layer of security is essential for protecting sensitive resources such as bank accounts, VPNs, or any other system. Instead of solely relying on a username and password combination, MFA mandates the provision of an extra authentication factor, significantly reducing the likelihood of unauthorized access by potential hackers. Implementing MFA strengthens the overall security posture of a system and is often a prerequisite for systems aiming to be deemed secure, such as those employed by financial institutions.

# Why MFA Is Important

Imagine a scenario where you have stored your bank account credentials in Google Keep, a note-keeping application. Now, suppose Mr. Professor gains access to your phone or obtains your Google ID and password. In such a situation, Mr. Professor would have complete access to your notes, including your bank credentials. This could potentially lead to unauthorized access to your bank account, allowing him to perform transactions or transfer money without your knowledge or consent.

However, this risk can be mitigated if multifactor authentication (MFA) is enabled. Even if Mr. Professor manages to log in to your bank account using your compromised credentials, MFA adds an additional layer of security. In addition to the password, an OTP (one-time password) is required, which is typically sent to your mobile phone. This means that Mr. Professor would not be able to transfer money or perform any sensitive actions without possessing both your password and the OTP from your phone.

Furthermore, if Mr. Professor attempts to change the phone number associated with the account, MFA still provides protection. Without the SMS OTP sent to your registered phone number, the change request would not be successful, thwarting any attempts to gain control over your bank account.

By enabling MFA, you significantly enhance the security of your sensitive information and financial assets, safeguarding them against unauthorized access and potential fraudulent activities.

# Types of MFA

Multifactor authentication (MFA) can be implemented through various methods, ensuring an additional layer of security beyond traditional username and password authentication. Here are some common ways MFA can be achieved:

1.  SMS OTP (one-time password): A unique password is sent to the user's mobile phone via SMS, which must be entered along with the regular login credentials to gain access. This password is generally valid for a few minutes.

2.  Email OTP (one-time password): Similar to SMS OTP, but the one-time password is sent to the user's registered email address instead.

3.  Time-based one-time password: This method involves the use of time-based algorithms to generate a unique password that changes periodically. Users need to enter this password, along with their regular login credentials, within a specified time window. This password is generated on the device and not sent via any network.

4. Hardware token–based one-time password: Users are provided with a physical device, often a small electronic token or key fob, which generates unique passwords that need to be entered during the authentication process.

5. Location-based authentication: This method uses the user's current location as an additional factor for authentication. It verifies if the user is logging in from a trusted or predefined location, adding an extra layer of security.

6. Google-based two-step verification: This method utilizes Google's two-step verification process, where users provide a secondary verification code generated by the Google Authenticator app or received via SMS or phone call.

These methods enhance the security of authentication processes by requiring users to provide additional information or verification beyond the traditional username and password combination. Implementing MFA helps protect against unauthorized access, as potential attackers would need to bypass multiple layers of authentication to gain entry.

# JSON Web Tokens

JWT (JSON Web Token) is a universally accepted and standardized token used to establish a secure and trusted connection between two parties. JWT is a compact JSON object that is digitally signed. The JWT is issued to the clients after successful authentication; the token contains relevant information such as the user's identity, access roles, token validity details, and expiration time. JWTs are commonly used for user authentication in modern, stateless applications.

To understand JWT, imagine it as a boarding pass for a flight. It includes your identity, details of the flight you are authorized to enter, and a barcode to prevent forgery by malicious individuals.

JWTs are encoded in base64 format, allowing the base64 decoder to read the JSON information contained within.

JWTs can be digitally signed using various algorithms such as RSA (Rivest-Shamir-Adleman) and HMAC (hash-based message authentication code). Additionally, they can be encrypted using the JSON Web Encryption (JWE) standard, which ensures the confidentiality of the claims contained within the token.

Overall, JWTs provide a secure and standardized approach to authentication, enabling the verification of user identities and the secure exchange of information between parties.

# JWT Authentication Flow

The API gateway plays a crucial role in the validation of JWTs. It examines the header information and expiration time contained within the token to determine its validity. If the token is found to be invalid, either due to an incorrect signature or expiration, the API gateway rejects the request immediately. This means that the request is halted at the API gateway level and never reaches the downstream services.

By performing this validation process, the API gateway ensures that only authenticated and valid requests are forwarded to the appropriate services. This adds an extra layer of security to the system by preventing unauthorized or tampered requests from reaching the backend services. Figure 2-2 illustrates the flow and system interaction.

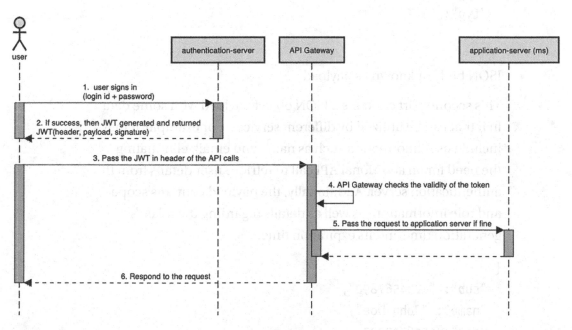

*Figure 2-2.* *The token validation mechanism on the API gateway*

# JWT Structure

Let's take the following JWT as an example to discuss the details of the token. By examining its components, we can gain a deeper understanding of its structure and purpose.

xxxx.yyyy.zzzz

The JWT contains three parts and is joined by the dot operator:

- Header

- The header contains two parts: the token type and the signing algorithm used. It specifies the type of the token and provides details about the specific signing algorithm, such as, HMAC, SHA256 or RSA.

```
{
  "alg": "HS256",
  "typ": "JWT"
}
```

- JSON body or known as payload

  This second part contains a JSON object payload with some data in it that can be utilized by different services. For example, it may include user information such as name and email, eliminating the need for an additional API call to retrieve user details from the authentication server. Additionally, the payload contains scope and role information, as well as details regarding the token's generation time and its expiration time.

```
{
  "sub": "1234567890",
  "name": "John Doe",
  "iat": 1516239022
}
```

- Signature

  This part is a crucial component of the JWT that serves the
  purpose of verifying the authenticity of the sender and ensuring
  the integrity of the payload. To generate the signature, the header
  and the payload parts are encoded in base64 format. The resulting
  encoded strings are then combined and signed using the specified
  signature algorithm from the header, using a private key. This
  process ensures that the signature can be validated using the
  corresponding public key to verify the integrity and origin of
  the JWT.

  The signature would be the following:

```
HMACSHA256(
    base64UrlEncode(header) + "." +
    base64UrlEncode(payload),
    256 bit secret
)
```

# Setting Up Authentication Using AWS Amplify

In this section, we will dive into the practical aspect and demonstrate the integration of
AWS Amplify Auth in our application. We will write code to implement this integration
and make our application ready for authentication using AWS Amplify.

Upon completion of this section, we will accomplish the following objectives:

1.  Creation of public and private pages: We will establish distinct
    pages in our application, some of which will be accessible to the
    public, while others will require authentication to access.

2.  Implementation of a sign-up page: Users will be able to register
    themselves by providing the necessary information, enabling
    them to create an account within our application.

3.  Development of a login page: Users will have the ability to log in
    and log out of their accounts securely, allowing them to access
    restricted features and personalized content.

4.  Provision of a manage password page: Users will be provided
    with a dedicated page where they can change their passwords,
    ensuring they have control over their account's security.

By accomplishing these tasks, we will have successfully integrated AWS Amplify
Auth into our application, enhancing its functionality and security through user
authentication and account management features.

---

**Note**   Prior to proceeding, please ensure that you have completed the setup
section outlined in the first chapter and that your machine is configured with AWS
Amplify. If you haven't done so yet, kindly follow the provided steps to set up AWS
Amplify before continuing from this point. It is important to have the necessary
configurations in place to ensure a smooth integration process. Once you have
completed the setup, you can resume the following steps.

---

# Creating Our React App

To initiate the development of a React application, we will employ the create-react-app
CLI, which offers a streamlined approach for setting up the project structure. By utilizing
this tool, we can create a foundation for our React app and subsequently enhance it with
additional features and functionalities.

```
npx create-react-app react-authentication
```

Upon executing the aforementioned command, a rudimentary "Hello World"
React application will be generated. This initial setup will encompass all the essential
configurations needed for running and building the application.

Once the repository is established, navigate to the corresponding directory, and we
can commence with the configuration of the authentication system.

```
cd react-authentication
```

To launch the React application, you can execute the script provided as follows. This
script will initiate the necessary processes to start the app and make it accessible for
interaction.

```
npm start
```

You can now open your web browser and enter the following URL in the address bar: `http://localhost:3000`. By doing so, you will be directed to the main page of the React application index page. Figure 2-3 illustrates the index page.

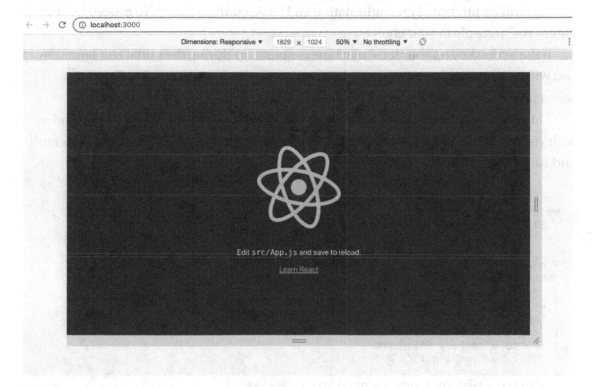

*Figure 2-3.* *The default index page of the newly generated React application*

# Configuring the Backend for Our React Application

Now that we have our web app up and running, we need to set up the necessary infrastructure and services that enable functionalities like login, logout, and user creation. We will leverage the power of AWS Amplify to streamline this process effectively.

To begin, navigate to the root directory of your project and execute the following command:

```
amplify init
```

Running this command will initiate the creation of a new app within AWS Amplify. This step is crucial as it prepares the backend infrastructure required for your application.

You will be prompted for confirmation and basic configurations. To proceed, simply enter "yes" to confirm your choices.

If the accessKey on your local machine is not set up during the initial configuration, you will be prompted to select an authentication method. As depicted in Figure 2-4, select the "AWS access keys" option.

This authentication method allows your local machine to establish communication with your authorized AWS account, enabling you to utilize Amplify services such as auth and REST API.

```
→  react-amplified git:(master) ✗ amplify init
Note: It is recommended to run this command from the root of your app directory
? Enter a name for the project reactauthentication
The following configuration will be applied:

Project information
| Name: reactauthentication
| Environment: dev
| Default editor: Visual Studio Code
| App type: javascript
| Javascript framework: react
| Source Directory Path: src
| Distribution Directory Path: build
| Build Command: npm run-script build
| Start Command: npm run-script start

? Initialize the project with the above configuration? Yes
Using default provider  awscloudformation
? Select the authentication method you want to use: (Use arrow keys)
❯ AWS profile
  AWS access keys
```

**Figure 2-4.** *The options provided by the init command to choose from*

Provide the authentication method you wish to use, if you have followed instructions in Chapter 1, you can select **AWS profile** option and select the profile you created, else you can select **AWS access keys** options and then enter the "accessKeyId" and "secretAccessKey" that you configured in Chapter 1, as shown in Figure 2-5. These credentials will authenticate your local machine and allow it to securely access and consume Amplify services.

```
? Initialize the project with the above configuration? Yes
Using default provider  awscloudformation
? Select the authentication method you want to use: AWS access keys
? accessKeyId:  ******************
? secretAccessKey:  **************************************
? region: ap-southeast-1
Adding backend environment dev to AWS Amplify Console app: d1oiz66742347w
: Initializing project in the cloud...
```

***Figure 2-5.*** *Entering the access key and secret key to authenticate the app*

These changes include the creation of an "amplify" directory, which contains all the necessary code to regenerate your backend infrastructure on AWS. As you continue to add more services such as Auth, REST API, and GraphQL, this directory will automatically expand, and any changes made to it should be committed to your Git repository. This approach exemplifies the concept of Infrastructure as Code (IaC), where your infrastructure can be easily replicated across different AWS accounts.

Once the Amplify CLI successfully initializes the backend for your new React application, several changes are made to your project repository. The changes are as follows:

1. A directory with the name "amplify" got created, which contains all the necessary code to regenerate your backend infrastructure and configurations in AWS. As you continue to add more services such as Auth, REST API, and GraphQL, this directory will grow automatically, and any changes made to it should be committed to your Git repository. This approach exemplifies the concept of Infrastructure as Code (IaC), where your infrastructure can be easily replicated across different AWS accounts.

   To illustrate this, let's consider a scenario where you have two different AWS accounts: one for basic proof of concept (POC) and testing and another for a different business or company's account. If you wish to recreate the Amplify app in the latter account, you simply need to update the access keys and secrets, and all the code within the amplify directory will replicate the Amplify services in the new AWS account. This future-proof approach ensures seamless deployment and management of your infrastructure.

2.  The Amplify CLI generates an "aws-export.js" file in the "src" directory, which contains all the necessary configurations for your services. It is important to avoid modifying any of the generated code directly. Instead, utilize the Amplify CLI to add or remove services, which will automatically update these files accordingly.

**Note**   Please do not modify any of these generated codes. We will use the Amplify CLI to add or remove services, and those will be added automatically to these files.

If you wish to view your Amplify app, you can log in to your AWS account and navigate to the Amplify service from the list of available services, as illustrated in Figure 2-6. There, you will find a detailed overview and management interface for your Amplify backend.

Congratulations on reaching this milestone!

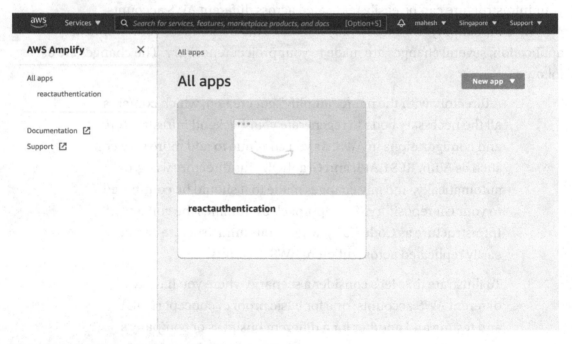

**Figure 2-6.**  *The Amplify app in the AWS console*

Now, let's proceed with setting up the authentication for your application.

# Setting Up Authentication

When setting up authentication for an application, there are several important components that need to be considered. Here is a list of the components required for a comprehensive authentication setup:

1. User management: Authentication revolves around allowing a predefined list of users to access the system. User management involves functionalities like user creation, blocking or removing users when necessary.

2. Role management: Different types of users may require different levels of access to resources. Role management allows the definition of roles and their assignment to users, ensuring appropriate access controls.

3. Registration link: To streamline user onboarding, it is essential to provide a registration feature where users can self-register. This eliminates the need for manual onboarding by administrators.

4. Unique identifier: Each user needs a unique identifier, such as an email, phone number, or username, to distinguish them from others. Verification of email or phone numbers can be done by sending a code for users to confirm their validity.

5. Login link: Users should have a secure login mechanism where they can authenticate themselves and receive a token or validation upon successful login.

6. Forget/reset password: As users are the owners of their passwords, the authentication system should provide options for password reset or generation as needed.

7. Logout: It is important to have a mechanism for users to terminate their active sessions or revoke the issued tokens if they wish to log out.

AWS Amplify provides all these features out of the box. It leverages Amazon Cognito, an authentication service for applications, to handle authentication-related functionalities. Cognito also offers a user interface dashboard for managing and monitoring user activities. By utilizing Amplify and Cognito, developers can easily implement a robust and secure authentication system for their applications.

Let's set up the authentication for our application.

# Creating an Auth Service

To add the authentication service to our app using Amplify, we can run the following command:

```
amplify add auth
```

As shown in Figure 2-7, this command will prompt us to configure the authentication settings for our app. We can choose the default configuration or customize based on our requirements. Amplify supports various authentication mechanisms such as username and password, social sign-in, multifactor authentication, and more. We can select the desired options during the configuration process.

```
→  react-amplified git:(master) ✗ amplify add auth
Using service: Cognito, provided by: awscloudformation

The current configured provider is Amazon Cognito.

Do you want to use the default authentication and security configuration? Default configuration with Social
Provider (Federation)
Warning: you will not be able to edit these selections.
How do you want users to be able to sign in? Username
Do you want to configure advanced settings? No, I am done.
What domain name prefix do you want to use? reactauthentication24f1ce07-24f1ce07
Enter your redirect signin URI: http://localhost:3000/
? Do you want to add another redirect signin URI No
Enter your redirect signout URI: http://localhost:3000/
? Do you want to add another redirect signout URI No
Select the social providers you want to configure for your user pool: Google

You've opted to allow users to authenticate via Google.  If you haven't already, you'll need to go to https
://developers.google.com/identi
ty and create an App ID.

Enter your Google Web Client ID for your OAuth flow:  7248322138-3tanld3cdq63s7njk87o5142jsqb4dha.apps.goog
leusercontent.com
Enter your Google Web Client Secret for your OAuth flow:  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
Successfully added auth resource reactauthentication24f1ce07 locally

Some next steps:
"amplify push" will build all your local backend resources and provision it in the cloud
"amplify publish" will build all your local backend and frontend resources (if you have hosting category add
ed) and provision it in the cloud
```

***Figure 2-7.*** *Options prompted by the CLI after the auth service add command is entered*

Once the authentication service is added, Amplify will automatically generate the necessary backend resources and update the relevant configuration files in the project.

Please expand the `amplify` directory in the root of your application; you will see auth being added in `/amplify/backend`.

To push the authentication configuration to our app on the cloud, we can use the Amplify CLI. Run the following command:

```
amplify push
```

During the execution of the `amplify push` command, AWS Amplify utilizes AWS CloudFormation to create the necessary infrastructure in the AWS cloud. CloudFormation is an AWS service that allows you to define and provision AWS resources using a declarative template.

By using CloudFormation, Amplify ensures that the infrastructure is created consistently. It automates the process of setting up the authentication service and its associated resources, such as user pools and identity pools, in a reliable and scalable manner.

---

**Note**   It is important to commit the changes made in the amplify directory, by the CLI. This directory contains the generated code and configuration files that define the infrastructure and services created by Amplify. By versioning the amplify directory along with your application code, you can track and manage the changes made to both the application and its underlying infrastructure. This approach ensures that the infrastructure and services are synchronized with your application code, making it easier to collaborate with other developers, revert changes if needed, and maintain a consistent deployment environment. Now, let's proceed by exploring some additional Amplify capabilities of React components to enhance our application further.

---

# Amplify UI React Components

The Amplify team has also published some React components to speed up the front development and integration with this service.

To streamline the frontend development and integration with the Amplify service, the Amplify team has provided a set of React components.

Let's begin by adding the necessary npm package to our application, by running the following command:

```
npm install aws-amplify @aws-amplify/ui-react
```

Once the package installation is complete, we can proceed to connect our React application with the Amplify backend. Let's now connect our React app with the Amplify backend.

Open the `index.js` file located in the `src` directory and call the `configure` function. This function will handle the configuration of the React app, ensuring that it is connected to the appropriate backend service. Open the index.js in the src directory and call the configure function. This will take care of pointing the React app to the correct backend service.

```
import { Amplify } from "aws-amplify";
import awsExports from './aws-exports'

Amplify.configure(awsExports);
```

## What If aws-exports Is Not Found?

Please note the aws-exports file will only be created after at least once the amplify push command is run. If you don't find the aws-exports file, please run the push command.

If you cannot find the `aws-exports.js` file in your project, it is likely because it has not been generated yet. This file is created after running the `amplify push` command at least once.

To generate the `aws-exports.js` file, please follow these steps:

1. Open your terminal or command prompt.

2. Navigate to the root directory of your project.

3. Run the following command: `amplify push`.

This command will deploy the backend resources defined in your Amplify project and generate the necessary configuration files, including the `aws-exports.js` file. Once the command completes successfully, you should be able to locate the `aws-exports.js` file in the `src` directory.

Note that the `amplify push` command should be run whenever you make changes to your Amplify backend configuration and want to deploy those changes to your AWS environment.

We have imported the AWS-amplify library which we installed and the AWS-export config file to point our app to amplify the backend.

And that's all we need to do for connecting our frontend app with the Amplify backend.

# Integrating Auth with React App

The AWS Amplify not only simplifies the process of creating the backend services for your application but also provides ready-to-use UI components that can be easily integrated into your React app.

## Login and Registration UI Components

By using these UI components, you don't have to build the authentication screens or components from scratch. Instead, you can leverage the prebuilt components provided by AWS Amplify to handle the user registration, login, and other functionalities.

To integrate the AWS Amplify login UI component into your React app, you can follow these steps:

**STEP 1:** Import the required component into your main app's file, typically `App.js`:

```
import { withAuthenticator } from '@aws-amplify/ui-react'
```

**STEP 2:** Wrap your main app component with the `withAuthenticator` higher-order component (HOC).

```
export default withAuthenticator(App);
```

**STEP 3:** Add the CSS file if you want to use the default styles and theme by AWS team. Add the following import command in your App.js file `import '@aws-amplify/ui-react/styles.css'`.

By wrapping your App component with withAuthenticator, you enable the authentication flow and automatically render the login UI component in your app.

---

**Note**   What is HOC?

A higher-order component (HOC) is a function that takes a component and returns a new component with additional functionality. It allows you to enhance or modify the behavior of a component without changing its underlying implementation.

---

In the context of React, an HOC is used to add or wrap a component with additional logic, state, or props. It helps in reusing code and separating concerns by abstracting common functionality into a separate function.

```
import React from 'react';

//HOC that adds a new prop extraProp
const withExtraProps = (Component) => {
    return class extends React.Component {
        render() {
            return <Component {...this.props} extraProp="Hii" />;
        }
    }
}

// The component that will receive the extraProp
const MyComponent = (props) => {
    return <div>{props.extraProp}</div>
}

export const WrappedComponent = withExtraProps(MyComponent)
```

**STEP 3:** Run the app.

```
npm start
```

As you launch the application, you will be presented with a login screen without having to create a separate login page or UI component. This login screen is provided by AWS Amplify, making it easy to incorporate authentication functionality into your app. Figure 2-8 provides a preview of the login screen, showcasing its appearance and layout.

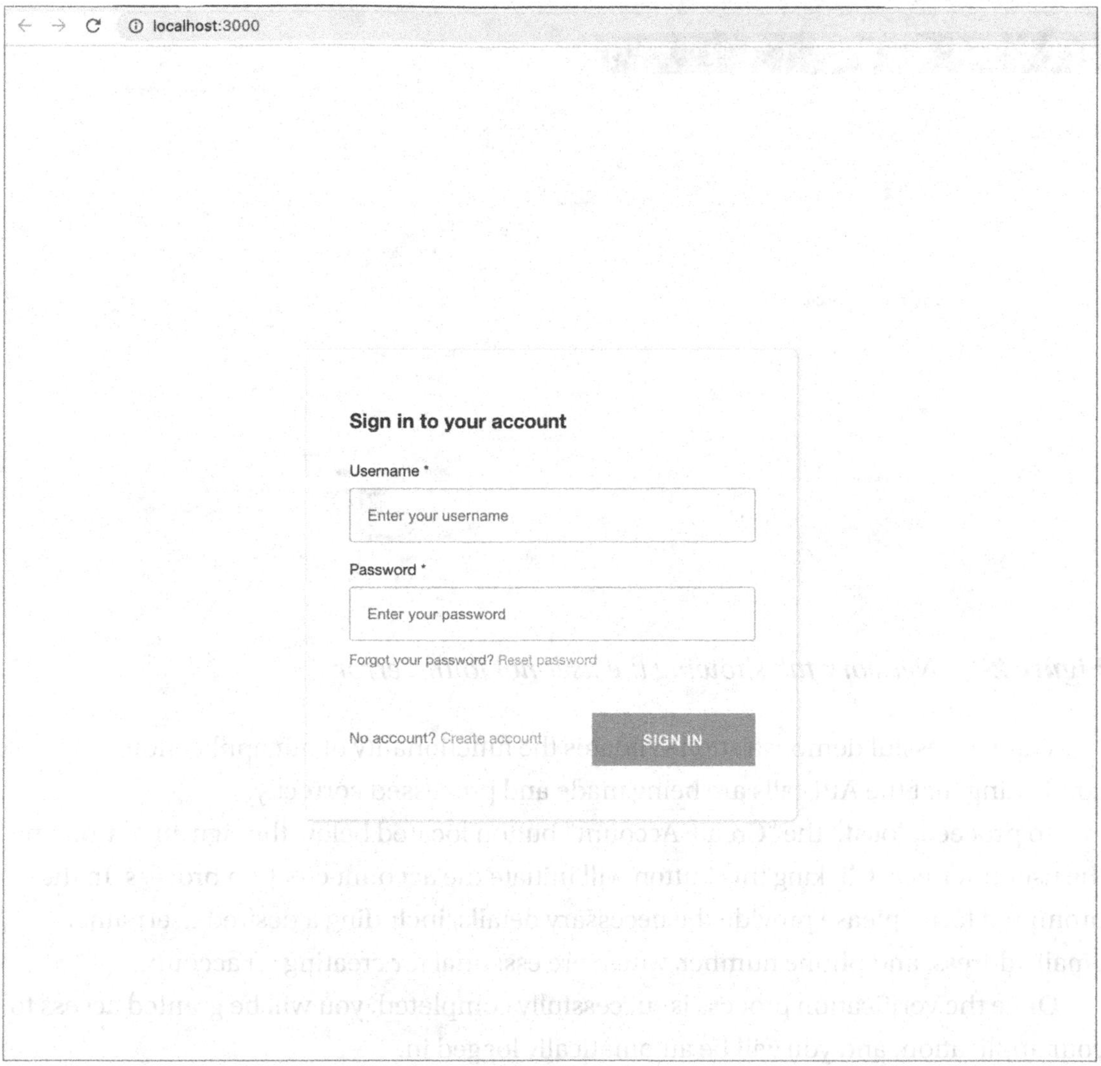

*Figure 2-8.* *The preview of the login screen for private pages*

Since we haven't created any users yet, a successful login won't be possible at this stage. However, you can still test the connection with the backend system by entering a random login ID and password. This should result in a "user not found" exception, indicating that the authentication process failed. Additionally, you can open the Network tab in your browser's developer tools to inspect the API call and response, gaining further insights into the authentication process; this is shown in Figure 2-9.

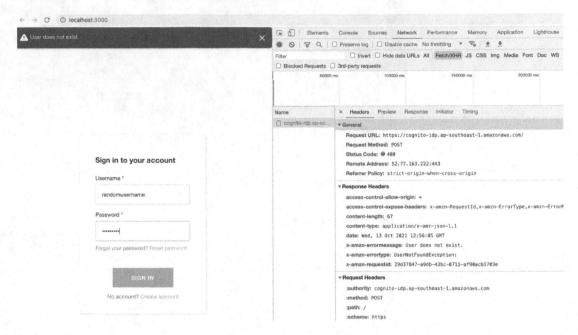

***Figure 2-9.*** *Network tab showing the user not found error*

This successful demonstration validates the functionality of our application, confirming that the API calls are being made and processed correctly.

To proceed, locate the "Create Account" button located below the sign-in button on the user interface. Clicking this button will initiate the account creation process. In the prompted form, please provide the necessary details, including a desired username, email address, and phone number, which are essential for creating an account.

Once the verification process is successfully completed, you will be granted access to your application, and you will be automatically logged in.

Congratulations on successfully creating your account and accessing your application.

## Logout UI

Once you have successfully logged in, you may notice that there is no visible "log out" button or option available. To enable the logout functionality, you have a couple of options.

Firstly, you can create a custom header component for your application that includes a profile section and a logout button, which triggers the logout API. This approach allows for more flexibility and customization according to your application's design and requirements.

Alternatively, AWS Amplify provides a prebuilt UI React component specifically for the logout functionality. By utilizing this component, you can easily integrate the logout feature into your application without the need for extensive coding. To add the logout UI component from AWS Amplify, follow these steps:

**STEP 1:** Import the Button component from the Amplify library.

```
import { Button } from "@aws-amplify/ui-react";
```

**STEP 2:** Add this imported button component in the app.js file and get the function to signOut as parameter in App passed by withAuthenticator HOC.

```
04: import { withAuthenticator } from '@aws-amplify/ui-react'
05: import { Button } from "@aws-amplify/ui-react";
06: import '@aws-amplify/ui-react/styles.css'
07: function App({ signOut }) {
08:   return (
09:    <div className="App">
10:     <Button onClick={ signOut }>Sign out</Button>
```

After you have logged in, the logout UI component will be rendered, as shown in Figure 2-10.

***Figure 2-10.***  *React application with logout component from the library*

By clicking the logout button, which calls the signOut function, the user will be successfully logged out, and the application will navigate back to the login screen.

The signOut component takes care of clearing the authentication information from the browser and handling the navigation back to the login screen.

# Logging In and Logging Out

After integrating the Amplify UI React component, which automatically generates the login UI and provides functionality for logging in and logging out, let's explore what happens behind the scenes. As mentioned earlier, to authenticate successfully, the client application needs a valid JWT access token, which will be used for future API requests from the frontend.

To understand where the generated tokens are stored, we can inspect the browser's developer tools. To do this, right-click the web page, select "Inspect," and navigate to the "Application" tab. Under the "Storage" section, click "Local storage." Here, you will be able to see the relevant information, including the storage of tokens, as shown in Figure 2-11.

***Figure 2-11.*** *View of local storage in the browser*

1.  If you are not logged in, please log in.

2.  The item with key `userData`, contains information about the currently logged-in user.

3.  The item with key `accessToken`, represents the JWT access token, generated by AWS Cognito. Additionally, there are other items such as `refreshToken` and `idToken`, which are also relevant tokens as discussed under the section of Auth2.0 protocols.

To further examine the contents of the access token, please copy the token value. Then, open a web browser and navigate to jwt.io. And paste the access token as illustrated in Figure 2-12.

51

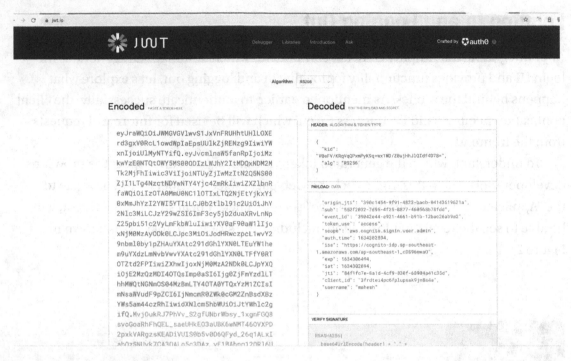

***Figure 2-12.*** *The decoding of the JWT token*

As shown in Figure 2-13, you can open the Cognito service in your AWS account and navigate to the list of users. There, you will find the users who have registered and interacted with your application through the authentication flow. The Cognito service provides a comprehensive dashboard for managing and monitoring user accounts and their associated information.

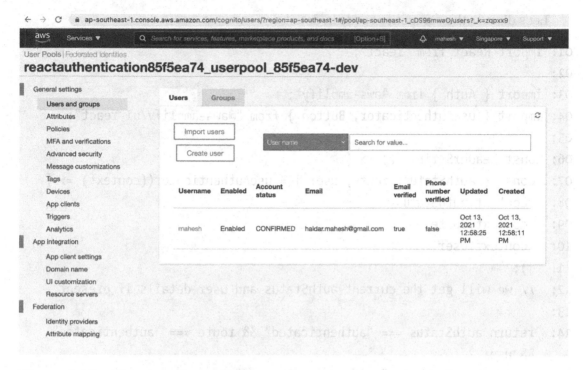

*Figure 2-13.* *The users list in AWS console*

# Getting Logged-In User Information

To display the username of the logged-in user in the header of our app, we will create a new React component called HeaderStrip. This component will be responsible for retrieving the user information and rendering the username.

Here are the steps to implement this:

1. Create a new file named HeaderStrip.js in the src directory.

2. Inside the component, import the necessary dependencies.

3. Add the logic to read the auth information for logged-in users.

Let's discuss the component code in detail.

```
01: import React from "react";
02:
03: import { Auth } from "aws-amplify";
04: import { useAuthenticator, Button } from "@aws-amplify/ui-react";
05:
06: const HeaderStrip = () => {
07:   const { authStatus, route, user } = useAuthenticator((context) => [
08:     context.authStatus,
09:     context.route,
10:     context.user,
11:   ]);
12:   // we will get the current authStatus and user details if present
13:
14:   return authStatus === "authenticated" && route === "authenticated"
       && user ? (
15:     <div className="App">
16:       Hi {user.username}
17:       <div style={{ width: "20%" }}>
18:         <Button
19:           onClick={async () => {
20:             await Auth.signOut();
21:           }}
22:         >
23:           Sign out
24:         </Button>
25:       </div>
26:     </div>
27:   ) : null;
28: };
29:
30: export default HeaderStrip;
31:
```

**LINE 7:** We are using useAuthenticator hook to get the current authState, route and details of the user.

Indeed, the different auth statuses provided by Amplify, such as "configuring", "authenticated" and "unauthenticated", allow us to identify and handle various user statuses within our application flow. The useAuthenticator hook exports the auth route context such as "authenticated", "confirmResetPassword", "confirmSignIn", "confirmSignUp", "confirmVerifyUser", "forceNewPassword", "idle", "resetPassword", and few others which helps us to control and customize the state of the application in the granular levels. These authStates and routes play a crucial role in determining the appropriate actions and rendering the corresponding UI components based on the current user state.

For example, when a user attempts to create an account, the signUp auth route is triggered. This enables us to display the necessary registration form and handle the registration process accordingly.

Similarly, when a user logs out, the signOut auth route is activated. In response, we can redirect the user to the login page or display a message indicating a successful logout.

On the other hand, when a user successfully logs in, the signIn auth route is triggered. This allows us to customize the user interface and provide access to authenticated features specific to logged-in users.

By leveraging these different auth statuses and routes, we can create a dynamic user flow that adapts to the current authentication status, enhancing the user experience and ensuring the application functions appropriately in each scenario.

**LINE 10:** We will get the current user's basic details from auth like username, phone number, etc., and store in variable user.

**LINE 14:** We check if the authStatus and route is "authenticated", we render the username.

**LINE 18-20:** We are rendering a sign out button if the user is authenticated, and calling the function signOut from Auth if this button is clicked.

```
JS App.js  M  ✕

src > JS App.js > ◌ App

                                                      > dropd

      You, 2 minutes ago | 2 authors (Mahesh Haldar and others)
1     import logo from "./logo.svg";
2     import "./App.css";
3     import { withAuthenticator } from "@aws-amplify/ui-react";
4     import HeaderStrip from "./components/HeaderStrip";
5
6     function App() {
7       return (
8         <div className="App">
9           <HeaderStrip />         You, a minute ago • Uncommitted changes
10          <header className="App-header">
11            <img src={logo} className="App-logo" alt="logo" />
```

*Figure 2-14.  Implementation of the HeaderStrip component*

**LINE 9:** Render the HeaderStrip component so that the logic of reading the user data and auth state can run, and we can show the logged-in username.

Congratulations! You have successfully implemented the functionality to read the logged-in user information; this is illustrated in Figure 2-15. By utilizing the Amplify authentication service and integrating it with your React app, you can now retrieve and display relevant user data such as the username, phone number, and other details.

This achievement allows you to enhance the user experience by personalizing the application based on the logged-in user's information. You can now customize the app's content, features, and interactions based on the specific user who is accessing the application.

By being able to read the logged-in user information, you have taken a significant step toward building a secure and user-friendly authentication system within your React app.

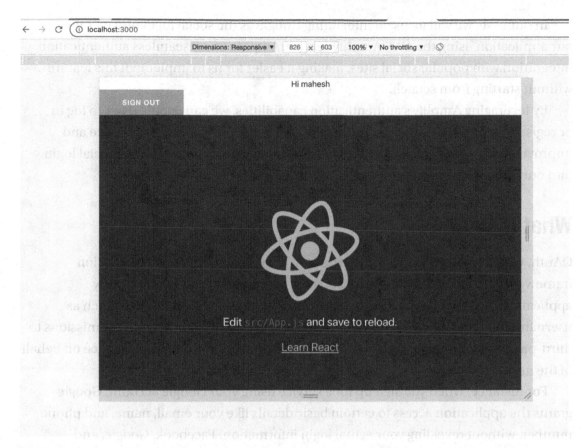

**Figure 2-15.** *The name of the logged-in user is shown in the implemented header strip*

Let us now proceed with implementing the social login feature in our application. This functionality allows users to log in using their social media accounts, such as Google, Facebook, or Amazon. By integrating social login, we can enhance the user experience and provide users with alternative authentication options.

# OAuth Social Login

Indeed, social login has become a common and convenient way for users to access various online applications. It eliminates the need for repetitive form filling by allowing users to log in or register using their existing social media accounts, such as Google, Facebook, Amazon, or Apple.

In our case, we will focus on integrating Google as the social login provider into our application using the AWS Amplify service. Amplify offers seamless authentication integration with popular social sites, making it easier for us to implement this feature without starting from scratch.

By leveraging Amplify's authentication capabilities, we can enable users to log in or register using their Google accounts, enhancing the onboarding experience and improving user convenience. Let's proceed with the integration of Google social login into our authentication app.

# What Is OAuth?

OAuth, which stands for Open Authorization, is a widely accepted authorization framework that facilitates the secure access of user information by third-party applications, without the need for users to disclose their login credentials, such as usernames and passwords. This framework allows users to grant specific permissions to third-party apps, enabling them to access limited data from a particular service on behalf of the user.

For instance, when you sign up for a service using your Google account, Google grants the application access to certain basic details like your email, name, and phone number, without revealing your actual login information. Facebook, Google, and GitHub are prominent examples of companies that have developed APIs (application programming interfaces) for other applications to leverage as authentication methods.

The OAuth protocol is openly available, and anyone can build APIs following its standardized specifications, as outlined in the publicly accessible RFC (Request for Comments) documentation. This allows developers to implement OAuth-based authentication in their applications and integrate with popular service providers for streamlined and secure user authentication.

There are different types of OAuth2.0 flows, though we will discuss one most commonly used when the authorization server is a third party, in our case Google.

Figure 2-16 illustrates the sequence of the OAuth2.0.

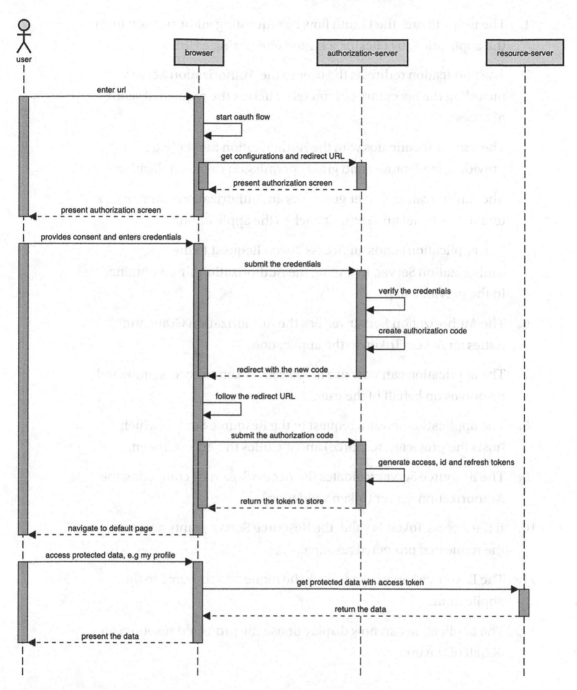

***Figure 2-16.***   *The high-level OAuth2.0 sequence flow*

1. The user initiates the OAuth flow by requesting authorization from the application, by clicking a button or entering a URL.

2. The application redirects the user to the Authorization Server, including the necessary parameters, such as the requested scope of access.

3. The user authenticates with the Authorization Server (e.g., providing credentials) and grants permission to the application.

4. The Authorization Server generates an Authorization Grant (e.g., a temporary code) and sends it back to the application.

5. The application sends an Access Token Request to the Authorization Server, including the Authorization Grant obtained in the previous step.

6. The Authorization Server verifies the Authorization Grant and issues an Access Token to the application.

7. The application can now use the Access Token to access protected resources on behalf of the user.

8. The application sends a request to the Resource Server (which hosts the protected resource) and includes the Access Token.

9. The Resource Server validates the Access Token by contacting the Authorization Server (token validation).

10. If the Access Token is valid, the Resource Server grants access to the requested protected resource.

11. The Resource Server sends back the requested resource to the application.

12. The application can now display or use the protected resource on behalf of the user.

This sequence diagram provides a high-level overview of the interactions between the user, application, Authorization Server, and Resource Server in the OAuth 2.0 flow. It showcases the delegation of authorization and the secure exchange of tokens to enable access to protected resources.

To integrate the social login with Google in our application, we are treating the auth server of Google as our authorization server, where we need to register our application, and our application's URL as a redirect URL, so that on successful authentication the user can be navigated back to our application.

Let's start with creating an application in Google Cloud to implement social login.

**STEP 1:** Create a Google app.

Go to `https://console.cloud.google.com/` and log in with a Google ID – as shown in Figure 2-17, you will see a similar dashboard – and click the highlighted drop-down.

***Figure 2-17.** Dashboard after logging in to the Google Cloud console*

**STEP 2:** Click New Project from the modal on the top-right corner, as shown in Figure 2-18, and enter the project name.

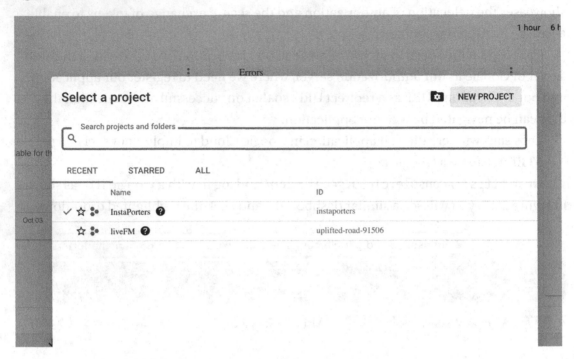

***Figure 2-18.*** *Modal to show the list of projects and create a new project*

**STEP 3:** Enter a valid project name and choose No organisation, if there is none, and click Create as shown in Figure 2-19.

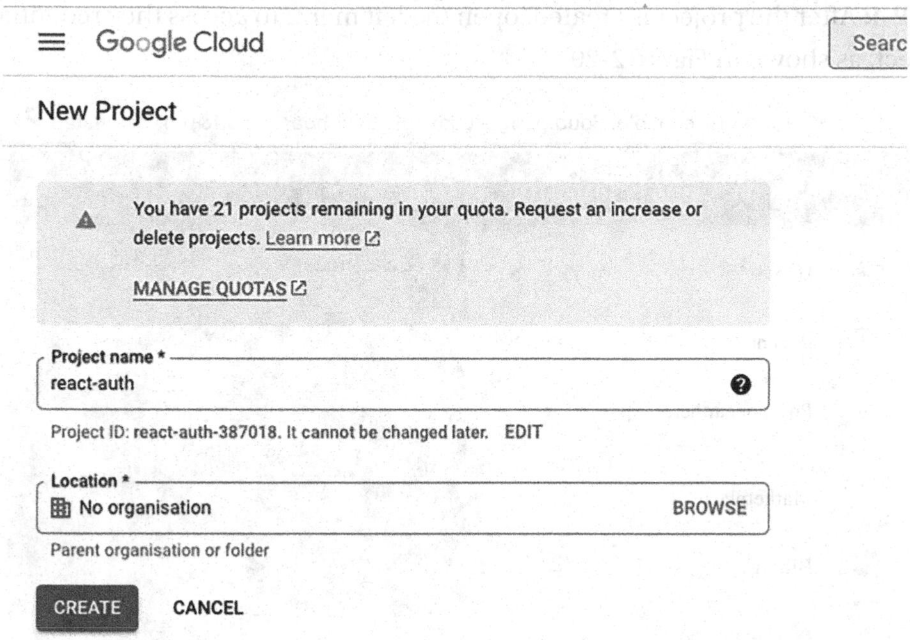


***Figure 2-19.** Create new project screen*

**STEP 4:** After the project is created, open the left menu to access the credentials of the project, as shown in Figure 2-20.

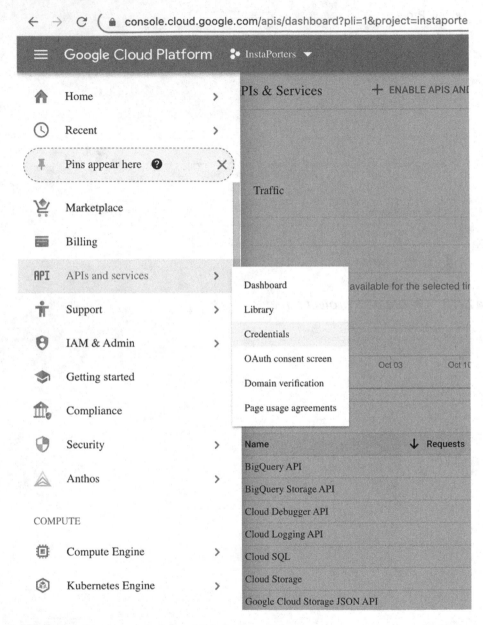

***Figure 2-20.*** *Menu to access the API credentials*

You might have no API keys and no client IDs; we will require to create a new set.

**STEP 5:** Creating the OAuth consent screenTo integrate Google as the social login provider in our application, we need to set up an OAuth consent screen. The OAuth consent screen is an important step in the OAuth 2.0 flow as it informs the user about the application's basic information and the user details that Google will provide to the third-party application. It ensures transparency and allows the user to give consent before providing their credentials.

As shown in Figure 2-21, choose the user type, and click Create. In the next screen, provide the app information and upload a logo and domain.

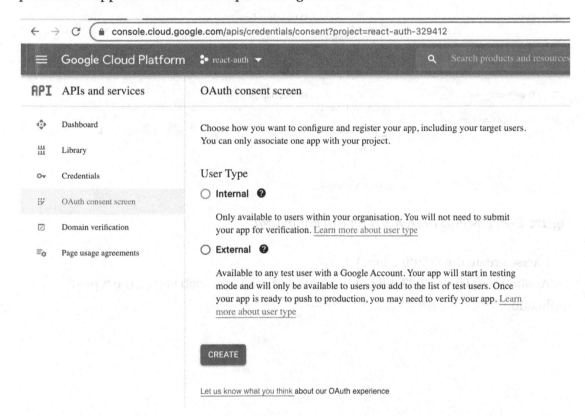

***Figure 2-21.***  *Creating the OAuth consent screen*

**STEP 6:** Creating the OAuth client ID

Follow Credentials from the left menu and click Create Credentials on top, as shown in Figure 2-22.

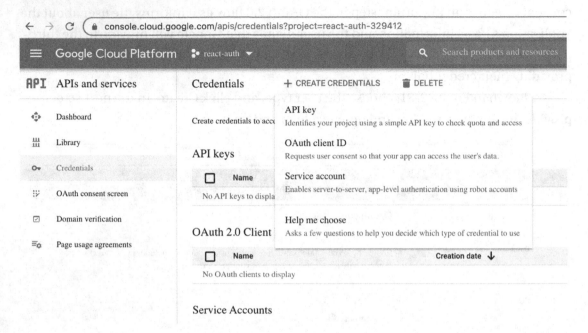

***Figure 2-22.*** *Menu to create a type of credential*

Please create the OAuth client ID.

As shown in Figure 2-23, fill out the form and select the web app as the type of application.

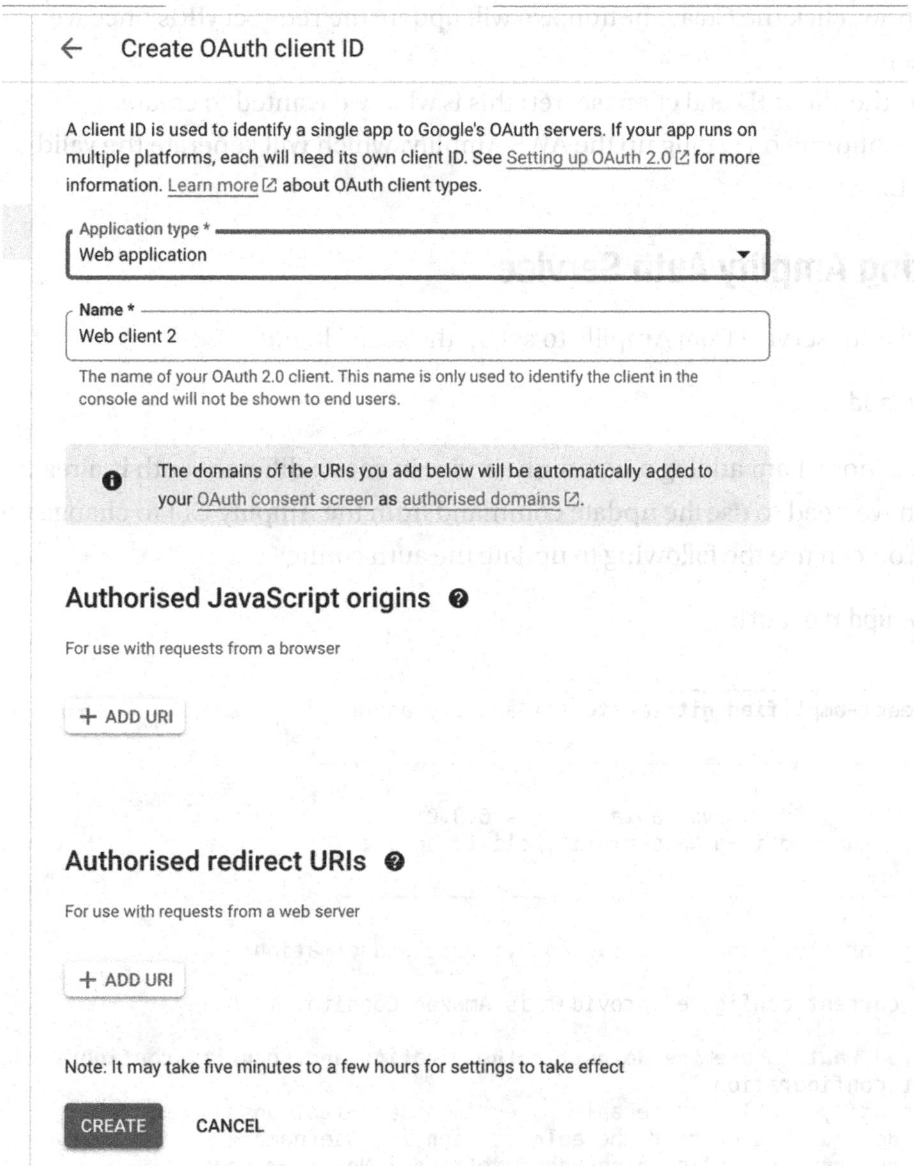

←     Create OAuth client ID

A client ID is used to identify a single app to Google's OAuth servers. If your app runs on multiple platforms, each will need its own client ID. See Setting up OAuth 2.0 ☑ for more information. Learn more ☑ about OAuth client types.

Application type *
Web application                                         ▼

Name *
Web client 2

The name of your OAuth 2.0 client. This name is only used to identify the client in the console and will not be shown to end users.

ℹ    The domains of the URIs you add below will be automatically added to your OAuth consent screen as authorised domains ☑.

## Authorised JavaScript origins ❓

For use with requests from a browser

＋ ADD URI

## Authorised redirect URIs ❓

For use with requests from a web server

＋ ADD URI

Note: It may take five minutes to a few hours for settings to take effect

CREATE     CANCEL

***Figure 2-23.*** *Creating OAuth client ID form*

We need to add the redirect URIs in the Google client app to let Google know which servers are allowed to log in. Once we add the auth configuration in Amplify, we will get the app URLs; we will use these URLs to add to the Google app.

For now, click the Create button; we will update the redirect URIs once we have them.

Copy the client ID and client secret; this is what we wanted to create.

Let's continue on setting up the AWS Amplify, which will generate the valid AWS URL.

## Updating Amplify Auth Service

Let's add auth service from Amplify to set up the social login:

```
amplify add auth
```

Please note, I am adding a new auth service in case a different auth is already set up, and then we need to use the update command from the Amplify CLI to change the auth config. You can use the following to update the auth config:

```
amplify update auth
```

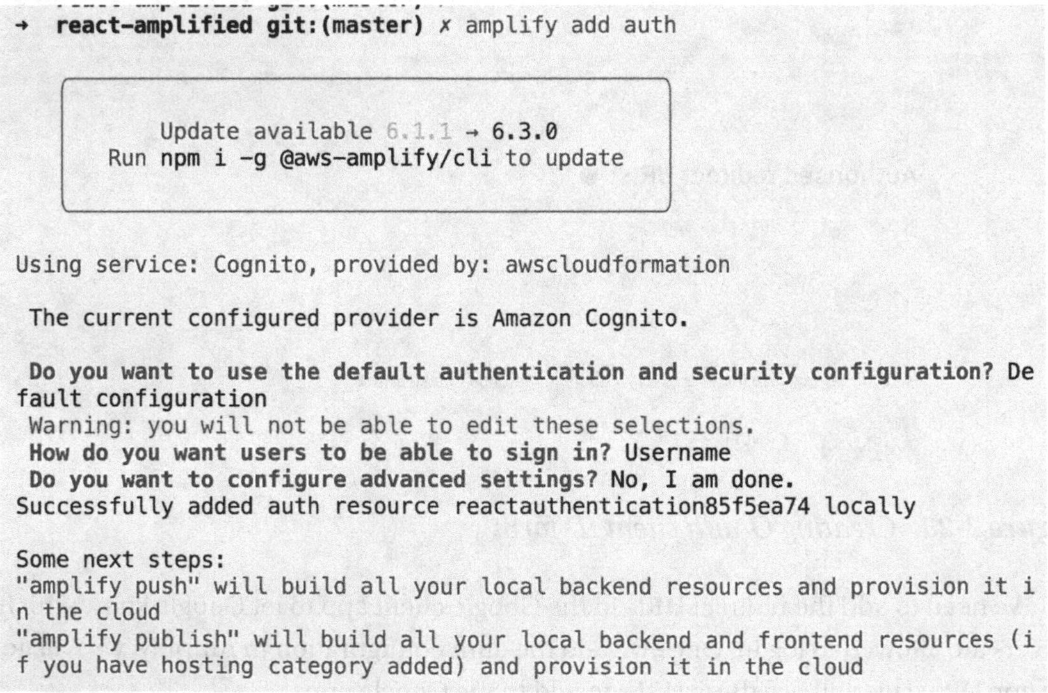

```
→  react-amplified git:(master) ✗ amplify add auth


        Update available 6.1.1 → 6.3.0
     Run npm i -g @aws-amplify/cli to update


Using service: Cognito, provided by: awscloudformation

 The current configured provider is Amazon Cognito.

 Do you want to use the default authentication and security configuration? De
fault configuration
 Warning: you will not be able to edit these selections.
 How do you want users to be able to sign in? Username
 Do you want to configure advanced settings? No, I am done.
Successfully added auth resource reactauthentication85f5ea74 locally

Some next steps:
"amplify push" will build all your local backend resources and provision it i
n the cloud
"amplify publish" will build all your local backend and frontend resources (i
f you have hosting category added) and provision it in the cloud
```

*Figure 2-24.* *Amplify add auth options*

Follow the options from the menus.

As we are going to run the application on localhost, we have added `http://localhost:3000/` as a redirect URI for sign-in and sign-out.

Select Google as the social provider.

Enter the client ID and secret generated on console.google.com when we created the OAuth client.

Let's push the configuration to our AWS cloud:

```
amplify push
```

## Adding the Redirect URIs

Once successful, our social login setup is done from the backend Amplify perspective; now we need to tell Google which URLs are allowed to log in or use these credentials to log in.

```
ion::Stack Wed Nov 10 2021 14:55:38 GMT+0530 (India Standard Time)
UPDATE_COMPLETE                  apitodos                        AWS::CloudFormat
ion::Stack Wed Nov 10 2021 14:55:39 GMT+0530 (India Standard Time)
UPDATE_COMPLETE                  functiontodosfunction           AWS::CloudFormat
ion::Stack Wed Nov 10 2021 14:55:39 GMT+0530 (India Standard Time)
⁝ Updating resources in the cloud. This may take a few minutes...

UPDATE_COMPLETE functioncreateTodos              AWS::CloudFormation::Stack Wed Nov 1
0 2021 14:55:40 GMT+0530 (India Standard Time)
UPDATE_COMPLETE amplify-reactauthentication-dev-175519 AWS::CloudFormation::Stack Wed Nov 1
0 2021 14:55:40 GMT+0530 (India Standard Time)
✓ All resources are updated in the cloud

Hosted UI Endpoint: https://reactauthenticationa10272a0-a10272a0-dev.auth.ap-southeast-1.am
azoncognito.com/
Test Your Hosted UI Endpoint: https://reactauthenticationa10272a0-a10272a0-dev.auth.ap-sout
heast-1.amazoncognito.com/login?response_type=code&client_id=7c2r9i5hvdp5g9ocapokm83bs4&red
irect_uri=http://localhost:3000/
```

*Figure 2-25.* *The hosted UI endpoints after the successful amplify push*

Copy the first URL generated by AWS Amplify from the console.

Go to Credentials and open the OAuth2.0 client we created, as illustrated in Figure 2-26.

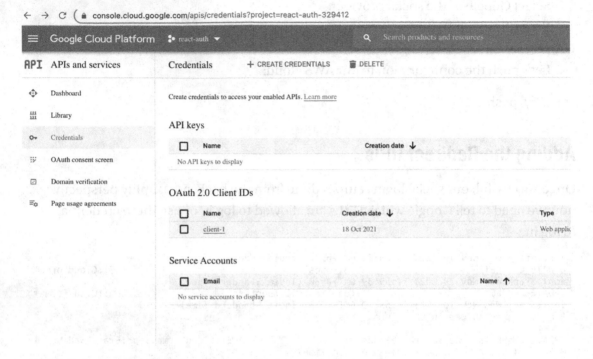

***Figure 2-26.*** *The OAuth2.0 client ID created a while ago*

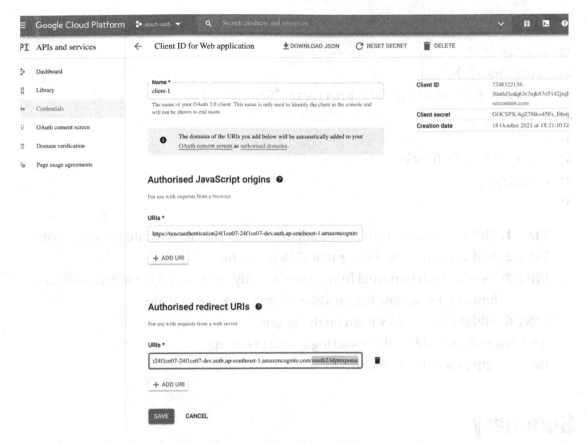

***Figure 2-27.*** *Updating the authorized URIs and redirect URIs*

Add the URL in both the text boxes, namely, `Authorised JavaScript origins` and `Authorised redirect URIs`.

Append `/oauth2/idpresponse` in the redirect URIs to get the user profile.

# Setting Up React App

To enable login with Google, in the login screen we need to add a button; when a user clicks this button, the Google login flow will be triggered.

Let's start with adding a button in our React app

```
1: <button
2:   onClick={() => {
3:     Auth.federatedSignIn({ provider: "Google" });
4:   }}
5: >
6:   Sign in with Google
7: </button>;
8:
```

**LINE 1:** This is a default button component; you can use any custom button as well.

**LINE 2:** Add a function on the event of click of this button.

**LINE 3:** Use the Auth imported from @aws-amplify/auth to call the federatedSignIn function by passing the provider; in this case, it is Google.

**LINE 6:** Add the title to be shown on the button.

And that's all in enabling the social login flow in our app.

Run the app to see this in action.

# Summary

The chapter started by introducing the concept of authentication and its importance in securing web applications. It highlighted the key components of authentication, such as user management, role management, registration, login, and logout.

Next, it explained how AWS Amplify simplifies the process of setting up authentication in a React app. The chapter walked through the steps of adding authentication to the app using the Amplify CLI and configuring the authentication service.

The Amplify library provides UI components that can be used to integrate the authentication flow into the app. The chapter demonstrated how to use these components to create a login and registration UI without writing custom components.

It further explored the storage of authentication-related data, such as access tokens, refresh tokens, and user information. The browser's developer tools are used to inspect the local storage and decode the access token to understand its contents.

The chapter also covered social login integration using OAuth with AWS Amplify. It explained the concept of OAuth and how it allows third-party applications to access user information without sharing passwords. It specifically focused on integrating Google social login into the app and provided step-by-step instructions for setting it up.

Finally, the chapter concluded by summarizing the key concepts covered, including the use of Amplify's authentication-related states and the storage of user information. It emphasized the convenience and improved user experience provided by social login features.

Overall, the chapter provided a comprehensive guide on implementing authentication and social login in a React app using AWS Amplify, empowering developers to enhance the security and usability of their applications.

# CHAPTER 3

# CRUD and REST APIs – Pillars of Efficient Data Exchange

*APIs are the conduits through which data flows, applications communicate and functionality is shared.*

—Akshat Paul

In today's world, the exchange of information and data between systems or devices is really important. As businesses and individuals continue to rely on digital technologies, the need for efficient and secure data transfer protocol becomes a necessity. REST APIs are one way to achieve this goal. REST APIs provide a set of standardized interface that allows systems to communicate with each other in a scalable and flexible manner.

CRUD (create, read, update, and delete) operations are some of the most common operations that any API must support. In this chapter, we will explore how to create a REST API using AWS Amplify that supports CRUD operations.

We will start by explaining what a REST API is and how it works. Then we will go through the steps defining endpoints, handling request and response, deploying the API, and testing it from Postman.

## API Overview

I am pretty sure you have connected your phone with some of your friends' Bluetooth speaker, where the speaker was not manufactured by the same company as your phone. Please think how these different components manufactured in different factories by different companies are able to connect and communicate with each other.

The answer is the standard protocol.

75

© Akshat Paul, Mahesh Haldar 2023
A. Paul and M. Haldar, *Serverless Web Applications with AWS Amplify*,
https://doi.org/10.1007/978-1-4842-8707-1_3

For Bluetooth connection, there is a standard protocol and set of rules; if the phone and speaker manufacturer follows it, they will be able to communicate to and fro. There are standard rules for USB connectors to be followed by adapters and cables. Similarly, we humans follow standard protocols of languages like pronunciations and grammars to communicate with other humans; if there is a mismatch, then they are not able to communicate. Imagine a French and a Chinese trying to communicate in their local languages. ☺

The protocols for computer programs are called application programming interfaces (APIs). An API is a software interface through which more than one software component interacts, sends commands, and receives responses.

When talking in terms of web development, from a high level, there are two big components, the frontend app and the backend server. Backend servers are a set of CPUs, which run programs and from a business point of view perform tasks. An API is the interface through which any application can request to perform some action; the server gets a request through these APIs, performs a defined action, and responds with the response and status after performing tasks.

Let's discuss the basic login flow from a user's point of view using Figure 3-1.

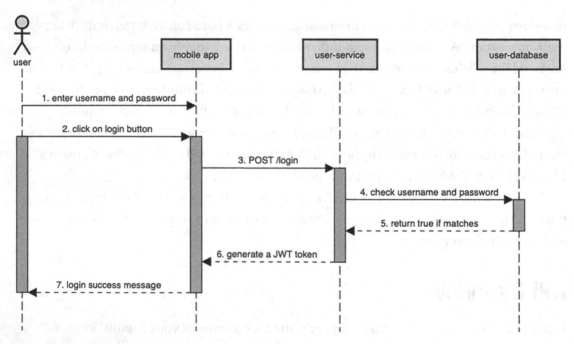

***Figure 3-1.***  *The system interaction when a user tries to log in*

When the user wants to log in via an app, following steps are followed:

**STEP 1:** The user enters the username and password.

**STEP 2:** The user clicks the login button.

**STEP 3:** The mobile app requests the server by sending a POST API request on the URL path `/login` with request parameters like username and password.

**STEP 4:** Then the server processes that request and checks in the database if the username and password are correct.

**STEP 5:** The database will return true or false on the find match query.

**STEP 6:** The server then responds that the job is successfully finished and responds with the answer; in this case, it will be a valid JWT token.

**STEP 7:** The mobile app now will understand this result and navigate the user to the dashboard.

This URL path, namely, `/login`, through which the server takes a request and performs actions is an API, that is, application programming interface.

APIs are the interfaces through which our own FE (Front-end) application or third-party applications interact with the server.

In software applications, APIs play an important role; as the important business logic and computation-heavy jobs are written in servers and exposed to multiple clients via APIs, these also help the whole system to reuse some code logic exposed via APIs. For example, for Facebook, all the code of authentication and friend recommendations can be reused for web and mobile apps via APIs.

Many companies sell the logic and important data via APIs; hence, APIs are also the baseline of many businesses.

# Why Do We Need an API?

The following are a few reasons about the usages of APIs:

1. **Connect with systems built with different technologies**

   APIs let systems communicate and interoperate with each other, even if they are built using different technology languages, for example, the Java microservice and Node.js microservice can communicate via JSON standard.

2. **Business logic abstraction**

   APIs let developers use the functionality of a system without needing to know the business logic or how it is built, for example, the weather API exposes the current weather status by wrapping the sensor and other logics.

3. **Enable automation**

   APIs enable the team to do the automation and integration with various systems and lead a path to innovation. For example, we can use Slack APIs to develop Slack apps to automate our daily tasks.

4. **Reduce the development time**

   Let's assume we have two frontend applications, a mobile app and a web app; it would be costly to have to maintain and write their individual servers and business logic. Maintaining separate servers and duplicating business logic for each application can be costly. By exposing APIs from servers, we can reuse the same business logic across multiple clients and platforms, such as mobile apps and web apps. Furthermore, APIs offer the flexibility to support multiple versions and ensure backward compatibility indefinitely.

5. **Improving the security**

   APIs encapsulate different private keys on the server side, ensuring that only the desired data is exposed to specific users. This approach enhances the overall security of applications, providing end-to-end protection.

6. **Extending features to multiple platforms**

   APIs enable us to extend the services to multiple platforms, for example, once we have written backend services they can be consumed by various form factors like web and mobile at the same time.

# API Design

Whenever the system's APIs are to be used by more than one client or more than one external platform, the API design is crucial. These APIs become the interface for the developers. Hence, the API should be

- Consistent
- Understandable
- Backward compatible

# Types of APIs

As API developers, we should be aware that APIs can be classified in terms of their availability. Let's discuss the different types:

- Public APIs: These APIs are publicly available and require no authentication or special access to consume.

- Private APIs: These APIs belong to a particular system and are not available for everyone to use. For example, the APIs by Facebook are only available to be used by Facebook web and mobile apps. There are various layers of security in place so that any anonymous user is not able to exploit and consume the APIs.

- Partner APIs: These are similar to private APIs, but generally shared with a third-party platform to consume, for example, a third-party wallet app integrated with an ecommerce platform for easy payment. These partners are registered and authorized to use the APIs mostly using JWT tokens, digital certificates, or secret keys.

# API Specifications and Protocols

- SOAP (Simple Object Access Protocol) APIs are based on XML format over a variety of transports, including HTTP, HTTPS, SMTP, TCP, and others. SOAP is commonly used in enterprises to exchange data from one system to another.

- gRPC (Remote Procedure Calls) is an open source RPC framework. It was developed by Google and uses HTTP/2 as the transport protocol. gRPC is designed to be highly performant, with a focus on low latency and low bandwidth usages. It can be used to build highly scalable distributed systems. One of its use cases is microservices, where the servers communicate via APIs.

- WebSocket is a protocol for a persistent, bidirectional, full-duplex communication over a single TCP connection. It is widely supported by web browsers and enables real-time interactive use cases like chat systems, collaboration tools, online games, etc. This lets the data flow in real time without needing the client apps to poll the data again and again for latest data.

79

- Message Queue Telemetry Transport (MQTT) is a lightweight messaging protocol for small sensors and mobile devices for high latency or unreliable networks. MQTT runs over the TCP/IP protocol. MQTT is often used in the Internet of Things (IoT), where low power consumptions and small message size make it suitable for various use cases.

- Representational State Transfer (REST) APIs are based on the HTTP or HTTPS protocol and use standard HTTP methods such as GET, POST, PUT, DELETE, and OPTIONS to perform operations on resources as requested over the URL. REST APIs are stateless and are often used to expose data from backend to frontend servers. The most common format of data used is JSON.

- GraphQL is a query language API that gives the control to clients. The clients can request the exact data they want. This solves the problem in REST APIs of overfetching and underfetching. Generally, GraphQL is used as an alternative of REST APIs.

# Introduction to Lambda

AWS Lambda is a serverless compute service that runs the code without provisioning or managing servers, allowing us to focus on our application business logic rather than infrastructure management. In this section, we will learn what AWS Lambda is, how to create a function using AWS Amplify, how to deploy it, how to invoke the function via an HTTP request, and how to configure triggers to execute those functions.

## Lambda Functions – The Serverless Functions

Let's assume you are starting up a restaurant and delivering the food online to your customers. We are quite aware that setting up a restaurant is a capital-heavy investment, which requires setting up a full-fledged commercial kitchen with commercial kitchen equipment, apart from arranging the chefs and raw material, preparing menus, renting a place, and marketing. The cost generally goes from $1000 to $15,000 just for commercial equipment.

In this case, it's not an easy question to estimate the time to get back the return on investment. If you are starting up and especially if you are not sure how many orders we might receive and how the customers are going to react to the launch of the restaurant, it can be a big risk.

Given the following two options, which one would you choose?

1. Buy all the commercial kitchen equipment and spend $5000–$10,000 on equipment.

2. Rent someone's commercial kitchen and pay a small amount on the amount of time you use to prepare food, which may cost up to $75 per hour.

I am not sure about you, but if I would be this person who is not sure about many aspects of starting up a restaurant, I would start slow and rent on an hourly basis.

Similarly, when we deploy applications, there are many operations jobs required before we can run our business logic, which include server setup, scaling, deployment, server management, security, etc. What if there was a service where we as developers only care about writing the business logic code and everything is taken care of, and there's no need to pay for the server instance's computation for the whole day if you run once a day for a few hours?

Yes, the AWS Lambda function is that service.

# Lambda Functions

In the AWS ecosystem, the Lambda function is a service that lets you and me run a piece of code on demand without worrying about the setup and operations of servers.

The service automatically manages the underlying operations of server management, handling high traffic, and security parts of it.

This service is capable of all the dynamic state changes and updates like adding items in a cart, making payments, listening to data from your sensor and adding in your database, or training your AI/ML models.

The Lambda function takes away all the overhead of running your piece of code and helps you to focus only on your business logic on highly available infrastructure. The Lambda function manages all the operations like provisioning of computing services, updating the security patch, operating system updates, monitoring, and logging.

# Use Cases of Lambda Functions

Lambda functions can be used in various scenarios; these functions are also capable of integrating with other available AWS services like DynamoDB or notification services.

Let's discuss some of the use cases of Lambda functions:

1. APIs for web development to read from databases and update data in the database

2. On-demand file processing operations like resizing of images or Excel sheet parsing

3. Various kinds of daily or weekly scheduled tasks, like parsing web pages to fetch news or job posting

4. Scalable backend for your web, mobile, or IoT apps

5. Training of AI/ML models

# Cons of Using Lambda Functions

- **No control over the underlying hardware**

  If your code requires to access some hardware capabilities like the GPU, you should not use Lambda functions.

- **Cost vs. computation time required**

  If your code requires a computation machine to run continuously most of the time during the day, then the Lambda function might be costly compared to having a dedicated server to run the code.

# How Lambda Function Works

The service requires you to upload the code, and then whenever triggered via the API, the function runs on a dedicated pool of servers managed by AWS and returns the response.

The function is the piece of code which runs on service AWS Lambda. This function can further integrate with third-party systems via APIs or integrate with other AWS services. After successful processing of code, this returns some value to the caller.

Let's take an example; you wrote a function that, when triggered, calls the Yahoo Finance API and gets the list of stocks.

Then you apply some business logic, for example, you do some sorting and some calculation to get the top five stocks.

You can then store that in the database and return the list of recommended stocks.

This can be easily represented in Figure 3-2.

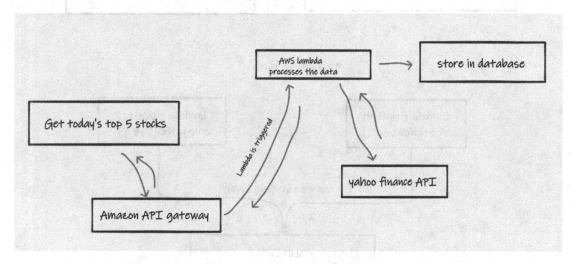

***Figure 3-2.*** *The steps involved when triggering the Lambda function via the REST API*

# What Is the Lambda Layer?

From AWS's perspective, we need to upload the function to Lambda service, and that gets deployed to service handled by AWS. The larger the function, the more time it takes to upload and be deployed. Many times, we may want to share a piece of code or library among more than one Lambda function. For example, there is a util function that generates UUID (Universally Unique Identifier) based on some input, and it also depends on the third-party npm package. If we want the same util function of generating UUID in more than one Lambda function, instead of duplicating the function we can create a Lambda layer that contains this logic and npm package and reuse it in more than one function.

The Lambda layer (as shown in Figure 3-3) is an abstraction of dependency or library, which can be further shared among more than one Lambda function. This is similar to creating a new npm module and using it in more than one project.

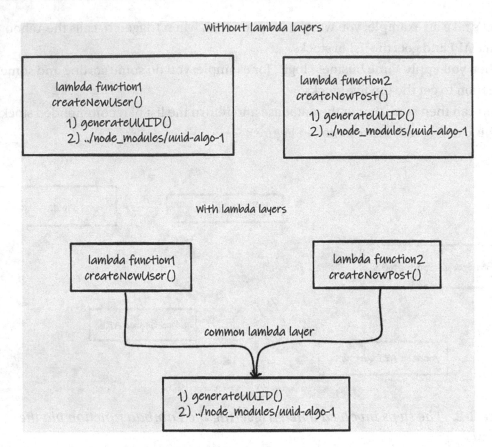

*Figure 3-3. Reusing code with Lambda layers*

# Why Lambda Layers Are Useful

1. **The function's code becomes smaller.**

   Using Lambda layers, we are able to split the main business logic code and the pure functions in a different layer; this makes the main individual function smaller and makes it lightweight.

2. **Reuse code across multiple Lambda functions.**

   More than one Lambda function can reuse these layers.

3. **Easy management and deployment of the main function.**

   Lambda layers make the root function smaller, and hence it takes lesser time to upload and deploy the functions; the other util logic is referred to using the location of the Lambda layer and version which gets called after deployment.

# Working with REST APIs

Let's get our hands dirty and see the REST APIs in action. In this section, we will create the REST APIs and create a Things Todo application. In this application, we should be able to do the following:

1. Get the list of todos

2. Create a new item in the list

3. Delete one item

To achieve these, we need the following APIs:

1. List of all todos:

   GET /todos

2. Create new item:

   POST /todos and metadata in the request body

3. Update the todo item:

   PUT /todos and metadata in the request body

4. Delete one item:

   DELETE /todos/{id}

**STEP 1:** To create a set of APIs, we will use the Amplify CLI tool shown here:

amplify add api

This will give us two options to choose from, as shown in Figure 3-4.

**STEP 2:** Let's select REST and press enter.

```
→  react-amplified git:(master) amplify add api
?  Please select from one of the below mentioned services: (Use arrow keys)
>  GraphQL
   REST
```

***Figure 3-4.*** *Add a new API using AWS Amplify*

85

**STEP 3:** The CLI will ask to give a label to the set of APIs; let's name it `todosapi` as shown in Figure 3-5.

```
→  react-amplified git:(master) amplify add api
? Please select from one of the below mentioned services: REST
? Provide a friendly name for your resource to be used as a label for this category in the
project: todosapi
```

***Figure 3-5.*** *Add a name to the API resource*

**STEP 4:** The CLI will ask for a path; as we know the best practices of REST APIs, we will name it `/todos` as shown in Figure 3-6.

```
→  react-amplified git:(master) amplify add api
? Please select from one of the below mentioned services: REST
? Provide a friendly name for your resource to be used as a label for this category in the
project: todosapi
? Provide a path (e.g., /book/{isbn}): /todos█
```

***Figure 3-6.*** *Provide the path to the API*

Now is the time to create a Lambda function; choose the option to create a new Lambda function, which will map all the CRUD API endpoints.

**STEP 5:** Add `todosfunction` as the name of the Lambda function as shown in Figure 3-7.

```
? Provide a path (e.g., /book/{isbn}): /todos
? Choose a Lambda source Create a new Lambda function
? Provide an AWS Lambda function name: todosfunction
? Choose the runtime that you want to use: NodeJS
? Choose the function template that you want to use:
  CRUD function for DynamoDB (Integration with API Gateway)
  Hello World
  Lambda trigger
> Serverless ExpressJS function (Integration with API Gateway)
```

***Figure 3-7.*** *Select the template for the Lambda function*

Then, the CLI will ask which programming language you want to use to serve the APIs; as we are JavaScript enthusiasts, we will choose Node.js. Please note, you can choose other languages as well from the list.

**STEP 6:** The Amplify CLI autogenerates the template functions for the APIs, which can be modified easily.

As we intend to have the CRUD APIs, let's choose the Express.js function.

---

**Note**  Express.js is a Node.js framework, majorly used to serve web-based HTTP APIs, where we write the API path and attach a set of functions against that path to fulfill the API request.

---

**STEP 7:** Select No for advanced settings for now.

**STEP 8:** Now we will like to see how our autogenerated function looks like; hence, select Yes for editing the Lambda function now and select your IDE.

The menu looks like Figure 3-8 with selected options.

```
? Choose the runtime that you want to use: NodeJS
? Choose the function template that you want to use: Serverless ExpressJS function (Integra
tion with API Gateway)

Available advanced settings:
- Resource access permissions
- Scheduled recurring invocation
- Lambda layers configuration
- Environment variables configuration
- Secret values configuration

? Do you want to configure advanced settings? No
? Do you want to edit the local lambda function now? Yes
? Choose your default editor: Visual Studio Code
Edit the file in your editor: /Users/maheshhaldar/Documents/personla/book/code/react-amplif
ied/amplify/backend/function/todosfunction/src/app.js
? Press enter to continue
```

***Figure 3-8.*** *Final selection of Lambda function configuration*

**STEP 9:** The file where the Lambda function is written will open automatically; if it doesn't open, you can navigate to the following location:

`amplify/backend/function/todosfunction/src/app.js`

If you note, we want to open the Lambda function generated by the Amplify CLI; hence, the directory structure depicts the same. Lambda function configurations are in the function directory, and we can create n number of APIs and functions to serve the API, hence there is todosfunction directory, this is the name we gave in **STEP 5** and create a group of functions with this name.

87

Let's check the autogenerated Lambda function and modify to achieve the required functionality as shown in Figure 3-9.

```
29    /**********************
30     * Example get method *
31     *********************/
32
33    app.get('/todos', function(req, res) {
34      // Add your code here
35      res.json({success: 'get call succeed!', url: req.url});
36    });
37
38    app.get('/todos/*', function(req, res) {
39      // Add your code here
40      res.json({success: 'get call succeed!', url: req.url});
41    });
42
43    /***************************
44     * Example post method *
45     **************************/
46
47    app.post('/todos', function(req, res) {
48      // Add your code here
49      res.json({success: 'post call succeed!', url: req.url, body: req.body})
50    });
```

**Figure 3-9.** *The autogenerated Express.js template*

As we selected the Express.js-based template, we have the app.get and path in line number 33.

**LINE 33:** This means whenever the get API with path `/todos` is requested, the response will be returned with a JSON object as

```
{
    success: 'get call succeed!',
    url: 'request string url'
}
```

**LINE 38:** This means whenever the GET API call with path `/todos/*` is requested, it will run the function and return the object. The `*` is from the regex family and means any string is valid.

For example, if you hit `/todos/89` or `/todos/my-name`, it will call the same function.

**LINE 47:** This means whenever the POST API call with path `/todo` is requested, it will call the callback function. In this case, it will return the JSON object, with the success key, the URL from the request using req.url, and the request body using req.body.

**STEP 10:** Press enter on your console to continue on the Amplify CLI.

**STEP 11:** Let's push these REST APIs and Lambda functions, so that we can check the working APIs as shown in Figure 3-10.

```
amplify push
```

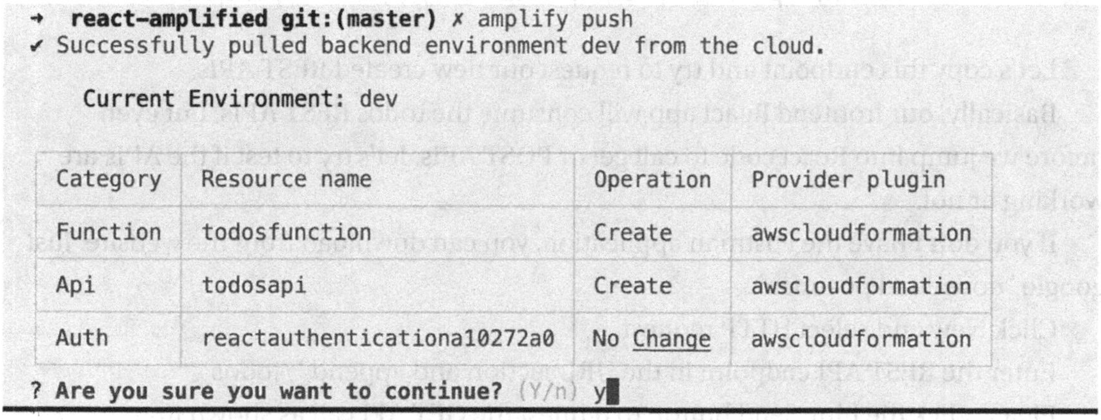

```
→  react-amplified git:(master) x amplify push
✓ Successfully pulled backend environment dev from the cloud.

    Current Environment: dev

| Category | Resource name             | Operation | Provider plugin   |
| Function | todosfunction             | Create    | awscloudformation |
| Api      | todosapi                  | Create    | awscloudformation |
| Auth     | reactauthenticationa10272a0 | No Change | awscloudformation |

? Are you sure you want to continue? (Y/n) y
```

*Figure 3-10.* Push the Lambda function to the cloud

The AWS Amplify CLI will ask for confirmation on pushing the changes; enter yes.

What we are pushing here is `todosapi` and the Lambda function `todosfunction`; hence, you see these two resources have create operations, while Auth has no change in operation.

Let's wait for CloudFormation changes, and we should be really good with REST APIs and running our first Lambda function.

When the push operation is successfully finished, you will be prompted with the REST API endpoint as shown in Figure 3-11.

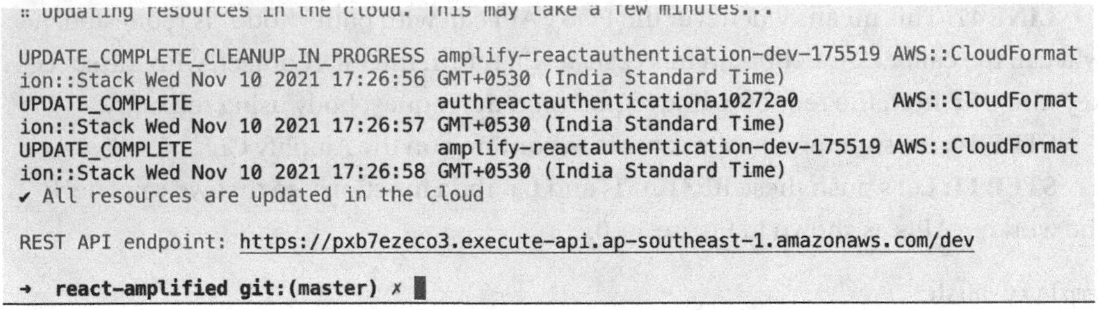

```
:: updating resources in the cloud. This may take a few minutes...

UPDATE_COMPLETE_CLEANUP_IN_PROGRESS amplify-reactauthentication-dev-175519 AWS::CloudFormat
ion::Stack Wed Nov 10 2021 17:26:56 GMT+0530 (India Standard Time)
UPDATE_COMPLETE                    authreactauthenticationa10272a0           AWS::CloudFormat
ion::Stack Wed Nov 10 2021 17:26:57 GMT+0530 (India Standard Time)
UPDATE_COMPLETE                    amplify-reactauthentication-dev-175519 AWS::CloudFormat
ion::Stack Wed Nov 10 2021 17:26:58 GMT+0530 (India Standard Time)
✓ All resources are updated in the cloud

REST API endpoint: https://pxb7ezeco3.execute-api.ap-southeast-1.amazonaws.com/dev

→  react-amplified git:(master) ✗ █
```

*Figure 3-11.   Successful prompt when the Lambda function is pushed*

Let's copy this endpoint and try to request our new created REST APIs.

Basically, our frontend React app will consume the todos REST APIs, but even before we jump into React code to call get or POST APIs, let's try to test if the APIs are working or not.

If you don't have the Postman application, you can download from the website. Just google `download postman`.

Click New and select HTTP request.

Enter the REST API endpoint in the URL section and append `/todos`.

Please click the blue Send button to request the GET API call as shown in Figure 3-12.

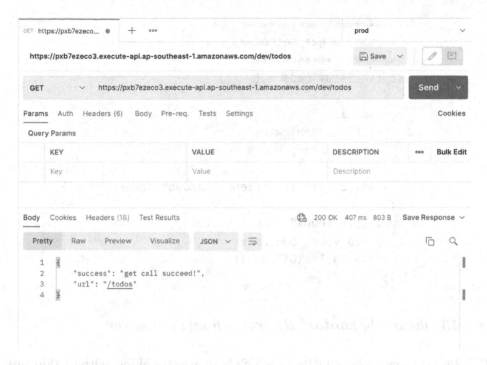

***Figure 3-12.*** *Response from the REST API*

You will see the response, as this is what we sent from the Lambda function.

Similarly, you can try the DELETE, PUT, or POST APIs, and you will get the expected response from all of these APIs.

**STEP 12:** Let's modify our Lambda functions to return a list of data, and also on the POST API call, we will add one item in the array. Open the todosfunction file to modify the Lambda functions as shown in Figure 3-13.

```
25   /**********************
26    * Example get method *
27    **********************/
28   const listOfTodos = [
29     {
30       id: 1,
31       title: "Review PR",
32       done: false,
33     },
34     { id: 2, title: "Attend standup", done: true },
35   ];
36   app.get("/todos", function (req, res) {
37     // Add your code here
38     res.json(listOfTodos);
39   });
40
```

*Figure 3-13.* *Return the hardcoded response from the function*

**LINE 28:** Add a variable listOfTodos which is an array of object with id, title, and done status.

---

**Note**   We have declared the variable which has the list of items; ideally, the data should be stored in any database; we will modify this function when we learn about using databases in later chapters.

---

**LINE 38:** Instead of static strings, return the array of todo items.

## Saving the File

**STEP 13:** Now that the function is modified, we need to save the file and push the changes to AWS also shown in Figure 3-14.

```
amplify push
```

```
→  react-amplified git:(master) ✗ amplify push
✔ Successfully pulled backend environment dev from the cloud.

   Current Environment: dev
```

| Category | Resource name | Operation | Provider plugin |
|----------|---------------|-----------|-----------------|
| Function | todosfunction | Update | awscloudformation |
| Auth | reactauthenticationa10272a0 | No Change | awscloudformation |
| Api | todosapi | No Change | awscloudformation |

```
? Are you sure you want to continue? Yes
⠿ Updating resources in the cloud. This may take a few minutes...
```

*Figure 3-14.* *Confirmation dialog when pushing the changes*

As you can see in the confirmation section, the function has an update operation. Once pushed, let's wait for the changes to be applied on AWS cloud.

**STEP 14:** Let's test our API again on Postman as shown in Figure 3-15.

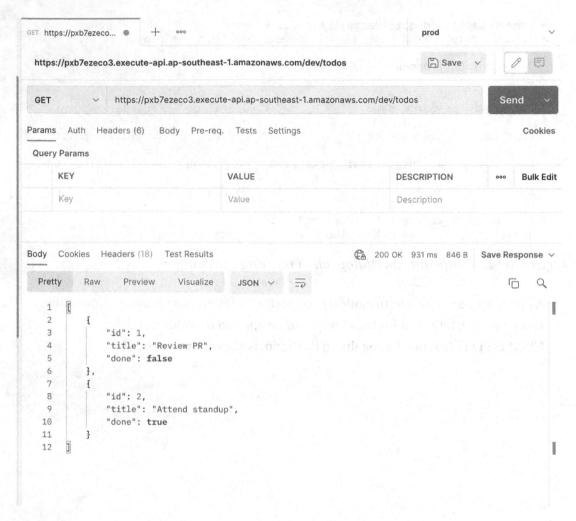

*Figure 3-15.*  *Response on Postman from the REST API*

Voila, as we can see, the changes are reflected on the same APIs.

**STEP 15:** Let's modify the add new item POST API.

```
46    /**************************
47     * Example post method *
48     **************************/
49
50    app.post("/todos", function (req, res) {
51        // Add your code here
52        const newItem = { id: listOfTodos.length + 1, ...req.body };
53        listOfTodos.push(newItem);
54        res.status = 201;
55        res.json(newItem);
56    });
57
```

---

**Note**   We have used a variable and updated the data in the variable which is in memory. Please be aware the new data added using the POST API will only be persisted until the same server is up and running; the moment you restart the server, the data will be reset to the actual value declared initially. Please note, we are running the Lambda functions which run the same functions in different machines; hence, if you hit the get all item API after some time, you will not receive the data added using the POST API, because the server picked to run the function by AWS will change, and hence the variable will return the initial value assigned to it.

---

To resolve this issue, as discussed earlier, we should have a database, which we will learn in later chapters, and we will replace the datasource from variable to database.

**LINE 52:** Get the request body and add a dummy id, using the total length of the array.

**LINE 53:** Push this new item in the same array.

**LINE 54:** Because we know the best practices of REST APIs, we are setting the HTTP response status code as 200, because technically this API is going to create a todo item resource.

**STEP 16:** Let's push the changes and test the API in Postman.

Change the request type to POST from GET in Postman, and add the request body as shown in Figure 3-16.

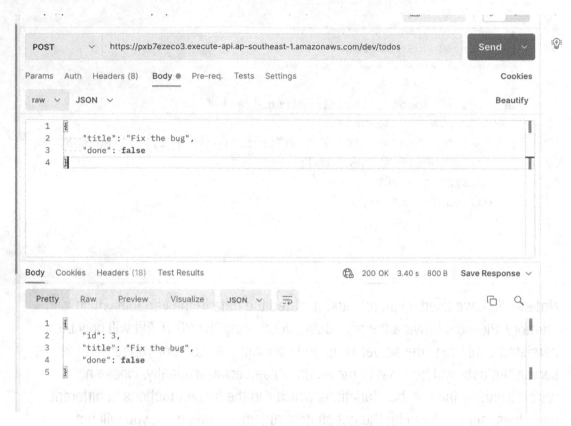

***Figure 3-16.*** *Response from the REST API after the modification of the response structure*

As we get the response 200 with the expected JSON response, let's test the get all todos; we are expecting to get one more item now.

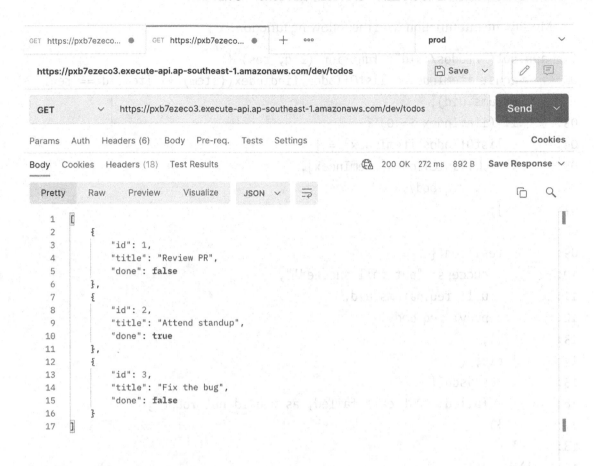

*Figure 3-17.* *Response when requesting all the todos*

As you can see in Figure 3-17, we got the new item in getting all API.

## PUT API to Update Items

Now that we can get all list of items, and add a new item in the list, let's try to update existing todo items.

The following function template is where we will customize it, so that we can edit the items by passing the id:

```
app.put("/todos/*", function (req, res) {
// Add your code here
res.json({ success: "put call succeed!", url: req.url, body: req.body });
});
```

Modify the put function with the following function:

```
01: app.put("/todos/:uid", function (req, res) {
02:     const itemIndex = listOfTodos.findIndex((item) => item.id == req.
        params.uid);
03:     if (itemIndex >= 0) {
04:       listOfTodos[itemIndex] = {
05:         ...listOfTodos[itemIndex],
06:         ...req.body,
07:       };
08:
09:       res.json({
10:         success: "put call succeed!",
11:         url: req.params.uid,
12:         body: req.body,
13:       });
14:     } else {
15:       res.json({
16:         failed: "Put call failed, as the id not found",
17:       });
18:     }
19:   });
```

To update the item by id, we have done the following changes in the preceding code snippet:

- **LINE 1:** We have replaced `` `*` `` with :uid; we are capturing the id of the item to be edited in a variable named uid.

  For example, when we want to update any item, we will hit the PUT API as follows:

  ```
  ```

  PUT /todos/3

  Request body: title to be updated

  ```
  ```

  Now we need the id in one variable, in this case, 3.

- **LINE 2:** We are finding the index of the item which has the id passed by the client; we can easily capture the id from the URL by req. params.uid, where uid is the named variable.

---

**Note** We are using `==` instead of `===`, as the uid will be in string and will fail if we use the triple equal operator. Either we can use `==` or transform the types from string to int or vice versa before comparison.

---

- **LINE 3:** If the item with the id is found, the function findIndex returns the index of the item from the array, and if not found, it returns –1.

- **LINE 4:** If the index is greater than or equal to zero, we know the item with the id is found, and now we can handle the positive edge case.

- **LINE 5:** We are updating the object in the found index with the request body data.

- **LINE 9:** Return with the success message.

- **LINE 15:** This case is a negative case when the passed item id is not found in the list.

Once you have modified the function, save the file and push the Lambda function changes to the AWS cloud so that we can test the API.

You can try the API in Postman to update the items.

# Using the Delete API to Delete an Item by ID

Now that we can get all list of items and add and edit items in the list, let's try to delete existing todo items.

The following function template is where we will customize it, so that we can delete the items by passing the id:

```
app.delete("/todos/*", function (req, res) {
 // Add your code here
 res.json({ success: "delete call succeed!", url: req.url });
});
```

The following is the modified function:

```
01: app.delete("/todos/:uid", function (req, res) {
02:     const itemIndex = listOfTodos.findIndex((item) => item.id === req.
        params.uid);
03:
04:     if (itemIndex >= 0) {
05:       list.splice(itemIndex, 1);
06:
07:       res.json({ success: "delete call succeed!", url: req.url });
08:     } else {
09:       res.json({
10:         failed: "Delete call failed, as the id is not found",
11:       });
12:     }
13:   });
```

- **LINE 1:** Capture the id in the variable named uid.

- **LINE 2:** Find the index of the item, searching by id.

- **LINE 5:** Remove the item from the index, using the splice function.

- **LINE 7:** Return a success message.

- **LINE 9:** This is handling a negative case when the item is not found in the datasource against the id passed in the delete API.

Once you have modified the function, save the file and push the Lambda function changes to the AWS cloud so that we can test the API.

# Summary

Congratulations, you have now successfully created a CRUD REST API and saw it working end to end. In this chapter, we explored on what REST APIs are and created CRUD APIs. We also discussed the best practices of REST APIs. We used Node.js and Express.js to create a sample CRUD REST API. We also discussed in depth about Lambda functions and what value they generate.

Throughout the chapter, we emphasized the importance of testing and showed how to use tools like Postman to verify whether our goal is achieved or not.

## CHAPTER 4

# Integrating REST APIs with a Frontend React App

*Building a powerful frontend is an art, but it becomes a masterpiece when it is integrated seamlessly with APIs.*

—Akshat Paul

In the previous chapter, we have created REST APIs which is ready to be consumed by client apps and client apps can render the user interface using these APIs. The next step is to add security enhancements, and we'll be ready to distribute our APIs to third-party apps as well. In this chapter, we will focus on React application to consume these APIs and render the UI components. In order to integrate these APIs with a React app, we will first create a basic todo application.

## Creating a Basic React ToDo App

Let's create a new file in the React app, where we will achieve the following:

1. Call the get all items API and render the items in an ordered list.

2. Strike the items, which are marked done.

3. Add a create new item button; on clicking it, we should be able to add one item to the todo list.

4. Add the check box button to update the status from done to not done and vice versa.

5. Add a delete button to delete one item.

© Akshat Paul, Mahesh Haldar 2023
A. Paul and M. Haldar, *Serverless Web Applications with AWS Amplify*,
https://doi.org/10.1007/978-1-4842-8707-1_4

**STEP 1:** Let's start with basic API integration; we will call the get all API and show the title in an ordered list in the UI. Figure 4-1 shows what we want to achieve.

*Figure 4-1.* *User interface for a todo application*

Let's create TodoPage.js and add the following code. Let's discuss the code line by line:

```
01: import React, { useState, useEffect } from "react";
02: import { API } from "aws-amplify";
03:
04: const TodoPage = () => {
05:    const [todoList, setTodoList] = useState([]);
06:
07:    useEffect(() => {
08:      API.get("todosapi", "/todos").then((data) => {
09:        setTodoList(data);
10:      });
11:    }, []);
12:
13:    return (
14:      <>
15:        <h1>Todo lists</h1>
16:        <ol>
17:          {todoList.map((item) => {
18:            return <li>{item.title}</li>;
19:          })}
20:        </ol>
21:      </>
```

```
22:   );
23: };
24:
25: export default TodoPage;
26:
```

**LINE 1:** Importing dependencies from React, we will use useState to manipulate the state, namely, after calling the API, we want to set it in React state to reflect in the UI. And useEffect to add a hook to call the API instantly after loading the page.

**LINE 2:** Import the API from aws-amplify; this will help us in the integration with the REST API we created and deployed in Chapter 3 and this also acts as the HTTP client to call the REST API and return the data asynchronously.

**LINE 5:** Define useState with a default empty array value. The setTodoList is the function which will help in setting the new data after we receive the data from the GET API call.

**LINES 7 and 11:** Consuming the useEffect React hook, this gets triggered as soon as the React page is loaded, as we want to call the API instantly. When we pass an array as the second parameter, the hook is triggered on change on the variables passed in the array. If you don't pass anything as the second parameter, the hook will be triggered infinite times, in this case, the get all API will be called infinite times, and we don't want this. We passed an empty array to call the API only once; technically, the array is empty; hence, the array will never change, guaranteeing the API to be called once.

**LINE 8:** Use the API from the aws-amplify package to call the API, by mentioning the HTTP method API we want to call. The first parameter is the API name, as we created by the name of todosapi, and the second parameter is the path of the API; in the case of get all, it is going to be /todos.

---

**Note**  The hostname will change with different environments, that is, different for the dev environment and different for production. Similarly, if we kill the AWS backend config and recreate in a new AWS account, the hostname will change; the API from aws-amplify handles this, so that the base host is not hardcoded in our application.

---

**LINE 9:** When the API call is finished or succeeded, the data is to be set in React state using the setTodoList function, so that the UI can rerender with the items.

**LINE 17:** Until the API call is not a success, the value of items will be an empty array; hence, nothing will be rendered on the UI.

---

**Note**   Here, you can show a loader component until the value of itemList is empty, and when the itemList is not empty, show the title. In this way, we can achieve the functionality of showing loader whenever there is an API call happening in the background.

---

**LINE 18:** Render the title from the item to show on the UI.

Run the server and load the page on the browser; you will see the list.

If you want to see the API getting called and response, open the Network tab, as shown in Figure 4-2.

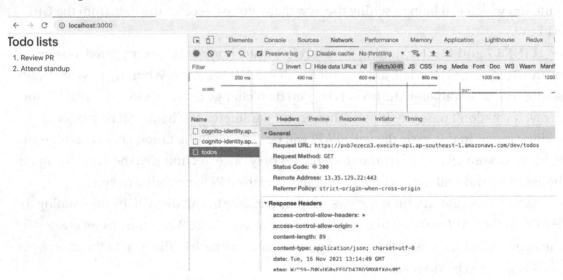

***Figure 4-2.***  *List of data from REST APIs*

Let's modify our application further to show the status of which item is done and which is not:

```
17:        {todoList.map((item) => {
18:          return (
19:            <li>{item.done ? <strike>{item.title}</strike> : item.
             title}</li>
20:          );
21:        })}
```

**LINE 19:** Add a ternary operator, and check if the item's status is done, then wrap the title in an HTML <strike> tag; if not done, then render without the strike tag.

The output will be like Figure 4-3.

**Figure 4-3.** *UI change indicating a completed todo task*

# Adding a New Item

Let's add a new button so that we can add a new item using the POST API call.

**STEP 1:** Add the button to add a new item.

```
24:      <div>
25:        <input type="text" />
26:      </div>
27:      <div>
28:        <button>+ Add new item</button>
29:      </div>
```

The preceding input field and button will render as shown in Figure 4-4.

**Figure 4-4.** *Button addition to the UI*

**STEP 2:** Let's now add the functionality on what happens on clicking this button.

```
01: import React, { useState, useEffect } from "react";
02: import { API } from "aws-amplify";
03:
04: const TodoPage = () => {
05:   const [newItemField, setNewItemField] = useState("");
06:   const [todoList, setTodoList] = useState([]);
07:
08:   const addNewItem = (title) => {
09:     API.post("todosapi", "/todos", { body: { title, done: false } })
10:       .then((data) => {
11:         console.log("Creation success with data", data);
12:       })
13:       .catch((err) => {
14:         console.log("ERROR while calling POST api call");
15:       });
16:   };
17:
18:   useEffect(() => {
19:     API.get("todosapi", "/todos").then((data) => {
```

```
20:         setTodoList(data);
21:      });
22:    }, []);
```

**LINE 5:** We want to create a new item, and the title is to be picked from the input box; hence, we need a variable to store the value of the new title typed in the input box. Hence, we use the useState.

**LINE 8:** We are writing an addNewItem function, which will call the POST API with the title passed to the function as a parameter. This function will be called when the add button is clicked.

**LINE 9:** We are going to use the API from AWS-amplify and pass the request body as a JSON object as a parameter.

**LINE 11:** If the response is a success, for now, let's log the response in the console.

**LINE 14:** The catch part will be triggered if the API fails; let's also log the failure.

**STEP 3:** Integrate the input box, and call the POST API on button click.

```
33:
34:        <div>
35:          <input
36:            type="text"
37:            onChange={(event) => {
38:              setNewItemField(event.target.value);
39:            }}
40:          />
41:        </div>
42:        <div>
43:          <button onClick={() => addNewItem(newItemField)}>
                 + Add new item
             </button>
44:        </div>
45:      </>
46:    );
47: };
48:
49: export default TodoPage;
50:
```

Now run your React app and try to add a new item; the expectation is we should be able to create a new item, and on success, it should show the result in the console.

Figure 4-5 shows the screenshot of the application.

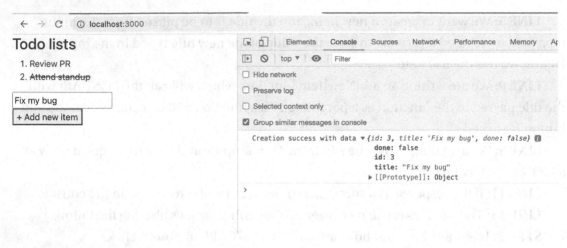

*Figure 4-5.*  *UI updated allowing a new todo item to be added from the page*

# Enhancing the User Experience

Now that API integration of getting all the data and adding new items is done, let's enhance the user experience.

As an end user, when I add a new item, I want the experience to be better than what we have achieved so far.

1.  When I add a new item, the new item should be added in the list.

2.  The text field should get clear so that I can add a new item.

Let's achieve these one by one.

## Enhancement 1

If we want to add the new item, when the POST API call is successful we will add the response in our list of todo item variables. Let's change what we should do in our React app:

```
08:    const addNewItem = (title) => {
09:      API.post("todosapi", "/todos", { body: { title, done: false } })
10:        .then((data) => {
11:          console.log("Creation success with data", data);
12:          setTodoList([...todoList, data]);
13:        })
14:        .catch((err) => {
15:          console.log("ERROR while calling POST api call");
16:        });
17:    };
```

**LINE 12:** We will use the function by the useState React hook to push the new item we received from the POST API call. And we achieve what we wanted. What it does is, as the list of todos is in the state, when the list gets updated, React also rerenders and shows our new item in the list.

# Enhancement 2

We want to reset the text field value when the POST API call is successful. Let's see how the React code will change to achieve this enhancement:

```
08:    const addNewItem = (title) => {
09:      API.post("todosapi", "/todos", { body: { title, done: false } })
10:        .then((data) => {
11:          console.log("Creation success with data", data);
12:          setTodoList([...todoList, data]);
13:          setNewItemField("");
14:        })
15:        .catch((err) => {
16:          console.log("ERROR while calling POST api call");
17:        });
18:    };
```

**LINE 13:** For capturing the value of text from the input field, we have used the useState hook; we will use the same set function to set the value of the field to an empty string.

The preceding change will have no impact on our text field because we are so far only capturing the value from the text field, but we have not set the value of the text field.

Let's set the value:

```
37:         <div>
38:            <input
39:              type="text"
40:              onChange={(event) => {
41:                setNewItemField(event.target.value);
42:              }}
43:              value={newItemField}
44:            />
45:         </div>
```

**LINE 43:** We are using the HTML attribute name 'value' to set the value from the state.

Let's run our React app and see the app in action.

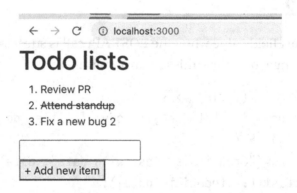

***Figure 4-6.*** *Input box emptied to add new item*

Now if you see, the moment an add new button is clicked, the item gets added in the preceding list as a third item and the input box is cleared to be ready to accept the new item.

Congrats, you have implemented a basic feature and also enhanced the user experience. Next, we will add delete and update features to our React application.

# Do It Yourself (DIY): Deleting and Updating

Still, our app is not complete; we have to add the feature of deleting one item and updating the status of the item from done to not done, so that the strike on the item goes off and on, depending on the item.

Please write your function to implement the APIs and write the React code to achieve the update status and delete one item functionality.

# GraphQL API

GraphQL is a powerful and flexible query language and runtime for APIs that was developed by Facebook. It allows clients to request and receive only the data they need, which can help solve the problem of overfetching and underfetching of data that occurs with traditional REST APIs.

With GraphQL, clients can send dynamic queries that specify exactly what data they want, and the server will respond with only that data. This gives clients greater control and power over the data they receive and can lead to faster and more efficient application performance.

In addition to its query capabilities, GraphQL also provides a strongly typed schema that defines the types of data that can be queried. This can help catch errors early in the development process and make it easier to maintain and evolve APIs over time.

GraphQL has gained widespread adoption in recent years and is now supported by many popular programming languages and frameworks. It's a powerful tool for building modern, scalable APIs, and I highly recommend it to anyone looking to build APIs for their applications. Let us understand GraphQL with the help of an example:

```
{
  author {
    firstName
    twitterHandle
  }
}
```

This schema will return the following structure data:

```
{
  author {
    "Andrew",
    "some_handle"
  }
}
```

if the query is modified to the following query:

```
{
  author {
    lastName
  }
}
```

This will return the following:

```
{
  author {
    "James"
  }
}
```

---

**Note**    GraphQL was initially developed by Facebook (now Meta) in 2012 and later published as open source in 2015.

---

**Why GraphQL?**

- It simplifies backend and frontend communication.

- Frontend developers can get exactly what they want, no under- or overfetching.

- Reduced number of HTTP API calls, compared to REST APIs.

- GraphQL allows an API to evolve by adding more keys without breaking existing queries. Not required to maintain versions like in REST APIs.

**Why not GraphQL?**

- Learning curve: GraphQL can have a steeper learning curve than traditional REST APIs, especially if you're not familiar with the GraphQL query language and its concepts.

- Small APIs: If you have a small API with simple data requirements, it may be overkill to use GraphQL. In such cases, a traditional REST API or a simpler solution may be sufficient.

- Caching: Caching can be more complex with GraphQL than with REST, as GraphQL queries are often dynamic and can have a wide range of possible responses. This can make it harder to implement effective caching strategies.

- Lack of tooling: While GraphQL has gained widespread adoption, some tools and libraries may not yet support it, which could make development more difficult.

- Security concerns: As with any API, security is a concern, and GraphQL has its own unique security considerations, such as query depth limits and input validation.

- Performance: While GraphQL can offer improved performance in certain cases, it can also have performance issues if queries are too complex or too many requests are made. This can require additional optimization and caching strategies to be implemented.

Now that we deeply understand the GraphQL APIs well, let's create all APIs for the todo list in GraphQL and run those in action, and we will modify our React app to consume the GraphQL APIs instead of REST APIs.

To create a set of APIs, we will use the Amplify CLI tool:

```
amplify add api
```

This will give us two options to choose from, namely:

**STEP 2:** Let's select GraphQL and press enter.

```
→  react-amplified git:(master) amplify add api
?  Please select from one of the below mentioned services: (Use arrow keys)
>  GraphQL
   REST
```

**STEP 3:** The CLI will ask to give a label to the set of APIs; let's name it todosgql.

```
→  react-amplified git:(master) x amplify add api
?  Please select from one of the below mentioned services: GraphQL
?  Provide API name: todosgql█
```

**STEP 4:** The CLI will ask the type of API authorization; let's choose the API key. There are other ways to authorize, but let's select the quickest of all options.

```
→  react-amplified git:(master) x amplify add api
?  Please select from one of the below mentioned services: GraphQL
?  Provide API name: todosgql
?  Choose the default authorization type for the API
>  API key
   Amazon Cognito User Pool
   IAM
   OpenID Connect
```

**STEP 5:** The CLI tool will ask for a description of the key; provide some text.

**STEP 6:** The CLI will ask for the number of days, after which one API key will expire. Select the default number, namely, 7.

```
→  react-amplified git:(master) x amplify add api
? Please select from one of the below mentioned services: GraphQL
? Provide API name: todosgql
? Choose the default authorization type for the API API key
? Enter a description for the API key: My gql key
? After how many days from now the API key should expire (1-365): (7)
```

**STEP 7:** Select no for additional settings option.

**STEP 8:** When asked if you have annotated GraphQL schema, select no. This will autogenerate from a template, which we can modify to fit our todo application use case. Though if you already have some schema you want to migrate to Amplify, you can select Yes and add your schema.

```
→  react-amplified git:(master) x amplify add api
? Please select from one of the below mentioned services: GraphQL
? Provide API name: todosgql
? Choose the default authorization type for the API API key
? Enter a description for the API key: My gql key
? After how many days from now the API key should expire (1-365): 7
? Do you want to configure advanced settings for the GraphQL API No, I am done.
? Do you have an annotated GraphQL schema? No
? Choose a schema template:
〉 Single object with fields (e.g., "Todo" with ID, name, description)
  One-to-many relationship (e.g., "Blogs" with "Posts" and "Comments")
```

This will lead to choose the template option; let's go simple with a single object and choose the todo template GraphQL schema.

**STEP 9:** The tool will ask if you want to edit the schema, select no. As from the previous section we know where this API file will be generated, we will navigate to the directory and edit the GraphQL API.

Let's check our amplify directory and check what code has been generated.

Given we want to modify the GraphQL API, it should be placed in the API directory. Follow the following path:

./amplify/backend/api/todosgql

---

**Note**   todosgql is the name we gave to this new gql API, hence the directory name. We can have more than one GraphQL API with different names, and the name of the directory will be created.

---

Open the schema.GraphQL file.

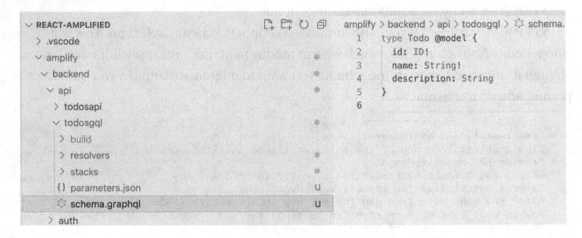

And we see the basic GraphQL schema is generated for Todo:

```
1: type Todo @model {
2:   id: ID!
3:   name: String!
4:   description: String
5: }
6:
```

**LINE 1:** The @model directive in the schema tells AWS to create a similar database schema in DynamoDB, so that the data can be stored and read from the database.

We will discuss in detail about database integration in later chapters; let's remove the @model directive from this schema.

Modify the schema to add a done field of type boolean for our todo item status and rename "name" field to "title", as our React app is using "title" key:

```
1: type Todo {
2:   id: ID!
3:   title: String!
4:   done: Boolean!
5: }
```

Let's add some operation type in our GraphQL schema so that the clients can perform some operations on the GraphQL API, like getting data, creating, deleting, etc.

In GraphQL, the operations can be of following types:

1. Query

   This operation is equivalent to the GET HTTP verb, where any get operations are grouped.

2. Mutation

   This operation is responsible for all the operation which mutates or changes the resource data, for example, all the creation, deletion, and update operations are written under this keyword.

3. Subscription

   This operation enables the clients to create a socket connection with the server, and any change on the resource will be delivered on real time to the clients.

We want to get a list of all todo items. Let's modify our schema using the keyword 'query':

```
6: type Query {
7:   todos: [Todo] @function(name: "")
8: }
```

**LINE 7:** The query returns a field 'todos' which returns the array of Todo items.

The @function directive helps us to quickly connect a Lambda function with a GraphQL API.

To explain further, the client will request 'todos', and to operate on this request, we need to connect a function, and @function helps us.

We also need a Lambda function, the following command will add a Lambda function and we need to pass the name of that function:

```
amplify add function
```

Provide a name to the function; you can give 'todosfunctiongql'.

Select Node.js and select a basic Hello World template:

```
amplify add function
? Select which capability you want to add: Lambda function (serverless
function)
? Provide an AWS Lambda function name: todosfunctiongql
? Choose the runtime that you want to use: NodeJS
? Choose the function template that you want to use: Hello World
```

Now we have the Lambda function, and we need to add the name of this in GraphQL API configuration, and this Lambda function will be our custom resolver.

Open the schema.GraphQL file, and modify as follows:

```
6: type Query {
7:   todos: [Todo] @function(name: "todosfunctiongql-${env}")
8: }
9:
```

**LINE 7:** @function expects the name of the function as a parameter to be able to resolve the query, and we need to provide '-${env}'.

# Custom Resolver

We want to control our function, so that we can have the confidence of ownership in our API. As we have already connected the GraphQL API controller layer with our custom Lambda function, let's modify the function to respond to the GraphQL query.

We will modify the Lambda function in a way, so that it returns some list of todo items from in-memory datasource.

Navigate to open the function file:

`./amplify/backend/function/todosfunctiongql/src/index.js`

```
01: const listOfTodos = [
02:   {
03:     id: 1,
04:     title: "Review PR",
05:     done: false,
06:   },
07:   { id: 2, title: "Attend standup", done: true },
08: ];
09:
10: const resolvers = {
11:   Query: {
12:     todos: (ctx) => listOfTodos,
13:   },
14: };
```

**LINE 1:** This is our in-memory variable, which will hold the items of todos.

**LINE 10:** The resolver map, which will have the GraphQL operation keywords like query, mutation, and subscription as keys and resolver function as value.

In this case, when the query todos is requested, it should resolve to return the list of todos.

The ctx variable holds the request contexts like header, params, or auth info.

# Modifying the Lambda Handler

To be able to resolve the GraphQL query, we need to handle the operation type in the Lambda handler.

Please replace the autogenerated handler with the following:

```
16: exports.handler = async (event) => {
17:   const typeHandler = resolvers[event.typeName];
18:   if (typeHandler) {
19:     const resolver = typeHandler[event.fieldName];
20:     if (resolver) {
```

```
21:        return await resolver(event);
22:      }
23:    }
24:    throw new Error("Resolver not found.");
25: };
```

Let's take the following two sample GraphQL queries to understand the preceding handler:

```
01: query {
02:    products {
03:      name
04:    }
05: }
06:
07: mutation {
08:    deleteCategory(id: 2) {
09:      name
10:    }
11: }
12:
```

**LINE 17:** The event contains some information about the incoming request, so that we can identify the GraphQL operation types.

event.typeName will return one of the operations, for example, query, mutation, or subscription, event.typeName would be query and mutation if the preceding two queries are passed.

**LINE 19:** The field name from the event map returns the field under an operation the client is requesting to. For example, the value of event.fieldName will be products and deleteCategory for the preceding two sample queries.

**LINE 21:** The same event is passed as ctx to our custom resolver function, so that in our resolver function we can get the request metadata like header, auth information, etc.

Congratulations, now we have successfully created a GraphQL API and connected a customer Lambda function to resolve the query. Let's push this change and test the API by running the following command:

```
amplify push
```

# Testing the API

There will be some configuration preference asked by the CLI tool; you can answer as follows:

```
? Do you want to generate code for your newly created GraphQL API Yes
? Choose the code generation language target javascript
? Enter the file name pattern of graphql queries, mutations and
subscriptions src/graphql/*
*/*.js
? Do you want to generate/update all possible GraphQL operations - queries,
mutations and s
subscriptions No
```

And wait for the CloudFormation script to generate the resources in AWS cloud.

Let's test our new GraphQL API; navigate to the Amplify console:

```
amplify console
```

You can choose the console option from the menu. This will open the console on the browser.

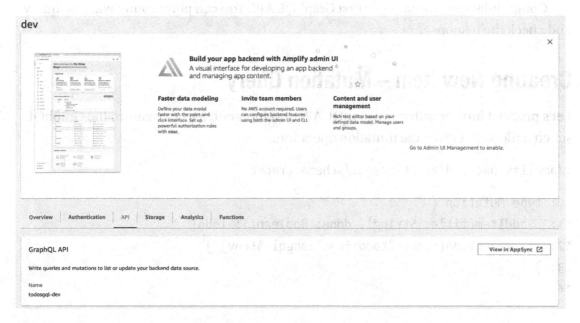

***Figure 4-7.*** *Amplify console*

Navigate to the API and click the View in AppSync button under the GraphQL API.

Click the Run a query option, which will open a console to add the GraphQL query.

Enter the todos query and hit the run button, the result is shown in Figure 4-8.

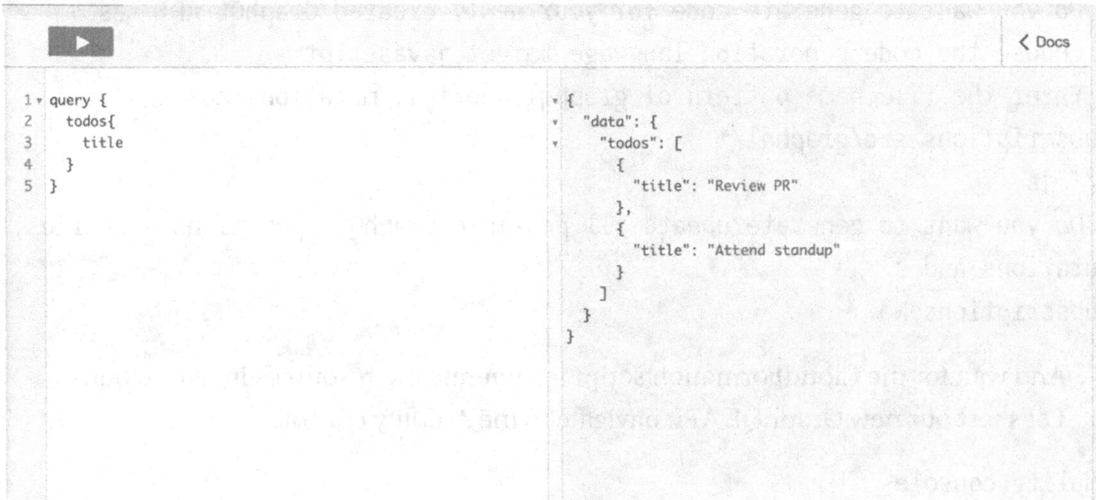

*Figure 4-8.* *AppSync to run the GraphQL query*

Congratulations, we have our first GraphQL API. You can play around with the query and check the response.

# Creating New Item – Mutation Query

Let's proceed further with our GraphQL API development; let's navigate to the GraphQL schema file and register the mutation operation:

./amplify/backend/api/todosgql/schema.graphql

```
10: type Mutation {
11:    addItem(title: String!, done: Boolean!): Todo!
12:       @function(name: "todosfunctiongql-${env}")
13: }
14:
```

**LINE 10:** Add the operation type as mutation to be able to mutate the resource.

**LINE 11:** The addItem is the subfield name in the mutation query, which expects two arguments title and done, and both of them need to be a valid value; it cannot be null. This returns an object of type Todo.

**LINE 12:** Connect the same Lambda function we created which has all the resolvers using the @function directive.

Modify the Lambda resolver function.

After connecting the Lambda function with the gql API, we need to add the support for the mutation operation and addItem field.

Navigate to the Lambda function, and let's start the modification:

```
10: const addNewItem = (title, done) => {
11:    const newItem = { id: listOfTodos.length + 1, title, done };
12:    listOfTodos.push(newItem);
13:    return newItem;
14: };
15:
16: const resolvers = {
17:    Query: {
18:       todos: (ctx) => listOfTodos,
19:    },
20:    Mutation: {
21:       addItem: (ctx) => addNewItem(ctx.arguments.title, ctx.
          arguments.done),
22:    },
23: };
24:
```

**LINE 10:** Create a new function, so that we pass the title and boolean value from the query to add the new item in our datasource, in this case the in-memory variable.

**LINE 11:** Generate the ID and create a new item object.

**LINE 20:** Add the mutation operation in the resolver map to be able to resolve whenever adding a new item in the list.

**LINE 21:** Read the arguments passed in the ctx variable and pass to the resolver function.

Let's push the changes and test the GraphQL mutation API:

```
amplify push
```

# Testing the Mutation

Please navigate to the GraphQL API console on a browser, and let's try to hit the mutation query. This is shown in Figure 4-9.

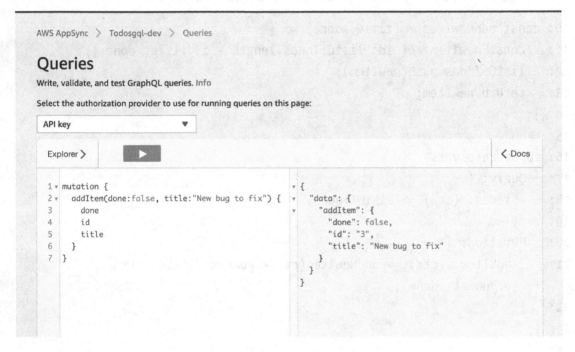

*Figure 4-9.*  *AppSync console*

In response, we created the new item. Let's again hit the get all items query, and the expectation is we should receive three items now.

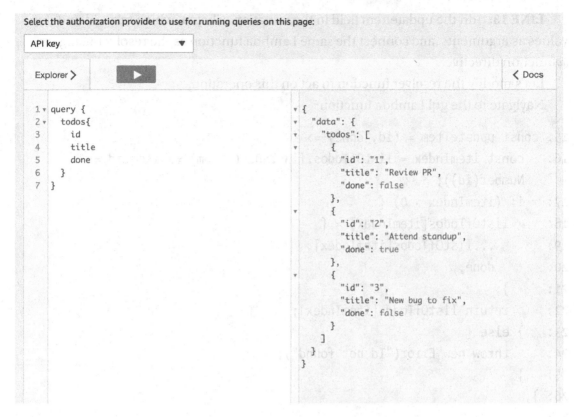

*Figure 4-10.* *Query to get all the items*

We now are able to add new items using the GraphQL API.

# Updating the Item by ID – Mutation Query

Let's now create one more mutation query, which should take the ID of the item, and we should be able to update the status of the item, with a boolean value.

Let's start with modifying the GraphQL schema:

```
10: type Mutation {
11:   addItem(title: String!, done: Boolean!): Todo!
12:     @function(name: "todosfunctiongql-${env}")
13:   updateItem(id: ID!, done: Boolean!): Todo!
14:     @function(name: "todosfunctiongql-${env}")
15: }
```

**LINE 13:** Add the updateItem field in the mutation schema, which takes id and done values as arguments, and connect the same Lambda function as the resolver using the @function directive.

Let's modify the resolver function to act on this operation.

Navigate to the gql Lambda function:

```
15: const updateItem = (id, done) => {
16:    const itemIndex = listOfTodos.findIndex((item) => item.id ===
       Number(id));
17:    if (itemIndex > 0) {
18:      listOfTodos[itemIndex] = {
19:        ...listOfTodos[itemIndex],
20:        done,
21:      };
22:      return listOfTodos[itemIndex];
23:    } else {
24:      throw new Error("Id not found");
25:    }
26: };
27:
28: const resolvers = {
29:    Query: {
30:      todos: (ctx) => listOfTodos,
31:    },
32:    Mutation: {
33:      addItem: (ctx) => addNewItem(ctx.arguments.title,
         ctx.arguments.done),
34:      updateItem: (ctx) => updateItem(ctx.arguments.id,
         ctx.arguments.done),
35:    },
36: };
```

**LINE 15:** Add the function which takes id and done values to update the item from the datasource.

The implementation is pretty much the same as we did in the REST API Lambda function. Find the item by id and update the value and throw an error if the id is not found.

**LINE 16:** Please note the type of id has changed from number to string, hence transposing to a number type using the Number keyword and then comparing to find the index.

Alternatively, we could use the == operator instead of === so that only a comparison could happen, ignoring the type.

**LINE 34:** In the mutation map, create a key with the same name as the query field, and read the arguments from the GraphQL query and pass to the function.

Let's push the changes to Amplify and test the GraphQL API in the AWS console.

The following is the negative scenario: when the id is not found, it should return an error; let's pass the id as a random number, which we are confident that it doesn't exist.

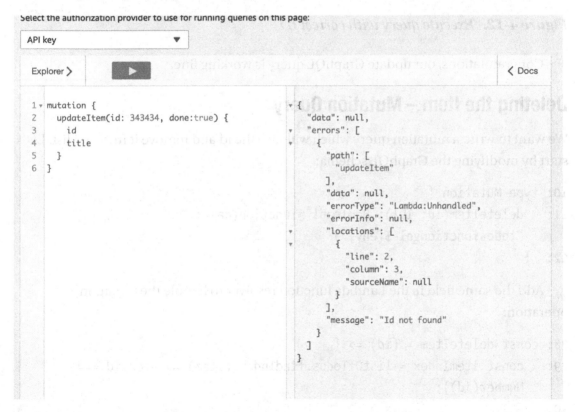

*Figure 4-11.* *Execute query with incorrect ID*

As expected, it throws an error. Let's pass the correct id to update the value.

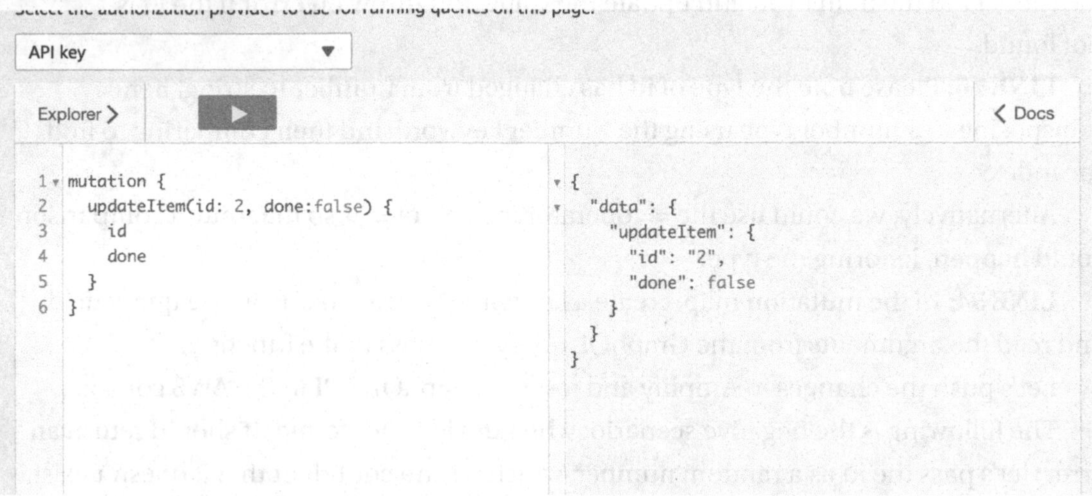

API key ▼

Explorer > ▶ < Docs

```
1 ▾ mutation {
2     updateItem(id: 2, done:false) {
3       id
4       done
5     }
6 }
```

```
▾ {
  ▾ "data": {
      "updateItem": {
        "id": "2",
        "done": false
      }
    }
  }
```

*Figure 4-12.* *Execute query with correct ID*

Congratulations, our update GraphQL query is working fine.

## Deleting the Item – Mutation Query

We want to write a mutation query which will take the id and remove it from the list. Let's start by modifying the GraphQL schema:

```
10: type Mutation {
11:    deleteItem(id: ID!): Boolean! @function(name:
       "todosfunctiongql-${env}")
12: }
```

Add the same field in the Lambda function resolver to handle the mutation operation:

```
28: const deleteItem = (id) => {
29:    const itemIndex = listOfTodos.findIndex((item) => item.id ===
       Number(id));
30:
31:    if (itemIndex >= 0) {
32:      listOfTodos.splice(itemIndex, 1);
33:      return true;
```

```
34:    } else {
35:      throw new Error("Id not found");
36:    }
37: };
38:
39: const resolvers = {
40:   Query: {
41:     todos: (ctx) => listOfTodos,
42:   },
43:   Mutation: {
44:     addItem: (ctx) => addNewItem(ctx.arguments.title, ctx.
         arguments.done),
45:     updateItem: (ctx) => updateItem(ctx.arguments.id, ctx.
         arguments.done),
46:     deleteItem: (ctx) => deleteItem(ctx.arguments.id),
47:   },
48: };
```

**LINE 28:** Add the delete function, which finds the item by id and removes it from the list.

**LINE 46:** Update the mutation resolver map with a field name and connect the resolver function.

Let's push the change to AWS and open the console to test the GraphQL API.

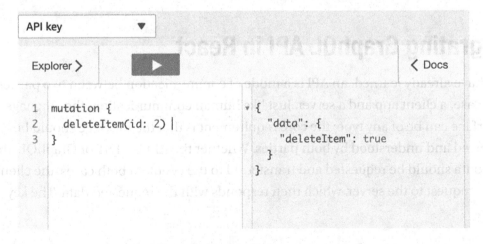

*Figure 4-13.* *Execute query to delete record*

The API returns a boolean true value, as expected, and let's hit get all todo items. Now we should get only one item.

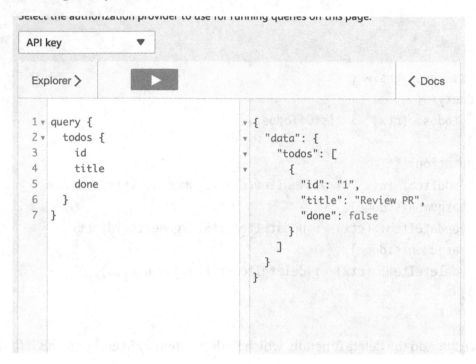

*Figure 4-14.* *Get all todo records*

Congratulations, now we are confident we have been able to delete an item.

# Integrating GraphQL API in React

As we have already learned, an API is a mode of communication between two parties, in this case, a client app and a server. Just like human communication, the language or interface can be of any type; the core requirement is that the message should be transferred and understood by both parties. Whether the API is REST or GraphQL, the actual data should be requested and transferred to the client. In both cases, the client sends a request to the server, which then responds with the requested data. The key difference between REST and GraphQL is in how the data is requested and how the server responds. With REST, the client specifies the endpoint, and the server responds with all the data at that endpoint. With GraphQL, the client specifies the data it needs using a query language, and the server responds with only the requested data. Both REST and GraphQL have their own strengths and weaknesses, and the choice between the two will depend on the specific needs of a given project.

Now that we have all the required set of GraphQL APIs for our todo application, we should integrate these in our application, we will not rewrite the React code from scratch, we will modify the existing client app to consume the GraphQL API, and the application should work as is.

Let's begin with our React hook where on load we call the API to get all lists of Todos and show them on the UI:

```
33:    useEffect(() => {
34:      API.get("todosapi", "/todos").then((data) => {
35:        setTodoList(data);
36:      });
37:    }, []);
```

The preceding code is the React hook integration to call the get all REST API; let's modify this so that it consumes the GraphQL query:

```
33:    useEffect(() => {
34:      API.graphql({
35:        query: `query {
36:          todos {
37:            id
38:            title
39:            done
40:          }
41:        }`,
42:      }).then((data) => {
43:        setTodoList(data);
44:      });
45:    }, []);
46:
```

**LINE 34:** Call the GraphQL function from the API to request the GraphQL query.

**LINE 35:** Pass the exact query from our query console.

Let's run, start the React server, and keep our eye on the Network tab of the browser.

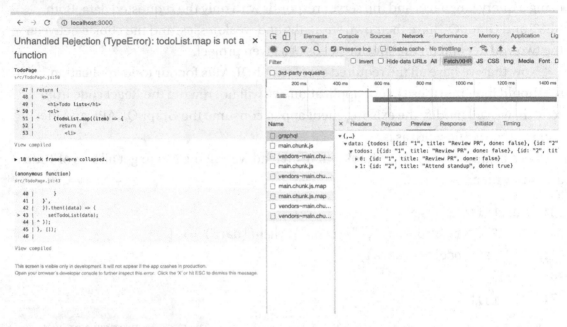

***Figure 4-15.*** *Integrating GraphQL with the React app*

Please note the GraphQL API is requested by the React hook; if you check the response, you will see we received the response.

But something failed on our React code.

It's nothing but the response structure. In the REST API, we got the response as an array; in GraphQL, we are getting the data wrapped in the data key and todos key.

Let's modify our response handler from the React hook:

```
37:            id
38:            title
39:            done
40:         }
41:      }`,
42:    }).then((data) => {
43:      setTodoList(data.data.todos);
44:    });
45:  }, []);
```

**LINE 43:** We are modifying to read the list of todos from the todos key wrapped under the data key.

Save and restart; voila, our new list of todos is getting fetched from the GraphQL API.

# Integrating GraphQL Mutation API

Let's start modifying the function on click of add item to call the mutation query, which will create a new item using our GraphQL mutation API:

```
08:    const addNewItem = (title) => {
09:      API.graphql({
10:        query: `
11:          mutation {
12:            addItem(done:false, title: "${title}") {
13:              id
14:              title
15:              done
16:            }
17:          }
18:        `,
19:      })
20:        .then((data) => {
21:          console.log("Creation success with data", data);
22:          setTodoList([...todoList, data.data.addItem]);
23:          setNewItemField("");
24:        })
```

**LINE 10:** Call the GraphQL function from the API to pass the GraphQL mutation query.

**LINE 11:** Pass the same mutation query for adding a new item, as we ran in the previous section from the AWS console.

**LINE 12:** Use the backtick to create a dynamic mutation query to pass the title to the query.

**LINE 22:** Read the response from the addItem key wrapped under the data key which is the response structure from GraphQL.

Save the file and run the server; voila, we are now able to add new items using the GraphQL mutation query.

# Do It Yourself (DIY): Modifying the React App

Modify the React application to integrate the update and delete mutation GraphQL queries.

## Subscription API

So far, we have implemented and consumed the traditional request-response model-based client-server interaction APIs, which uses the HTTP protocol. In this model, the client opens an HTTP connection to the server and sends a request, and the server responds with the requested data on the same connection. Once the response is complete, the HTTP connection is closed. This is true for all the methods of REST APIs, as well as for GraphQL queries and mutations.

Many times, we require receiving real-time data pushed from the server to the client. For example, while booking a cab on Uber, we want to receive notifications from the server when the cab is near us or receive messages on a chatting application. If the server does not push the data to the client, we would be required to refresh again and again to get the new status of the cab or get new messages.

Outside of the GraphQL realm, this can be achieved in various ways. One common approach is setting up a WebSocket connection between the server and client. This creates a two-way connection and enables the server to send the data without requiring the client to poll the data.

Now, given that we want to discuss GraphQL functionalities, let me introduce you to GraphQL subscription APIs. Subscriptions are a GraphQL feature that enables real-time data streaming from the server to the client over a WebSocket connection. With GraphQL subscriptions, the client can specify a subscription query to the server, which the server uses to push relevant data to the client in real time. Subscriptions provide a powerful and efficient way to implement real-time features in GraphQL APIs and can be particularly useful for applications like chat apps, stock tickers, and real-time gaming.

The GraphQL team has done an amazing job by providing the subscription feature. As the name suggests, clients can subscribe to events and receive real-time data from those events. For example, a client could subscribe to a Todo item mutation event. Every time a new Todo item is created, the subscribed client will receive the data in real time and can choose to update the list on their UI.

GraphQL subscriptions are a wrapper of WebSockets and handle all the edge cases under the hood. The client initiates a WebSocket connection with the server, and the server uses the connection to push data to the client in response to subscription queries. GraphQL subscriptions provide a powerful and efficient way to implement real-time features in GraphQL APIs and can be particularly useful for applications that require live updates, such as chat apps, social networks, and stock tickers.

With GraphQL subscriptions, clients have greater control over the data they receive and can choose to receive only the data they need. This can help reduce the amount of data transferred over the network, leading to faster and more efficient application performance. Overall, GraphQL subscriptions are a great addition to the GraphQL ecosystem and provide a powerful tool for building real-time applications.

As you can see in Figure 4-16, let's assume Mr. Bob subscribed to a Todo item mutation event, and Larry from a different browser created a new item in todo; Mr. Bob will instantly receive the details of the new item created.

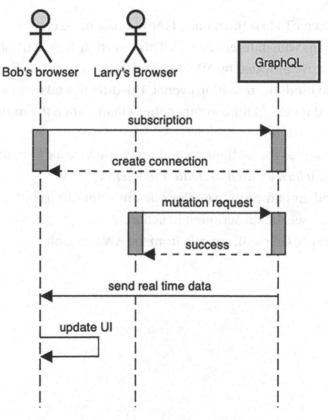

***Figure 4-16.*** *GraphQL subscription high-level workflow*

Let's create the subscription API and see the end-to-end flow in action.

We need to add the subscription in our GraphQL schema and connect to the event.

Open the schema.GraphQL file from the following location:

```
./amplify/backend/api/todosgql/shema.graphql
```

And add the following in the schema:

```
18: type Subscription {
19:   OnCreateTodo: Todo @aws_subscribe(mutations: ["addItem"])
20: }
```

Let's discuss what we wrote in the schema.

**LINE 18:** We are mentioning that we want to define a subscription type operation in our schema.

**LINE 19:** OnCreateTodo is the name of the operation; we can have n numbers of such subscriptions with different names. This returns a Todo type object. @aws_subscribe is a directive provided by AWS Amplify which automatically adds some functionalities and binds the mutation events. The directive takes an array of mutation, which returns the data in real time to subscribed clients when the mutation events are triggered.

Here, we have added the addItem mutation. *Please note we have already defined the addItem mutation, which we used to create Todo items.*

Please save and amplify push to deploy our subscription GraphQL API.

Once done, let's see the subscription in action.

Open the AppSync GraphQL console from the AWS console.

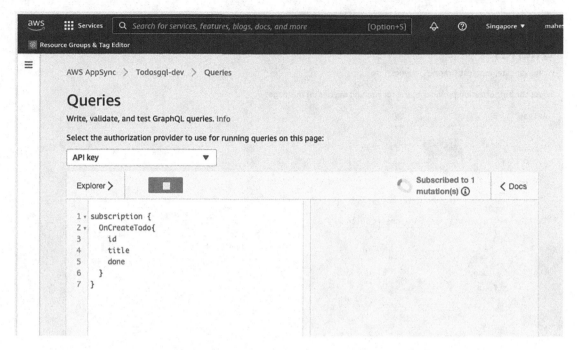

*Figure 4-17.   AppSync GraphQL console*

Enter the subscription query and click the play button, and please note on the right top, it shows the client is subscribed to one mutation.

Now open the same console on a new tab. We will run the mutation and create a new Todo item.

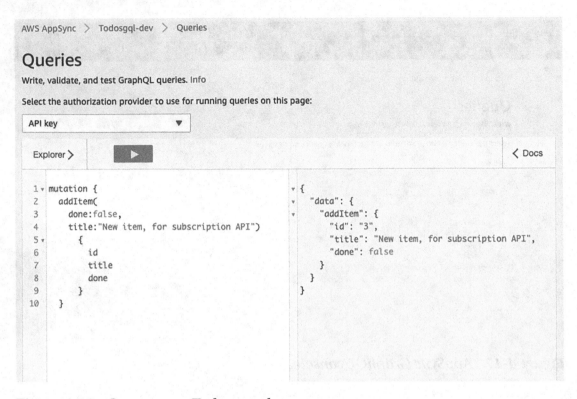

*Figure 4-18.*  *Creates new Todo record*

Add a new item using the addItem mutation and click play; as you can see, the new item is created and new id has been assigned.

Let's switch to the tab, which has subscribed to the addItem mutation.

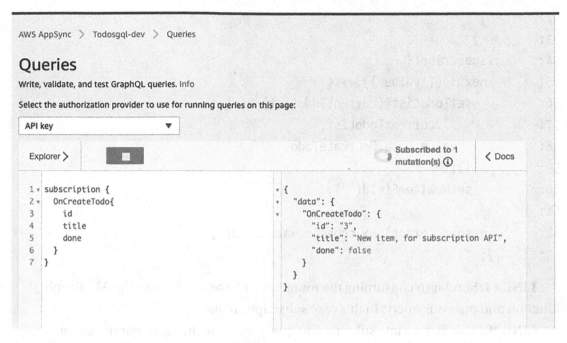

**Figure 4-19.** *Subscribed tab to see data*

Voila, as you can see, the same item is shown here, which was created now.

This is the magic of subscription.

# Integrating Subscription API with React

In the previous section, we tested the GraphQL subscription API over two different clients. Let's modify our React code to list real-time changes.

Let's switch to our React code and add the subscription in the useEffect hook:

```
43:    useEffect(() => {
44:      API.graphql(
45:        graphqlOperation(`
46:        subscription {
47:          OnCreateTodo{
48:            id
49:            title
50:            done
51:          }
```

```
52:        }
53:        `)
54:      ).subscribe({
55:        next: ({ value }) => {
56:          setTodoList((currentTodoList) => [
57:            ...currentTodoList,
58:            value.data.OnCreateTodo,
59:          ]);
60:          setNewItemField("");
61:        },
62:        error: (error) => console.warn(error),
63:      });
```

**LINE 44:** Similar to consuming the mutation API, we need to use the API.GraphQL function and pass our query, in this case subscription query.

**LINE 46:** This is the same subscription query we wrote in the previous section, and we tested it from the AppSync query console in the browser.

**LINE 54:** As this query is subscription based, there would be some events, and we need to react on certain events; hence, we would subscribe using the subscribe function and attach a listener, in this case, next and error.

**LINE 55:** On success event, we would receive a value; there are also other metadata we receive on success event, but for now we are not going to discuss those.

**LINE 56:** When we receive a new item on success event, we need to reflect it on the UI; hence, we are using the useState hook function to set the value, so that it can reflect on the UI.

**LINE 60:** We are setting newItemField to empty to clear the item label that we type.

***Figure 4-20.***  *Updated user interface for the Todo app*

Once you add via the mutation subscription event, the new item gets reflected to the list.

We can use this trigger point to notify or for a bunch of other activities.

**Use cases of subscription:**

- **All sort of real-time updates**

  Let's assume you are building your own Facebook; when the user's friends like or comment on a post, the user should instantly get the notification of who has liked or commented on the post, and instantly the like count should increase. If you are live streaming videos, and you want to continuously show the current number of live users watching the video.

- **Payment status updates**

  Whenever you are integrating a payment system via banks or cards, you will definitely be integrating the application with a third-party system, and payment APIs may take more than five seconds, and there may be a retry required due to failures, so keeping the customer waiting on the loading screen is not a good idea; hence, we might use the subscription APIs to notify the customer from the server to the client app when the payment status changes to success or failure.

# Why APIs Throw 401 Error

APIs pushed via Amplify are exposed via AppSync service by AWS. For security purposes, APIs need to have an API key.

If you inspect the element and check the Network tab from the React app, you will see the API key in action.

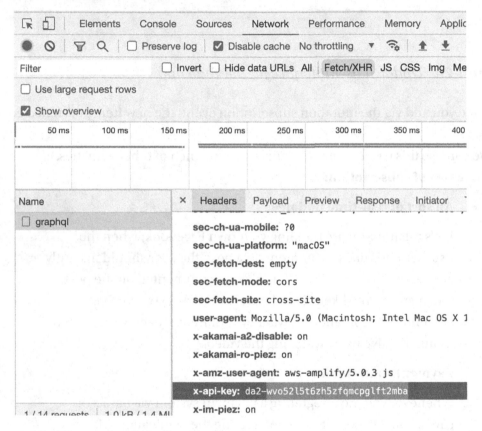

***Figure 4-21.*** *Network tab in DevTools*

If you recall, this was also shown on the console when you pushed the new API via amplify push.

This API key comes with an expiry date; when the key is expired, the application will stop working, and the APIs will throw a 401 error.

To check the current API key and its expiry

1.   Open and log in to the AWS console.

2.   Open the AWS AppSync service.

3.   Click the Amplify project.

4.   From the left pane, open the Settings tab.

5.   Scroll down to authorization mode; you will see the API keys and expiry date.

*Figure 4-22.* *Amplify project settings*

If the API key is expired, we need to rotate the keys.

Follow the steps to recreate the key:

1.   Open the parameters.json file located in amplify/backend/api/<api-name>.

2.   Add a key with "CreateAPIKey": 0.

For example:

```
{
  "AppSyncApiName": <api-name>,
  "DynamoDBBillingMode": "PAY_PER_REQUEST",
  "DynamoDBEnableServerSideEncryption": false,
  "CreateAPIKey": 0
}
```

143

3. The value 0 means to delete the existing key.

4. Run amplify push, and accept the changes.

5. After the successful push, open the same file and change the value to 1, which denotes create the key.

6. You can now choose from the CLI menu how long you want the key to be alive.

7. Run amplify push to recreate the API key with a new TTL.

# Summary

This chapter covered the process of integrating a REST API with a frontend React app. We started by creating a basic React todo app and then learned how to get data from a REST API using the fetch() method in JavaScript. Next, we introduced GraphQL as an alternative to REST APIs and discussed its pros and cons. We then moved on to using GraphQL with AWS Amplify, setting up the API for CRUD operations and creating custom resolvers for complex data operations.

We also covered testing GraphQL APIs with the Amplify console, adding new items to our GraphQL API using mutation queries, and integrating our GraphQL API with React. We then introduced GraphQL subscriptions and learned how to define them in our schema and integrate them with our React app using the Apollo client library.

Throughout the chapter, we covered a range of topics related to integrating APIs with React, including both REST and GraphQL APIs. We discussed the benefits and drawbacks of each approach and provided practical examples and code snippets to help readers implement the concepts covered in the chapter. By the end of the chapter, readers should have a good understanding of how to integrate APIs with React and how to choose the best approach for their specific needs.

# CHAPTER 5

# Offline-First App

*Offline-first is not just a feature, it's a mindset. It's about building resilient systems that empower users, no matter their connection status.*

—Akshat Paul

Most of the web or mobile applications require an Internet connection to work. This especially has changed in the last decade when the world adapted the client and server model, and both of these instruments interact using APIs, and the server will be on the cloud and require an active Internet connection to interact with, which makes the client more mobile and decouples itself with the physical location; In the late 1990s, applications used to be more client side, that is, on the desktop you install the software, and without any Internet, all the operations were allowed and all the user data were stored in the machine itself, in the hard disk. This model used to be much different than applications we use nowadays. These client-side applications never supported more than one user and also did not support multidevice features, because nothing was on the cloud and the data, device, and users were tightly coupled.

## Benefits of the Client-Server Model

The reason why the client-server architecture has tons of benefits and the world has shifted to the cloud is because of the following:

1.  Privacy: The server is secured and is not publicly accessible, unlike the client app; hence, we can keep valuable business logic and keep secret keys on the backend server.

2.  Multitenancy: We can design the server architecture in a way that we can support more than one user and add some security policies, namely, one user will not be able to see other users' data; this is known as a multitenant application.

© Akshat Paul, Mahesh Haldar 2023
A. Paul and M. Haldar, *Serverless Web Applications with AWS Amplify*,
https://doi.org/10.1007/978-1-4842-8707-1_5

3.  Easy updates: As the code is deployed on the server, it can be
    updated any number of times and doesn't depend on the client
    whether the customer has updated or not; it gives the flexibility
    of updating the server code as much as required, and changes are
    reflected instantly.

4.  Multidevice support: Given the user data is mostly stored on
    the server side, the application can be simultaneously logged
    on multiple devices, and the same data gets replicated instantly
    without any manual steps involved.

5.  Accessible anywhere: Given the server is on the cloud, this model
    reduces the dependency of specific devices; if it is a web app, just
    open any browser irrespective of the operating system you get the
    access to; if the device is mobile, then all you need is to install the
    app and log in. This model allows users to use any device.

We understand this solves a lot of problems, but it takes away some of the benefits
which client-only apps had.

There can be times when the Internet is not active but you still want to access the
app. As per the Internet stats data, still 63% of the world population don't have access to
the Internet.

Sometimes, the business requires offline apps and expects the Internet is not
available in some isolated areas or secured areas.

If we can make the web app also work without an Internet, and later sync with the
cloud when the Internet is back, then it can be labeled as an offline-first app.

This will give the benefit of both worlds.

# Use Cases of Offline Apps

Let's discuss some of the real-life use cases of offline apps to better understand why we
are even discussing this:

1.  Deep tunnel application: Suppose you are creating an application
    to record data for workers in a deep tunnel. If there is no Internet
    available in the tunnel, then the data cannot be recorded. In this
    case, having an offline-first app would solve the problem, allowing
    data to be recorded even without an Internet connection.

2. Lift or pipeline inspection app: Similar to the previous example, if you are part of a lift inspection application, you cannot expect the Internet to work with high bandwidth. Hence, an offline app would solve the problem by allowing data to be recorded without a reliable Internet connection.

3. Application for tourists when traveling outside the country: Imagine if you could not download Google Maps for offline use or could not access a tourism guide. As a tourist, this would cause a lot of problems, especially if Internet access is expensive. Hence, an offline-first app is valuable in such scenarios.

4. Improving user experience: Many times, even if the user has an Internet connection, there can be obvious Internet breakages due to various reasons such as Internet issues or unexpected jammers. This can negatively impact the user experience. By implementing an offline-first strategy, the user experience can be drastically improved. For example, the first screen can appear instantly, and the user would not have to wait for all the JavaScript, CSS, and images to load. Additionally, the user's data can be cached on the browser to minimize the number of loaders and improve overall performance.

5. Field service applications: Imagine if you are a field service engineer who needs to access customer data, work orders, and service manuals while in remote locations with poor connectivity. With an offline-first app, you can download all the necessary information beforehand and access it offline, ensuring that you have everything you need to do your job.

6. Point-of-sale systems: In busy retail environments, network connectivity can be unpredictable. An offline-first app for point-of-sale systems allows transactions to be processed offline and synced with the server when a connection is reestablished, preventing loss of sales and customer frustration.

7.  Learning and educational applications: Students and educators
    in remote areas may not have reliable Internet connectivity. An
    offline-first learning app can provide access to course materials,
    videos, and other educational content even without an Internet
    connection, enabling continuous learning.

8.  Remote and rural health applications: In remote and rural areas,
    Internet connectivity can be scarce or expensive. An offline-first
    health app can enable healthcare providers to collect and store
    patient data offline, ensuring continuity of care and enabling
    remote consultations when an Internet connection is available.

# The Offline App – Design Overview

Even before we make our hands dirty with code, let's discuss how the offline feature
would work in general, and let's together create a mental map of the same.

## Goal

Let's list down the goals we want to achieve:

1.  When the application is connected to the Internet, the application
    should work as expected.

2.  When the Internet is not available, we should be able to interact
    with applications.

3.  When the Internet connection is back, the data gets synced with
    our backend systems.

To achieve the preceding goals, when the Internet connection has failed, instead of
crashing the application and acting helpless, the application needs to be smarter.

We can keep track of when the Internet connection has failed, then we can store the
data local cache with a flag that the items are local only, and when the Internet is back,
we replicate the behavior and remove it from our local cache.

We can refer to Figures 5-1 and 5-2 to represent what we just discussed.

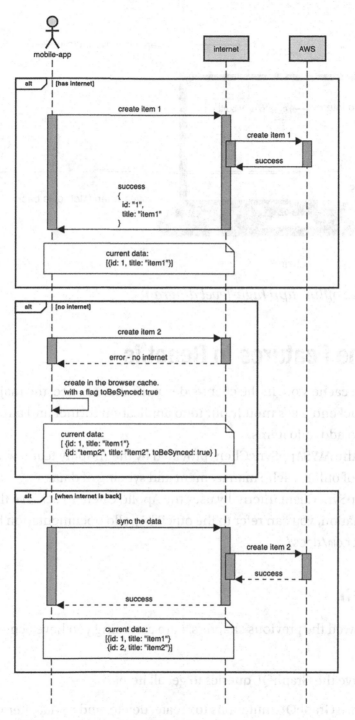

***Figure 5-1.*** *The offline app sequence diagram*

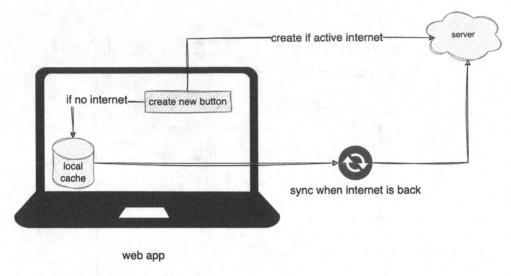

**Figure 5-2.** *The offline app high-level diagram*

# Add Offline Features in React.js

We will keep the cache store in the client-side application; hence, the majority of effort will be on the backend. Let's modify our todo application further and already created GraphQL APIs to add todo items.

We will use the AWSAppSyncClient provided by the Amplify team, which provides all the capabilities of offline cache management and syncing of data.

The AWSAppSyncClient internally uses the Apollo Client to achieve the functionality; for more information, you can refer to the official Apollo documentation `https://www.apollographql.com/docs/`.

## Assumption

If you have followed the previous chapters, I am assuming you have achieved the following:

1. We have the GraphQL queries to get all items.

2. We have GraphQL mutations to create, delete, and update items.

3. We have the React code which integrates with the preceding APIs.

4. And our React app looks similar to Figure 5-3.

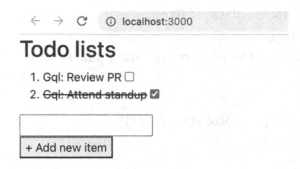

*Figure 5-3.* *Demo of the React application output*

# The Page Render Function

```
153:          <div>
154:             <button onClick={() => addNewItem(newItemField)}>
155:                + Add new item
156:             </button>
157:          </div>
```

When the add new button is clicked, we call the function addNewItem.

In this function, while trying to create an item on the server, there are two possibilities:

1.  The Internet connection is stable and the API call is a success; voila, we already have this working end to end.

2.  The device is not connected to the Internet and the API call fails; in this case, our smart app should handle the edge case and do the caching stuff to sync it when the Internet connection is back.

Let's see #2 in action:

```
70:   const addNewItem = async (title) => {
71:     let data;
72:     try {
73:       console.log("Trying to add through internet");
74:       const response = await addItemWithOnlineClient(title);
```

```
75:        data = response.data.addItem;
76:        console.log(
77:          "You are online now, hence added via network with response",
78:          data
79:        );
80:        setTodoList([...todoList, data]);
81:      } catch (err) {
82:        console.log(
83:          "The api call failed, may be you are offile, trying
             offline client"
84:        );
85:        console.log(">>> CALLING ADD WITHOFFLINE");
86:        const response = await addItemWithOfflineClient(title,
             setTodoList);
87:        data = response.data.addItem;
88:        console.log(">> Data stored in localstorage to sync when
             online", data);
89:      } finally {
90:        setNewItemField("");
91:      }
92:    };
```

**LINE 74:** Notice the function addItemWithOnlineClient; this is the client which will try to create items via the Internet, and this client doesn't have cache integration.

**LINE 75:** If the creation API is successful, we will get data; if the Internet is not there, then an error will be thrown. That's why we have wrapped this function with a try-catch block so that we can handle the cases when the Internet connection is not present and the app is offline.

**LINE 80:** If we get a response, this is the happy case, and we set the response in our state to rerender the UI with a new set of lists.

**LINE 81:** If the creation failed, then the error thrown will be caught here.

**LINE 86:** Then we try a different HTTP client using the function addItemWithOfflineClient; this client has all the capability of caching and syncing of data.

**LINE 89:** As discussed in the previous chapter, we want to reset the input field, hence resetting to the empty field via the useState function.

# Real-Time Online HTTP Client

We have already done this in the previous chapter; let's still check the function:

```
53: async function addItemWithOnlineClient(title) {
54:   return API.graphql({
55:     query: `
56:     mutation {
57:       addItem(done:false, title: "${title}") {
58:         id
59:         title
60:         done
61:       }
62:     }
63: `,
64:   });
65: }
```

**LINE 54:** It integrates with the API instance from the AWS-amplify plugin and calls the mutation GraphQL query.

# Offline HTTP Client

Let's discuss how we use the Amplify prebuilt HTTP client to achieve most of the offline capabilities:

```
07: import awsconfig from "./aws-exports";
08: import AWSAppSyncClient, { AUTH_TYPE } from "aws-appsync";
09:
10: const client = new AWSAppSyncClient({
11:   url: awsconfig.aws_appsync_graphqlEndpoint,
12:   region: awsconfig.aws_appsync_region,
13:   auth: {
14:     type: AUTH_TYPE.API_KEY,
15:     apiKey: awsconfig.aws_appsync_apiKey,
16:   },
```

```
17:   cacheOptions: {
18:     dataIdFromObject: (obj) => `${obj.__typename}:${obj.id}`,
19:   },
20: });
```

**LINE 7:** Import the aws config like the GraphQL endpoint and apikeys to be used to communicate with the servers.

**LINE 8:** We will install the aws-appsync package to get the appsync client.

**LINE 10:** Create a new instance of the client and pass the required configurations.

**LINE 17:** This configuration is for creating the entries in local cache; when the Internet connection is not there, then under which key the objects will be stored. In our case, we are forming the keys by combining the typename and id of the object, so that there is no conflict.

## Handling Errors in Real-Time API Clients with Offline Clients

As discussed in the previous section, this offline client will be used when the real-time API client fails and throws an error; hence, we catch and call the function to handle via the offline client.

Let's expand and discuss the function we wrote in the previous section:

```
20: async function addItemWithOfflineClient(title, setTodoList) {
21:   return client.mutate({
22:     mutation: gql(`mutation {
23:         addItem(
24:           done:false,
25:           title: "${title}")
26:             {
27:                id
28:                title
29:                done
30:             }
31:        }`),
32:     update: (cache, { data }) => {
33:       setTodoList((currentTodoList) => {
34:         let newListOfTodos = currentTodoList;
```

```
35:          if (!data.addItem) {
36:            newListOfTodos = [
37:              ...newListOfTodos,
38:              {
39:                title,
40:                done: false,
41:                isOffline: true,
42:              },
43:            ];
44:          } else {
45:            newListOfTodos = currentTodoList.filter((item) => !item.
                 isOffline);
46:            newListOfTodos = [...newListOfTodos, data.addItem];
47:          }
48:          return newListOfTodos;
49:        });
50:      },
51:    });
52: }
```

**LINE 21:** The mutate function is called when we want to do the mutation operation.

**LINE 22:** The mutation key takes the mutation query as a string. This query is the same as the one we developed in the previous chapter.

**LINE 32:** The update key requires a function to be operated. This function gets called two times: the first time when the Internet is off and the mutation is successful in the cache, and the second time again when the app is online and when syncing is done and, actually, mutation is successful on the server.

**LINE 33:** When the mutation is done in local, then we also want to reflect the data in the list of items, hence we are using the setTodoList which is the useState function.

**LINE 35:** If the response comes from the server, the data is defined; if it is stored in local, the data.addItem response is undefined; we are using this value to identify whether the data is stored locally for later syncing or is created in the server.

**LINE 41:** When we are confident the data is stored in the local cache for later syncing, we are updating the list with a flag isOffline to true, so that we can identify which data is offline and which is not.

**LINE 45:** When again the update function is called, with a valid data.addItem response from the server, we know the data is synced to the server; hence, we are removing the item which has an isOffline flag and setting the new data to our list.

# Rendering the Offline and Online Items in the List

To improve the user experience, we should flag the offline data and show the synced data differently.

Figure 5-4 is the screenshot of when we tried to add one item in the absence of an Internet connection.

***Figure 5-4.*** *React application screenshot rendering the item added in offline mode*

And the moment we connect to the Internet, the item should be synced, and the red color should be gone, and the wifi icon should also disappear.

Let's modify our render function to achieve this:

```
123:    return (
124:      <>
125:        <h1>Todo lists</h1>
126:        <ol>
127:          {todoList.map((item) => {
128:            return (
129:              <li style={{ color: item.isOffline ? "red" : "black" }}>
130:                {item.done ? <strike>{item.title}</strike> : item.title}
131:                <span>
132:                  {" "}
```

```
133:                <input
134:                  type="checkbox"
135:                  defaultChecked={item.done}
136:                  onChange={(event) => updateItemStatus
                      (item.id, event)}
137:                />
138:              </span>
139:
140:              <span>{item.isOffline ? <BsWifiOff /> : ""}</span>
141:            </li>
142:          );
143:        })}
144:      </ol>
```

This is the extend render function from the previous chapter.

**LINE 127:** todoList is the current list of items from useState, which initially is populated from the get all item API using useEffect.

**LINE 129:** If the data has isOffline as true value, we set the color in style to red, else black for non-offline data.

The React code we have already discussed in the previous chapter, if you skipped that, even then also its simple code to render some components.

**LINE 140:** We also wanted to render a wifi off icon, hence one more check and render icon for offline data.

# Testing Offline Feature

Let's start our server and open our landing page.

Figure 5-5 shows what is expected; the list will have two items already rendered if you are consuming the same get all query.

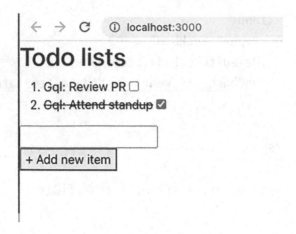

***Figure 5-5.*** *Screenshot showing different states of data*

Let's make our app offline.

Open the inspect element or developer tool on a browser, and navigate to Network; click the arrow which has No throttling as shown in Figure 5-6.

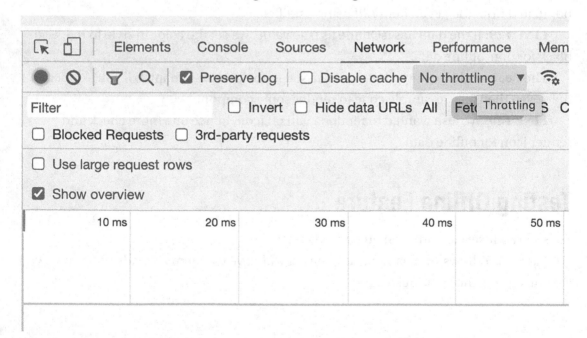

***Figure 5-6.*** *Screenshot of the Network tab to control the throttling configuration*

Click the Offline option as shown in Figure 5-7.

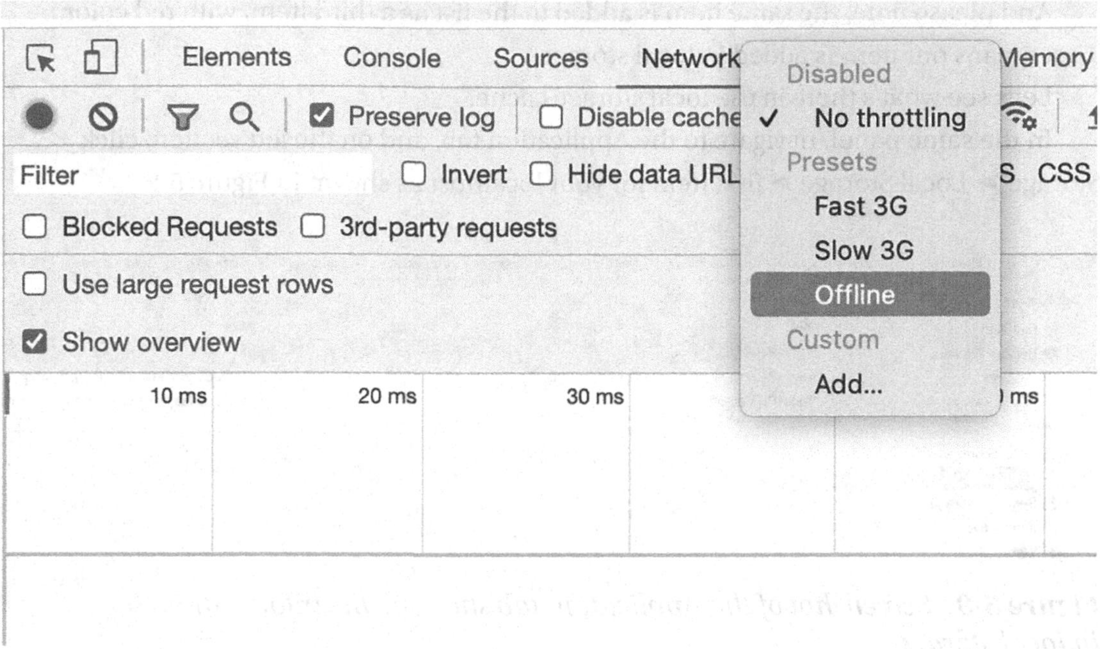

***Figure 5-7.*** *Screenshot of the Network tab to switch to offline mode*

Basically, this throttling tool is for developers to test your application and replicate scenarios of low Internet bandwidth or no Internet.

Once your app is offline, let's try to add an item in our todo list application.

As you can see in Figure 5-8 in network logs, one GraphQL API tried to communicate, but it failed as our app is offline.

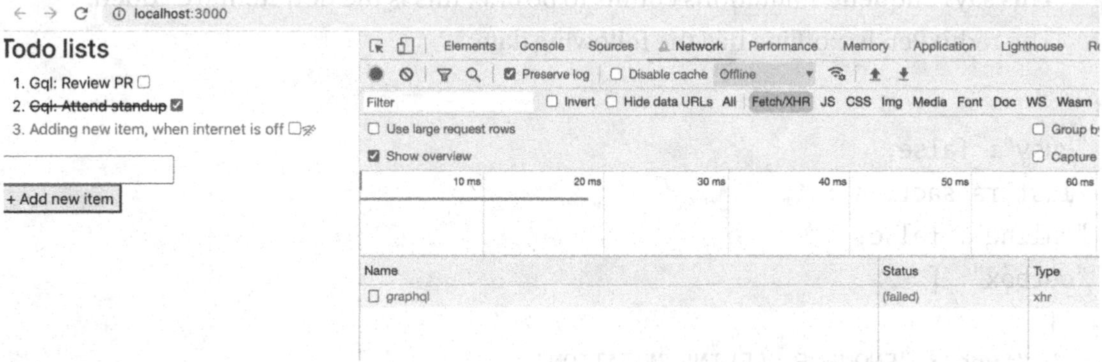

***Figure 5-8.*** *Screenshot of the Network tab and application to show the failed API call due to offline mode*

And please note, the same item is added in the list as a third item, with red color. That means our item is added in local storage.

Let's see what's there in the local storage cache.

In the same panel, navigate to the Application tab, and on the left section, click Storage ➤ Local Storage ➤ first item for your localhost as shown in Figure 5-9.

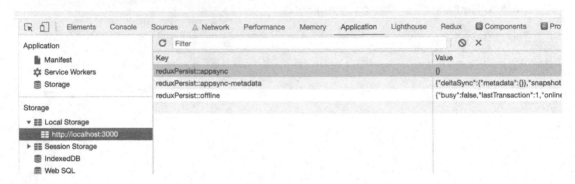

***Figure 5-9.*** *Screenshot of the Application tab showing the information in local storage*

You see some data is there; this data is added by the aws-appsync client, as we expected.

Let's see what type of data is added in this local storage.

The appsync-metadata has the following data:

```
{"deltaSync":{"metadata":{}},"snapshot":{"enqueuedMutations":1,"cache":{}},
"idsMap":{}}
```

This says enqueuedMutations counts to be one; this is the new item we added.

The reduxPersist::offline has the following data:

```
{
  "busy": false,
  "lastTransaction": 1,
  "online": false,
  "outbox": [
    {
      "type": "ENQUEUE_OFFLINE_MUTATION",
      "payload": {},
      "meta": {
```

```
    "offline": {
         "query": {
            "kind": "Document",
            "definitions": [
                {
                    "kind": "OperationDefinition",
                    "operation": "mutation",
                    ...

                        {
                            "kind": "Argument",
                            "name": { "kind": "Name", "value": "title" },
                            "value": {
                                "kind": "StringValue",
                                "value": "Adding new item, when internet
                                is off",
                                "block": false
                            }
                    },
                    "transaction": 1
                }
            }
        ],
        "retryCount": 0,
        "retryScheduled": false
    }
```

I have removed a few keys and values from the preceding code to make it short; you can navigate to your browser to see the data in detail.

If you check data, it stores some information like online: false.

The operation kind is mutation and also stores the data which needs to be synced when the app goes online.

Well, this shows we have successfully stored the data in the local cache when the app is not connected to the Internet.

# Testing the Online Syncing Feature

Now that we have offline data, let's replicate the situation when the app gets back the Internet connection and see the online syncing process in action.

Before making your application to the online state, let's navigate back to the Network tab and set the throttling to No throttling in developer tools.

As you can notice in Figure 5-10, in network log, the moment we made the network throttling to no throttling, there is a new API request which is successful with a 200 HTTP status.

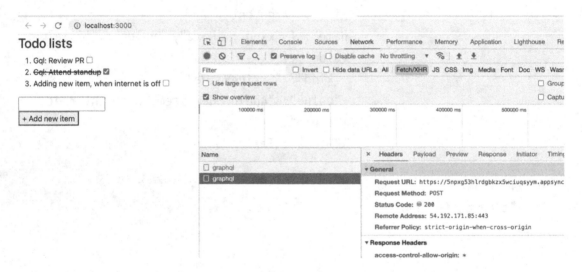

***Figure 5-10.*** *Screenshot of the Network tab showing a successful API when the Internet is connected*

And our list got refreshed with a new item, and the red color and wifi icon are also gone.

Voila, congratulations, our first offline storage and online syncing feature is working as expected.

# Things to Consider While Creating Offline Apps

Developing and maintaining offline features for an application is not an easy task; the major problem lies in making the data consistent across the system. The complexity is directly proportional to various parameters, like a number of features to have the offline capability and a number of users trying to modify the same data parallelly when offline.

The following steps should be taken when planning to build an offline-first app:

1.  Well-thought-of use case for offline scenario

    The scope of offline use cases should be well planned and handled. The user should be informed which data is not synced and also when the app is running in offline mode.

2.  API standard error codes

    The API should throw the correct and meaningful error codes, so that the client can respond accordingly.

3.  Error handling

    When we switch to offline, all the APIs will start breaking; hence, the client app should gracefully handle these errors and perform the actions of the offline journey.

4.  Data syncing strategy

    The application should subscribe to an Internet connection state, and the moment the Internet is back, the data should instantly start syncing.

5.  Mindful deleting of local cache data

    The application should mindfully remove the unsynced data only after a confirmation from the server, if the data is synced to the server. If this is not handled, then the user will end up losing the data forever.

6.  Testing

    The application should be thoroughly tested for all the use cases before going live on production.

# Summary

In this chapter on building offline applications, we learned to create an application which can function without a reliable Internet connection. This is an important consideration for any application which needs to work even when the Internet connection is guaranteed.

First, we discussed the limitations of a traditional web application and how they can be improved with offline functionality. We also discussed about various use cases in real life, where the offline-first application can really help the business to generate value and also get the benefits of the client-server model. We also explored the use of AWS Amplify services which helps in achieving the offline-first app.

Throughout the chapter, we provided the examples of how to use AWS Amplify and React.js to build offline functionality to create a todo application.

# CHAPTER 6

# Data Storage

*Data really powers everything that we do.*

—Jeff Weiner, CEO of LinkedIn

In the previous chapters, we have discussed how to create the backend and frontend of the application using the AWS Amplify service. The server and frontend interacted via REST and GraphQL APIs. However, we still need a place to store our data. This is where the data storage systems like databases or file storage come into the picture and play an important role in data-centric applications. In this chapter, we will explore the ways to store and retrieve data efficiently and reliably.

We will start with understanding the requirements of such systems, types of data and storages, and AWS services, and then we will do some coding to provision data storage and integrate with our APIs.

## Introduction

In computing context, the data is a piece of information that has some meaning and some value to a particular business or process; the data represents the state or information about an individual or a process. The data can be in different languages and different formats, like text, numbers, images, or videos. For example, the transactional data from a bank account can help the banks to calculate how much money is remaining in a particular bank account, and the ticket number, name, and photographs can help a person to get entry to the airport and travel from one place to another.

If we can store these data in a particular structure and store them in a computer to make it easy to search, filter, and readable by different systems and machines, this is termed a database. For example, a ticket number is the data, and the database is the computer where this is stored. Databases are the most important element in the human world. The database in the modern world is generally associated with the storage part

© Akshat Paul, Mahesh Haldar 2023
A. Paul and M. Haldar, *Serverless Web Applications with AWS Amplify*,
https://doi.org/10.1007/978-1-4842-8707-1_6

of any computer software. We interact with them almost every day, whenever you log in, search for products, view product reviews, or watch YouTube videos – all of these are possible because of databases.

The database has been existing way before computers and the Internet became reachable to humans. Before computing databases, humans used libraries, journals, and cabinets to store data in files. Even the shares in the stock market were traded on paper before the Internet. And, physical records were maintained in files by a bunch of humans to keep the process on.

Given the records were kept on paper, the challenge was searching for the right data; it took a lot of physical space and backup if something goes wrong, for example, accidental fire and rats chewing, wiping off the data records in minutes. Like many other problems in the world, the computer and the Internet solved the data storage problem as well. Data storage became digital, and it was a blessing to humanity.

## Types of Data to Store

Broadly, all the data in the world can be categorized into two buckets that are valuable for businesses or processes to run smoothly:

- Files: File-based data are an important part of the storage, for example, if we want to create and store a copy of our ID card in our phone, it has to be an image; if we want to store the memory of our travel, it has to be photos or videos. These data are raw file based. Other examples are Excel sheets, pdf, etc.

  If we upload these files on the cloud and generate a URL, we need not carry over a hard disk or pen drives anymore.

  We can control the access policy to make these files public or private. For example, your passport photo can be a public URL, but your driving license needs to be private and not public for security concerns.

- Data: The data is any other information that is not a file, for example, a list of students' names and addresses. These are generally strings, numbers, or special characters – basically, a combination of whatever keys you have on your keyboard.

These data are stored in databases in a particular manner and style, so that searching and filtering can be easier. We can interact with the data via a query language, which helps to easily search, filter, delete, or create data.

# Cloud Storage As a Service

Even after humans got the computerized database and solved all the problems with data storage, before the Internet, the data was still stored in floppy disks, pen drives, and hard disks. With applications going over the Internet and solving a bunch of problems, it was obvious and required to make the data storage available on the cloud and accessible via the Internet. Especially, AWS solved both problems with their services. The file-based storage and database are available as a service.

1. Amazon Simple Storage Service: Also known as AWS S3, it is a service offered by AWS to store and share raw files, for example, images, videos, sheets, pdf, etc. There are other similar service providers like Azure Blob Storage and Dropbox.

2. Amazon DynamoDB: DynamoDB is a fully managed NoSQL database service by AWS.

The Amplify CLI has the capability to provision and manage these services for our application. In the upcoming sections of this chapter, we will follow a hands-on guide to provide this data storage and make our application interact with these services.

# Database Provision and Integration

In the last couple of chapters, we have been successfully able to create RESTful and GraphQL APIs, and also we have created our Todo items React application to consume these APIs. Until this chapter, in our Todo application, the data was stored in in-memory variables, because we did not introduce the databases. Now we should extend our backend APIs to integrate with the database and fetch and store the data in the database.

# Provisioning Database

Even before we modify our APIs to integrate with the database, let's start with
provisioning our database and check if we got our database up and running or not. Let's
start with our Amplify CLI on the terminal with following command to add storage in our
Amplify application:

```
amplify add storage
```

The CLI will ask some questions for the new database that we are going to create;
let's answer them:

```
01: ? Please select from one of the below mentioned services: NoSQL
    Database
02:
03: Welcome to the NoSQL DynamoDB database wizard
04: This wizard asks you a series of questions to help determine how to set
    up your NoSQL database table.
05:
06: ? Please provide a friendly name for your resource that will be used to
    label this category in the project: todolist
07: ? Please provide table name: todos
08:
09: You can now add columns to the table.
10:
11: ? What would you like to name this column: id
12: ? Please choose the data type: string
13: ? Would you like to add another column? Yes
14: ? What would you like to name this column: title
15: ? Please choose the data type: string
16: ? Would you like to add another column? Yes
17: ? What would you like to name this column: status
18: ? Please choose the data type: boolean
19: ? Would you like to add another column? No
20:
21: ? Please choose partition key for the table: id
22: ? Do you want to add a sort key to your table? No
```

**LINE 6:** I have provided todolist as the data storage name, which is basically the database resource name.

**LINE 7:** I have named my database table todos; we can create more than one table in one database.

**LINES 11–19:** I have added the id, title, and status column, as these are what our todo application requires.

**LINE 21:** We choose the column id as the partition key.

**LINE 22:** Given that our database structure is quite simple and flat, we choose no for the sort key.

Let's push these changes to the AWS cloud, by running the following command:

```
amplify push
```

Once done, let's navigate to the browser on our AWS cloud console to verify these changes. Open the DynamoDB from the service list and open the tables (Figure 6-1).

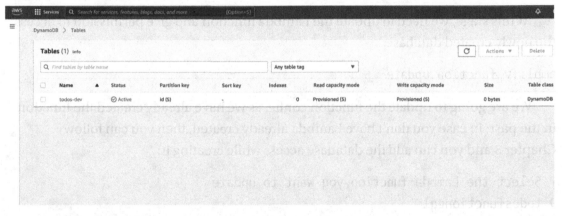

***Figure 6-1.*** *Screenshot of our newly provisioned database from the AWS console*

We can confirm that our todos table is created.

# Integrating the Database with APIs

In the chapter where we learned to create REST and GraphQL APIs, we skipped the database integration with our APIs and temporarily stored data in memory. Now that we have our Amplify database, we should modify our APIs to integrate with our database, so that our function deployment becomes stateless.

The Lambda functions and databases we created in the previous section are two different entities and live in two different servers; if our Lambda function wants to access the database, it has to be provided the access to the database by the admin, in this case, us. This makes our Amplify entities' boundaries more secure, and hence without the admin's permission, no one can access the services like the database.

We are assuming you are following the chapters sequentially, and so far you have the following in your Amazon console and in your local codebase:

1.  The todo React.js application.

2.  The GraphQL or REST endpoints, integrated with the React.js code.

3.  The Lambda function gets triggered on operations like create new, delete, or update.

4.  The Lambda function gets and updates the variable in memory.

At this stage, we need to update the Lambda function and give permission to access the newly created database:

amplify function update

We are going to update the function config, as we have already created the function in the past; in case you don't have Lambda already created, then you can follow Chapter 3 and you can add the database access while creating it:

```
? Select the Lambda function you want to update
> todosfunctiongql
```

The CLI will show all the list of Lambda functions you have created, and you can choose one to start updating it.

We are going to modify our GraphQL APIs; hence, we choose the todosfunctiongql function.

If you have more than one function, change your selection using the up or down arrow key.

Press enter to select the function.

```
? Which setting do you want to update?
> Resource access permissions
  Scheduled recurring invocation
```

```
Lambda layers configuration
Environment variables configuration
Secret values configuration
```

The next question the CLI asks is what kind of setting we want to update for our Lambda; this time, we are going to modify the access-related settings for the function; hence, as shown above choose the `Resource access permission`.

Press enter to move to the next question.

```
? Select the categories you want this function to have access to.
  ◯ auth
  ◯ function
  ◯ api
❯ ◉ storage
```

The next question is about the kind of access we want to modify or add to our functions.

The database falls under the storage category; hence, move to storage and press the space bar to select the option.

Note that this is a multi-option menu; hence, you can navigate to more than one option and press the space bar to select more than one option.

Hit enter once you select the storage option.

```
Storage has 2 resources in this project. Select the one you would like your
Lambda to access (Press <space> to sel
ect, <a> to toggle all, <i> to invert selection)
  ◯ thumbnail
❯ ◉ todolist
```

The next option will show which storage resource name we want to add the access policy; in my case, we created functions named thumbnail and todolist. The todolist is our DynamoDB resource; hence, we select this and hit enter.

```
? Select the operations you want to permit on todolist
  ◉ create
  ◉ read
  ◉ update
❯ ◉ delete
```

The next option pops up with what kind of operations we want to permit to our Lambda functions.

As we have CRUD APIs and we want our Lambda function to be able to create, read, update, and delete, we will select all using the space bar and hit enter.

```
? Do you want to edit the local lambda function now? (y/N)
```

When the CLI asks to edit the local Lambda function now, you can choose Yes if you are not sure about the location of the function.

Given we already discussed the pattern of the directory structure of Amplify files, I will choose N and continue to navigate the file and edit.

Congratulations, the policy to access the database is added to our Lambda function. Let's now start modifying our Lambda function attached to the GraphQL APIs, so that we can create the items in our database.

Please note, we create this function in Chapter 4.

## Assigning IDs to New Items

When we create new items in our database, we need unique ids to assign to the items. We will use the npm package named UUID which will guarantee uniqueness.

In the terminal, navigate to the directory where package.json is located by running the following command:

```
cd amplify/backend/function/todosfunctiongql/
```

And install the UUID npm package:

```
npm install uuid
```

## Modifying the Create Todo Item Function

Navigate to the Lambda function by opening the following file:

```
amplify/backend/function/todosfunctiongql/src/index.js
```

Modify the file to create a new DynamoDB instance client from the AWS-SDK:

```
8: const AWS = require("aws-sdk");
9: const dynamodbClient = new AWS.DynamoDB.DocumentClient();
```

Let's modify our addNewItem function which gets called when the GraphQL creation query is triggered:

```
21: const addNewItem = async (title, done) => {
22:   const id = uuid.v4();
23:   const item = { id, title, done };
24:   await dynamodbClient
25:     .put({
26:       TableName: "todos-dev",
27:       Item: item,
28:     })
29:     .promise();
30:   return item;
31: };
```

**LINE 22:** Get a new id for our new item to be created.

**LINE 23:** The new item to be created will be the new id, title, and done status from the params.

**LINE 24:** Use the same dynamodbClient to create the item. As we are using the async-await syntax, we need to add the async keyword in line 21.

**LINE 25:** Use the put function from the client to create the item.

**LINE 26:** We need to pass the table name, followed by env, for example, todos-dev; for now, we are hardcoding the env, but please note that we should pick the env from the env variables, which we will discuss in the upcoming chapters; otherwise, when we deploy this function to prod, it will still try to connect to the dev env database, which we don't want.

**LINE 30:** If creation is successful, we will return the item to the client, and if something fails, the exception will be thrown to the clients.

Let's push the changes and test our API:

```
amplify push
```

If you followed all the steps before pushing, you will see the Lambda function's access changes and Lambda function code updates.

Let's now run our React application and add a new item and hit the add button.

If you track the Network tab, you will notice the GraphQL mutation API was hit and the response looks as we expected, along with our new UUIDs, as shown in Figure 6-2.

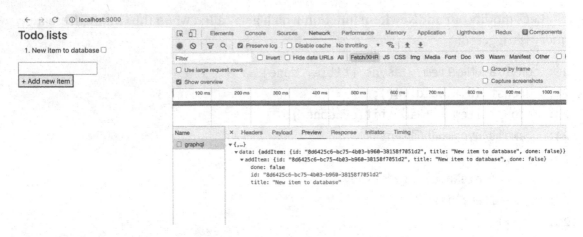

*Figure 6-2.* *Network tab showing the GraphQL mutation request*

## Modifying the Get All Items API

Instead of now returning the data from the in-memory variable, we will read from the database and return the data list, let's see how the query resolver function will change:

```
56: const resolvers = {
57:   Query: {
58:     todos: async (ctx) => {
59:       const data = await dynamodbClient
60:         .scan({
61:           TableName: "todos-dev",
62:         })
63:         .promise();
64:       return data.Items;
65:     },
66:   },
```

**LINE 59:** Use the dynamodbClient to read the list of data.

**LINE 60:** The DynamoDB client exposes the scan function to read all data.

**LINE 61:** We need to pass the table name, in this case, todos-dev where dev is the env name.

**LINE 64:** The response from the DB client has a few other options apart from the data, for example, total count and scanned count; the data list is under the key Items; hence, we are returning data.

Let's hit refresh on our React app, and we should get all the data loaded from the database.

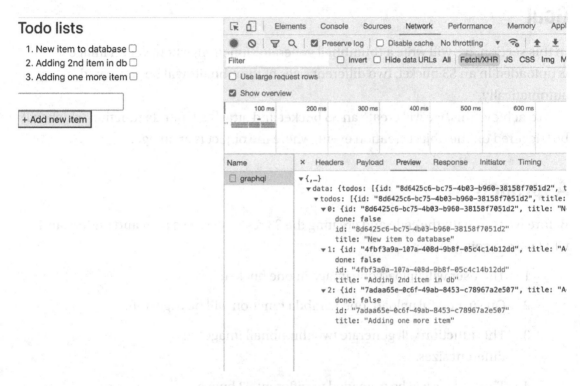

*Figure 6-3.* *GraphQL request showing get all todos*

If you notice the Network tab, in Figure 6-3, reloading the query returns all the data from the database. Congratulations on this integration.

# Do It Yourself (DIY)

Similarly, you should now modify the delete APIs and update APIs.

# File Storage – S3 Bucket

As we introduced already, AWS provides a service to manage the raw file of almost all file types. The service is named S3 or Amazon Simple Storage Service. The service offers all the capabilities required to manage the files of formats like jpg, png, video, pdfs, and documents which are scalable, highly available, secured, and cost-effective.

## Goal

In this section, we will write a thumbnail generator function; whenever an image is uploaded in an S3 bucket, two different sizes of thumbnails will be generated automatically.

To achieve this, we will create an S3 bucket and attach a Lambda function which will be triggered on the object creation event, where the object is an image.

## Approach

Before we start with the code and creating the S3 resources, let's plan and understand what we are going to do:

1. The user will upload one image in one bucket.

2. On successful upload, one Lambda function will be triggered.

3. This function will generate two thumbnail images of different sizes.

4. The images will be uploaded to different S3 buckets.

Figure 6-4 is the depiction of the processes we are going to follow.

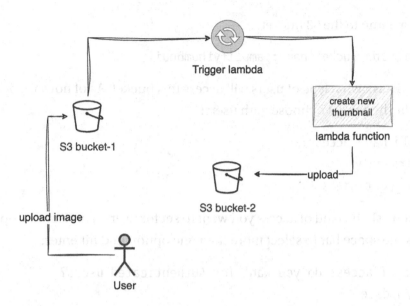

*Figure 6-4.* *The Lambda trigger flow on image upload*

## The Need for Two S3 Buckets

If you notice, the user uploads in one bucket, and the thumbnails are uploaded in a different bucket. If we don't do this, on upload of the generated thumbnail, it will trigger the Lambda again, and the S3 Lambda function will fall into infinite recursive calls, which will result in unwanted flow.

## Provision S3 Bucket

```
amplify add storage
```

This will ask what type of storage we want to create; choose the content, and hit enter:

```
Please select from one of the below mentioned services: (Use arrow keys)
> Content (Images, audio, video, etc.)
  NoSQL Database
```

Provide a name to this resource; we are going to name it amplifythumbnail:

```
? Please provide a friendly name for your resource that will be used to
label this category in the project: amplifythumbnail
```

Provide a name to the S3 bucket:

```
? Please provide bucket name: amplifythumbnail
```

Then it will ask what type of users will access this bucket. As of now, we don't plan to make it public; hence, let's choose auth users:

```
? Who should have access:
> Auth users only
  Auth and guest users
```

It will then ask the kind of access you want to set for users. This is multi-option; hence, press the space bar to select more than one option and hit enter:

```
? What kind of access do you want for Authenticated users?
 ◉ create/update
 ◉ read
>◉ delete
```

Enter yes to add a Lambda trigger for this bucket:

```
? Do you want to add a Lambda Trigger for your S3 Bucket? (y/N) y
```

Given we want to create a new function, choose the following option:

```
? Select from the following options
  Choose an existing function from the project
> Create a new function
```

Enter no for editing the function now; let's test this trigger, and later we will edit the function to add the capability:

```
? Do you want to edit the local S3Trigger8b84f142 lambda function
now? (Y/n) n
```

```
amplify push
```

Once you approve the changes, let's wait for this push to complete.

Now let's verify these resources on console.amazon.com.

# Verifying the Resources on Amazon Console

Log in to the console, and from the services, the section opens the Lambda service.

From the list of functions, select the one which starts with the S3Trigger name.

You will see the Lambda function is connected to S3 in the representation; this is proof that the Lambda function and the S3 buckets are connected via some event, as shown in Figure 6-5.

***Figure 6-5.*** *Screenshot from the AWS console showing the Lambda function and triggers*

In the function overview, click S3, as shown in Figure 6-6 and Figure 6-7.

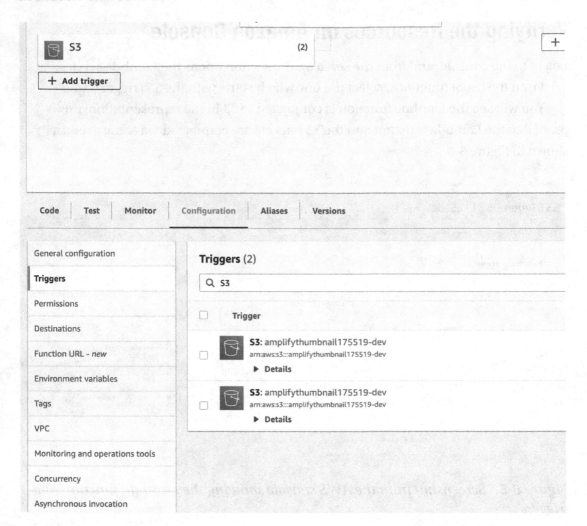

***Figure 6-6.*** *Screenshot from the AWS console showing the trigger details*

This will open the triggers; as shown in Figure 6-7, you will notice two triggers. Let's check the details.

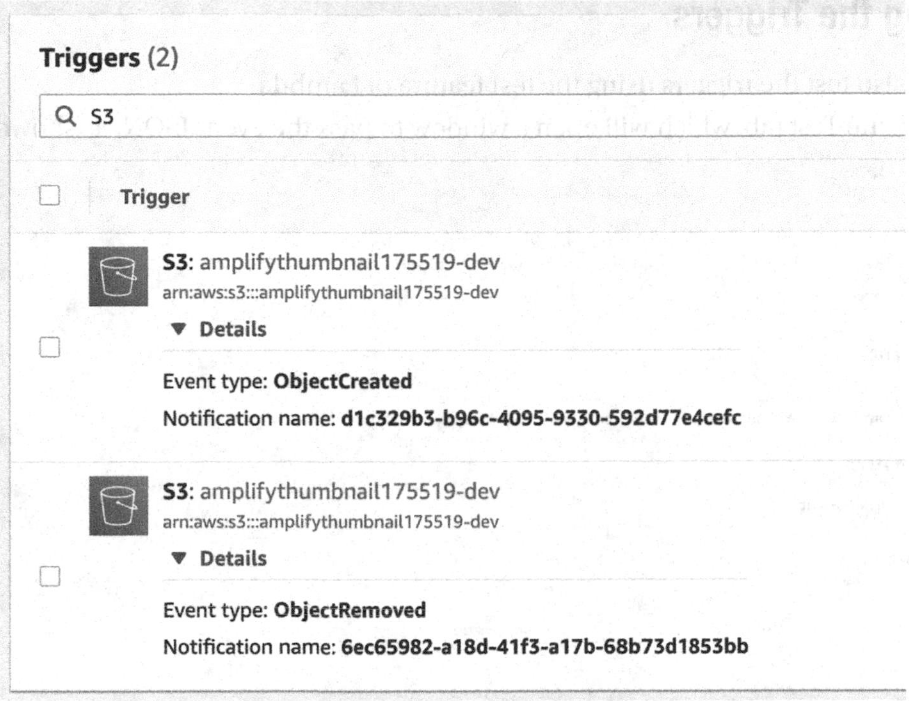

**Triggers** (2)

Q  S3

☐    Trigger

☐    **S3**: amplifythumbnail175519-dev
     arn:aws:s3:::amplifythumbnail175519-dev
     ▼ Details

     Event type: **ObjectCreated**
     Notification name: **d1c329b3-b96c-4095-9330-592d77e4cefc**

☐    **S3**: amplifythumbnail175519-dev
     arn:aws:s3:::amplifythumbnail175519-dev
     ▼ Details

     Event type: **ObjectRemoved**
     Notification name: **6ec65982-a18d-41f3-a17b-68b73d1853bb**

***Figure 6-7.*** *Screenshot from the AWS console showing the name and ids of the triggers*

The Amplify CLI has added two triggers on event types Object Created and Object Removed.

# Testing the Triggers

We can also test the triggers using the test feature of Lambda.

Click the Test tab, which will open a window to pass the event JSON, as shown in Figure 6-8.

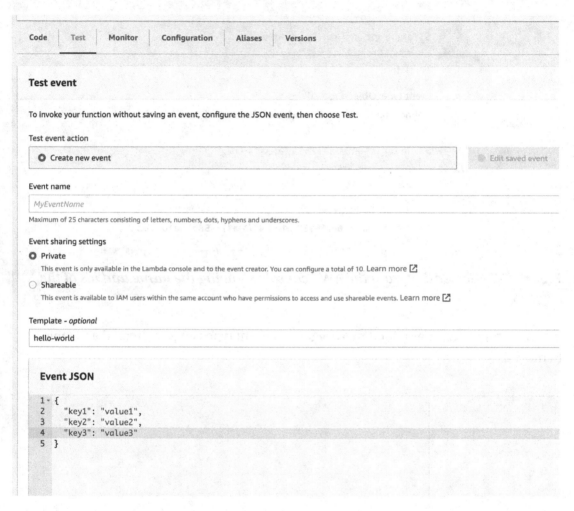

***Figure 6-8.*** *Trigger test console from the AWS console*

Let's see what our default function is doing now.

Navigate to the Lambda path to see function details:

`/amplify/backend/function/S3Triggere0581125/src/index.js`

```
1: // eslint-disable-next-line
2: exports.handler = async function (event) {
3:   console.log('Received S3 event:', JSON.stringify(event, null, 2));
4:   // Get the object from the event and show its content type
5:   const bucket = event.Records[0].s3.bucket.name; //eslint-disable-line
6:   const key = event.Records[0].s3.object.key; //eslint-disable-line
7:   console.log(`Bucket: ${bucket}`, `Key: ${key}`);
8: };
9:
```

The default function generated by the CLI simply reads the event object and logs the bucket name and key.

Let's replicate this event and test our trigger; in the browser test window, modify the event JSON to the following:

```
{
    "Records": [
        {
            "s3": {
                "bucket": "test bucket name",
                "object": {
                    "key": "test key"
                }
            }
        }
    ]
}
```

Pass this event and hit the Test button, as shown in Figure 6-9.

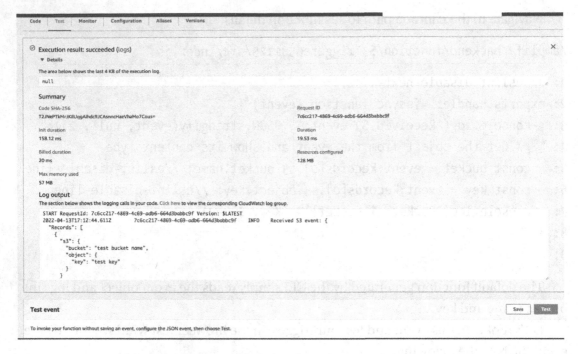

***Figure 6-9.*** *Screenshot of the result from the test console of triggers*

You will see the execution result to be a success.

You can also see the logs in a dedicated window to monitor.

Click the Monitor tab and then navigate to logs; you will see the same log there as well.

# The Lambda Function

Given the Lambda trigger function is working as expected, now let's write code to create the thumbnail image of a smaller size and upload it in the same bucket.

## Resizing the Image to Create a Small Thumbnail

We will use the npm package named sharp to resize our images. Sharp is a high-speed Node.js module that helps in various image operations.

The following is how we can resize an image to 320x240 size and create a new image file:

```
sharp(inputBuffer)
 .resize(320, 240)
 .toFile('output.webp', (err, info) => { ... });
```

You can refer to the sharp npm package for more APIs and capabilities.

# Lambda Function to Create Small Thumbnails

Let's open the Lambda function in VS Code and add the thumbnail creation code:

```
cd amplify/backend/function/S3Triggere0581125/src
```

Please note S3Triggere0581125 is the Lambda function name in my system; it can be a different name in your machine.

As discussed in Chapter 3 about Lambda functions, this is a self-sufficient node project which has its own package.json and package-lock.json.

Let's install the sharp npm package:

```
npm install --arch=x64 --platform=linux sharp
```

Please note we are passing architecture and platform information while installing; if we don't do this, by default it installs the package by detecting the system, in my case macOS, and it will install the macOS binary; given our Lambda function will run on Linux machines which have x64 processors, we need to pass this.

Open index.js and we will add the following snippet:

```
01: const sharp = require("sharp");
02: const aws = require("aws-sdk");
03: const s3 = new aws.S3();
04:
05: const THUMBNAIL = {
06:   width: 100,
07:   height: 100,
08: };
09:
10: const THUMBNAIL_DIRECTORY_NAME = "thumbnails";
11:
12: exports.handler = async function (event, context) {
13:   const BUCKET_NAME = event.Records[0].s3.bucket.name;
14:   const KEY = event.Records[0].s3.object.key;
15:   const DIRECTORY_LIST = KEY.split("/");
16:   const BASE_FOLDER = DIRECTORY_LIST[0];
17:   if (BASE_FOLDER === THUMBNAIL_DIRECTORY_NAME) {
18:     console.log(
```

```
19:        ">> Stopping the function execution, as the event is for new
           thumbnail file."
20:      );
21:      return;
22:    }
23:    console.log(">> The new file uploaded by customer");
24:    let FILE_NAME = DIRECTORY_LIST[DIRECTORY_LIST.length - 1];
25:    try {
26:      const image = await s3
27:        .getObject({ Bucket: BUCKET_NAME, Key: KEY })
28:        .promise();
29:
30:      const resizedImage = await sharp(image.Body)
31:        .resize(THUMBNAIL.width, THUMBNAIL.height)
32:        .toBuffer();
33:
34:      await s3
35:        .putObject({
36:          Bucket: BUCKET_NAME,
37:          Body: resizedImage,
38:          Key: `${THUMBNAIL_DIRECTORY_NAME}/thumbnail-${FILE_NAME}`,
39:        })
40:        .promise();
41:
42:      return;
43:    } catch (err) {
44:      context.fail(`Error resizing files: ${err}`);
45:    }
46:    console.log(`Bucket: ${BUCKET_NAME}`, `Key: ${KEY}`);
47: };
48:
```

**LINES 1 and 2:** Require the sharp npm module to resize the image and AWS SDK.

**LINE 3:** Assign the s3 instance to get an object from s3 and create new images in the bucket.

**LINE 5:** The constants for the width and height of the thumbnail to be generated.

**LINE 10:** The name of the directory to store the thumbnails.

**LINE 12:** The handler function that will run whenever the event is triggered, in this case, the upload event.

**LINE 13:** Get the current bucket name.

**LINE 14:** The key is the file name we uploaded; this key will be used to fetch the object from this bucket.

**LINE 15:** We are going to split the file path by "/" when the thumbnail will be created, and the event will be triggered again; we want to keep track of the directory path whether the file is a thumbnail or an actual image.

**LINE 17:** We are checking if the directory is a thumbnail or not.

**LINE 21:** If the file is from the thumbnail directory, we will exit the function by calling return, just to avoid creating a thumbnail from the thumbnail.

**LINE 25:** Here, we are confident we are not processing a thumbnail image; hence, we will start resizing in a try-catch block to handle any failure like corrupted file or access issues.

**LINE 26:** We are getting the actual image from the bucket using the key.

**LINE 30:** We will use the sharp module to resize our image.

**LINE 34:** We are uploading the thumbnail in the thumbnail directory.

**LINE 38:** We are creating a file with a new name by prepending the thumbnail word.

**LINE 44:** Let's log if there is any kind of error to debug later.

## Deploying the Function

Once done, save the file and push the changes, by running the following command:

```
amplify push
```

Approve the changes and let the CLI push and deploy the function.

# Testing the Thumbnail Creation by Lambda Trigger

Let's see our trigger in action. Open console.aws.amazon.com and log in using your credentials. Click the search bar and search for S3 service, as shown in Figure 6-10, and click it.

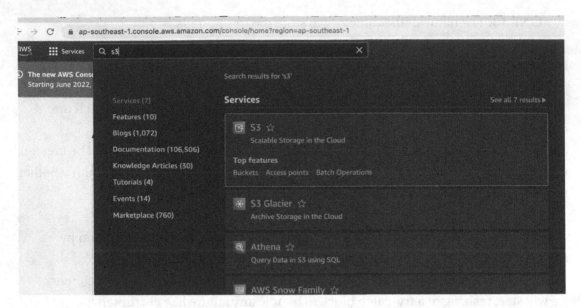

***Figure 6-10.*** *Screenshot of the AWS console from the search result of services*

You will land on your bucket list, and click the bucket where the Lambda trigger was set up, the reference is shown in Figure 6-11.

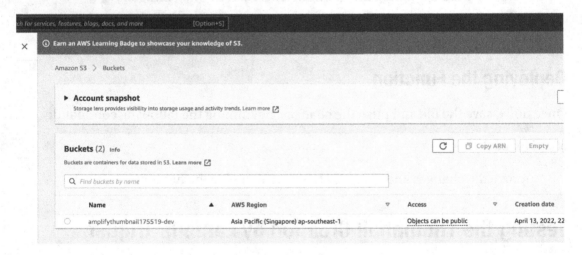

***Figure 6-11.*** *AWS console listing the S3 buckets*

You will see an empty bucket, as no files have been uploaded yet, refer Figure 6-12.

***Figure 6-12.*** *Screenshot of an empty S3 bucket*

Let's check the Lambda trigger by uploading one image. Click the Upload button, choose the image file, and click Upload.

After the upload is successful, come back to the bucket and refresh the page, as depicted in Figure 6-13.

***Figure 6-13.*** *Screenshot of the S3 bucket after an image is uploaded with a new directory*

You will see the image is uploaded, and the thumbnail directory is also created. Congratulations, the directory is created; it looks like our trigger worked. Let's open the directory, refer Figure 6-14.

***Figure 6-14.*** *S3 bucket showing a list of files under the new directory*

The smaller size file with the same name prepended with a thumbnail is also created. Congratulations, you can open the file to cross-check the file width and height. Now let's check our Lambda function logs.

## Checking the Lambda Function Logs

Click the search bar and search for Lambda service, the search result is shown in Figure 6-15 and Figure 6-16.

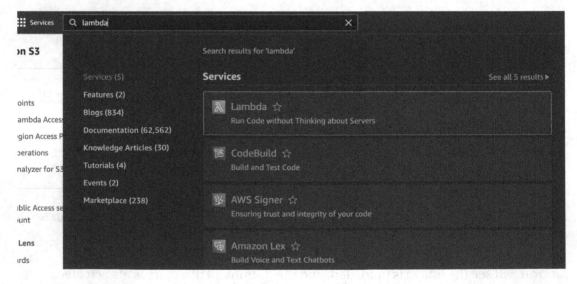

***Figure 6-15.*** *AWS console search result*

Lambda > Functions > S3Triggere0581125-dev

# S3Triggere0581125-dev

ⓘ This function belongs to an application. Click here to manage it.

▼ **Function overview** Info

λ S3Triggere0581125-dev

⬙ Layers                                            (0)

🪣 S3                                                (2)

+ Add destination

+ Add trigger

| Code | Test | Monitor | Configuration | Aliases | Versions |

| Metrics | **Logs** | Traces |

View logs in CloudWatch ☑        View X-Ray traces in ServiceLens

**CloudWatch Logs Insights** Info

Lambda logs all requests handled by your function and automatically stores logs generated by your code through Amazon CloudWatch Logs. To validate your code. instrumen

***Figure 6-16.*** *The Lambda function overview showing the bucket and triggers*

Open the S3 trigger function, and click Monitor ➤ Logs.

Depending on the number of files uploaded, you will see invocation logs, as shown in Figure 6-17.

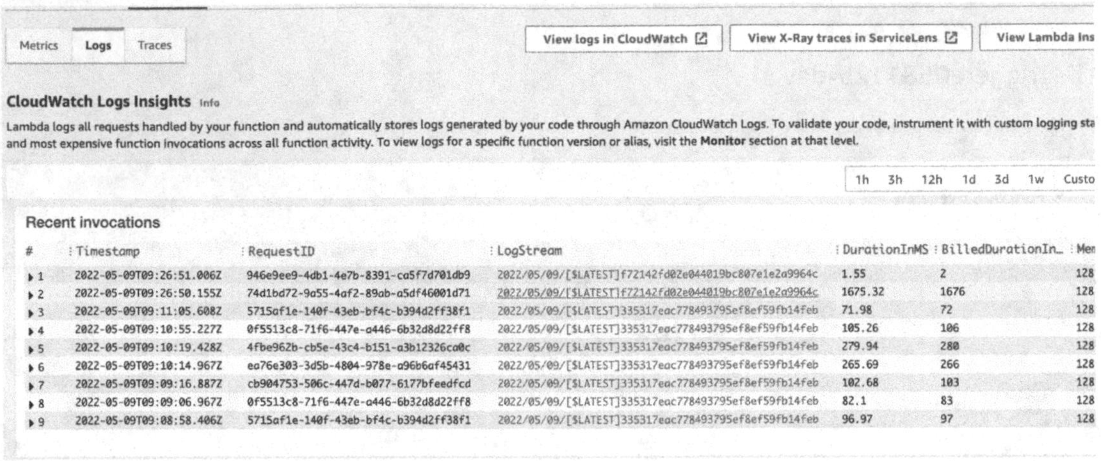

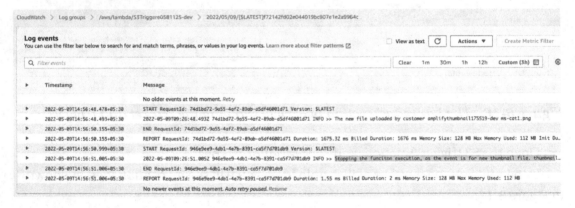

*Figure 6-17.* The log of the Lambda trigger function

Open the function invocation logs and try to read the logs which we added using console.log, the screenshot of logs are shown in Figure 6-18.

*Figure 6-18.* The log from the trigger function

In Figure 6-18, if you notice the highlighted line of logs, this is the second invocation of the trigger, when the thumbnail was created, and using the thumbnail directory condition, we were able to stop the function from falling in an infinite loop. Please refer back to the code snippets of this trigger function.

# Summary

This chapter covered the importance of data and storage required and gave a detailed hands-on guide to procure the database using AWS Amplify. This chapter also discussed the different ways to store and transfer data via a network.

This chapter also discussed in detail how to integrate our APIs with databases, and we wrote code to implement the use case of creating different-sized thumbnails from a parent image.

By the end of the chapter, readers should understand the basics of data storages, ways to implement the methodologies in their own problems, and how to debug issues to find the root cause of problems they face.

**CHAPTER 7**

# Analytics

*Analytics will not replace decision-makers, but decision-makers who use analytics will replace those who do not.*

—Akshat Paul

Analytics is essentially a framework that is used to gain insights into the behavior of end users. By analyzing data related to user behavior, businesses can gain valuable insights and know which products or services are popular among different groups of users, as well as which aspects of their application may be causing users to leave.

The data collected through analytics helps businesses in many areas, such as marketing, sales, user experience, and prioritizing features, to make informed decisions about how to improve their products and services. By analyzing user behavior, businesses can gain a deeper understanding of what is working and what is not and use this information to improve their offerings.

With analytics, we can do systematic analysis of data to find patterns and correlations. This can be achieved through various techniques such as data mining, predictive analytics, and machine learning. This chapter is intended to provide a deeper understanding of analytics and how it can be used to gain valuable insights into user behavior and ultimately help businesses make better decisions using technologies we have discussed so far along with new AWS services we will explore in this chapter.

In short, analytics is the systematic analysis of data available to find similar patterns across. In this chapter, we'll take a deep dive into analytics, understand it, and start writing code, but before we do, let's take a step back so that we see a panoramic picture.

## A High-Level View of Analytics

Data analytics is a powerful tool that can help businesses gain valuable insights into their operations, customers, and competition. With the right analytics framework in place, businesses can make informed decisions and improve their bottom line. Whether it's

© Akshat Paul, Mahesh Haldar 2023
A. Paul and M. Haldar, *Serverless Web Applications with AWS Amplify*,
https://doi.org/10.1007/978-1-4842-8707-1_7

improving sales, streamlining processes, or gaining a competitive edge, analytics can help businesses achieve their goals and outperform their competitors.

By analyzing data from various sources, such as sales figures, customer behavior, and market trends, businesses can gain a deeper understanding of their operations and identify areas for improvement. They can use this information to optimize their processes, develop more effective marketing strategies, and make better decisions about product development and pricing.

Moreover, analytics can help businesses build customer loyalty and improve retention by understanding their customers' preferences and behavior patterns. By analyzing customer data, businesses can personalize their offerings, anticipate their customers' needs, and provide them with a seamless, personalized experience.

In short, analytics is a powerful tool that can help businesses of all sizes make smarter, data-driven decisions. With the right analytics framework in place, businesses can unlock the full potential of their data and gain a competitive edge in today's fast-paced business environment.

In the past, businesses heavily relied on customer feedback collected on physical paper or forms on tablets, which were then grouped together to identify problems and discuss solutions. However, this traditional approach to collecting customer feedback presents several challenges in a modern business context.

Firstly, not all customers are willing to provide feedback, resulting in a limited and biased dataset. This makes it difficult to accurately identify areas for improvement and make informed decisions.

Secondly, even when feedback is collected, it may not be accurate or comprehensive. Customers may rush through the process or simply tick boxes without fully understanding the question or considering their response. This can lead to incomplete or misleading data, which may hinder the business's ability to make informed decisions.

Thankfully, with the advancement of technology, businesses now have access to a wide range of tools and platforms that make it easier to collect, analyze, and act on customer feedback. By leveraging the power of data analytics and machine learning, businesses can gain deep insights into customer behavior and preferences, identify trends, and develop more effective strategies to meet their customers' needs.

While traditional methods of collecting customer feedback may have served their purpose in the past, modern businesses need to embrace new technologies and data-driven approaches to stay competitive and meet the evolving needs of their customers.

I have talked to a few friends and family, and in my sample, most of the people do the same. Hence, we cannot depend on this, and we will never be able to find the real customer pain points. We need a more robust and automated way to visualize customer activities on our application, gather those data points, and analyze them to find problems. For example, we need to know how many customers are active and when and why they drop off from the app; if we are an ecommerce app, then we need to know how many customers visit products and why they don't end up buying. And the problems and use cases are infinite.

There are four steps to solve a problem:

1. Finding the current problems

   Using analytics data, businesses can identify problem areas and understand the root causes behind them. This allows them to develop more targeted and effective solutions to address the problems.

2. Proposing a few solutions

   Once the problems have been identified, businesses can brainstorm and propose various solutions to address them. This may involve collaboration with cross-functional teams, stakeholders, and customers to ensure that the proposed solutions are feasible and aligned with the business's goals.

3. Finding which solution works and which doesn't

   To determine the effectiveness of different solutions, businesses can leverage A/B testing, where two groups of users are provided with different solutions and their behavior is analyzed. This allows businesses to compare and contrast the effectiveness of different solutions and make data-driven decisions about which solutions to deploy.

4. Deploying the solution in which we have gained more confidence

   Based on the results of A/B testing and other data analyses, businesses can confidently deploy the solutions that have been shown to be effective. By deploying proven solutions, businesses can optimize their operations, improve customer satisfaction, and gain a competitive edge.

In summary, data analytics can provide businesses with valuable insights into their operations and customers, allowing them to identify problems, propose effective solutions, and make data-driven decisions. By leveraging analytics and A/B testing, businesses can gain a competitive edge and improve their bottom line.

## Analytics Fundamentals

Let's understand the whole fundamental of analytics by one use case. Let's say we have launched a new product, baby shampoo.

There are two aspects of this business:

1.  Marketing: Via various channels like Google Ads and blogs, which will increase customer reachability

2.  Ecommerce portal: One where customers can visit and buy the product by placing an order

Both of the preceding steps are crucial for a business. If marketing is not successful, customers will never know about the product and won't land on the website to make a purchase. And if the ecommerce portal's user experience is poor, customers will not buy, which is the only point where businesses generate revenue. The crucial aspect is measuring the effectiveness of our strategies to ensure they are working.

For instance, suppose we market using both Google Ads and blogs. How do we determine which of the two methods is generating the maximum impact? By analyzing the data, we can quantify the effectiveness of each approach. For example, if we find that for every $100 spent on blog marketing, we generate 10 leads, while for every $100 spent on Google Ads, we generate only 1 lead, we can make an informed decision to focus solely on blog marketing and discontinue Google Ads.

This is an example of the quantification process, which involves using data and analytics to measure the effectiveness of various strategies. By adopting this framework, businesses can make data-driven decisions and optimize their operations to achieve their goals.

Let's zoom in further on the marketing strategy, and let's assume the following list is the outcome from our analytics framework:

1.  90% of the users are women.

2.  80% of the users are between the ages of 28 and 38.

3.  75% are from metro city locations.

The business can use this outcome to improve its marketing strategy and attract more customers. The business will now focus on writing more blogs, targeting only women customers, targeting the age range which buys more, and also targeting only the metro locations.

This is called targeted marketing, and there will be points where the marketing strategy is so precise that any marketing campaign will produce best results.

Analytics can be used to identify patterns in available data, allowing businesses to gain insights and make data-driven decisions.

Google Analytics is a powerful and widely used tool that can be easily integrated into your website or mobile application. It requires only a few lines of code and a few simple steps to set up, after which you can gain valuable insights into user behavior and website performance. Most of the features are available for free, making it an accessible option for small companies and website owners to quickly analyze user behavior and optimize their operations.

# Terminologies

Before delving into the details, it's important to have a basic understanding of key terms that will be used further in this chapter. This will provide a foundation for better comprehension and prevent confusion in the future.

- User segments: The segmentation is basically breaking down the data by different dimensions – by age, sex, location, etc. For example, males and females are two user segments, and users from Tokyo is another segment.

- Events: Every user action that needs to be recorded is an event. For example, click a button is an event, and close the app is another event. Events have a name and some metadata. For example, the CLICK_BUTTON event will have metadata like button title and page name metadata so that data analysts can identify which button was clicked.

- Sessions: A session is a sequence of user actions that are performed by the same user in the app in a given time frame. The same user's activity on the app defines the session.

- Amazon Kinesis: This is the AWS service that will help us in streaming the user analytics data and storing it. Later, we can use these data to do our analysis and find various patterns.

- Amazon Pinpoint: This is an AWS service that enables businesses to engage with their customers through various channels. It offers personalized campaigns and in-depth analysis of customer behavior to improve engagement. With powerful A/B testing tools, businesses can optimize their campaigns for better results.

# Setting Up Amplify Analytics Backend

Let's start setting up our analytics backend so that it can start receiving the events and record them for our analysis to understand our users better.

Just like adding any other Amplify service, we will use the CLI to add analytics:

```
amplify add analytics
```

This will ask us to choose the analytics provider we want to use.

We will go ahead with pinpoint:

```
? Select an Analytics provider (Use arrow keys)
> Amazon Pinpoint
  Amazon Kinesis Streams
? Select an Analytics provider (Use arrow keys)
> Amazon Pinpoint
  Amazon Kinesis Streams
```

Press enter for Amazon Pinpoint.

This will ask you to give a name to the pinpoint resource; let me name it analyticsreactapp, and hit enter.

```
? Provide your pinpoint resource name: analyticsreactapp
```

You will get a success message, and that's all required to set up our analytics backend; it is that simple.

Now we only need to push the changes, and we can start recording the event from our React application and various kinds of information.

Let's publish our changes:

```
amplify push
```

Confirm the changes after reviewing by pressing `y` and pressing enter.

Voila, our backend is ready to start recording the events and the user actions and show us the data.

# Recording Events and Actions

Let's open the dashboard on the Amazon cloud console. Log in with your credentials and search for the Amazon Pinpoint service. You will see the screen in Figure 7-1 with different project IDs or names.

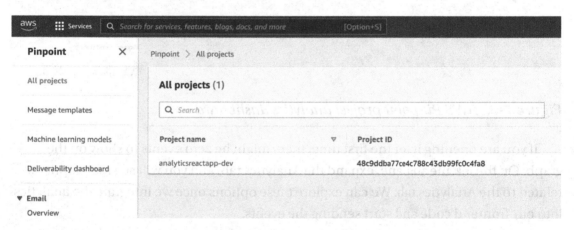

***Figure 7-1.*** *AWS console pinpoint service*

Click the project; you will land on the analytics dashboard, this is shown in Figure 7-2.

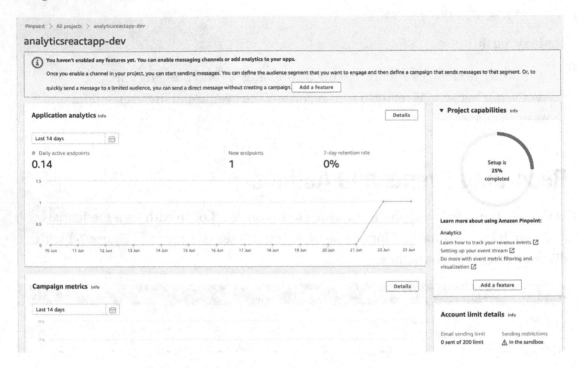

***Figure 7-2.*** *AWS Pinpoint project analytics dashboard*

If you are opening it for the first time, there might be zero events to show on the graph. On the left menu pane, expand the Analytics tab, and you will see more options related to the Analytics tab. We can explore these options once we integrate the analytics into our frontend code and start sending the events.

Let's jump to our React app and integrate the analytics service.

# Recording Events from our React App

In order to collect and analyze user data, it's essential to have a fully functional application with multiple pages and different types of pages. The application should also offer users a variety of options to choose from.

Continuing to add records in our todo application may not provide the full flavor of analytics in a production app due to its small use case. To replicate a production type of app, let's create a dummy page and smaller components, where we will treat each component as a page.

We will have three pages for this app. Refer to Figure 7-3.

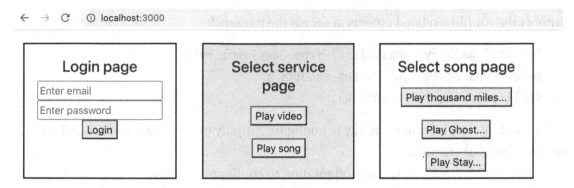

**Figure 7-3.** *UI design for the analytics application*

In our React application, the preceding three cards represent three different pages, and when the mouse hovers over the card, it glows with a yellow color that represents the user has visited the page; in the real-world web application, the page view is counted when the URL changes and the user navigates from one URL to another on the browser.

In this application, on clicking buttons nothing happens; we will only record events. The goal here is that with a very small and simple imitation of a real-world application, you will be able to understand the fundamentals of analytics easily.

As application owners, we want to know in our dashboard about various user actions we need to name the event, and call an API to create an entry in our analytics backend system.

Let's define our goal and outcome for page/card 2:

**Goal:** We want to know how many times users click the Play video button vs. the Play song button.

**Result:** As business owners, we will know users' behavior whether they like playing videos or listening to music. Accordingly, we can take a decision to further build on either of the options as investments.

**How to achieve this:** On every button click, call the record function from Amplify, for example:

```
Analytics.record({ name: "playVideoButtonClicked" });
```

where name is the unique key of the event.

# Recording Button Clicks on the Sign-In Page

Import the Amplify-related objects to access the backend:

```
2: import { Amplify, Analytics } from "aws-amplify";
3: import awsconfig from "./aws-exports";
4: Amplify.configure(awsconfig);
```

**LINE 2:** We will require Amplify to configure Amplify on this page and Analytics to record events or sessions.

**LINE 3:** Get the AWS export configuration to configure Amplify.

**LINE 4:** Configure Amplify.

The following is our React login page component:

```
01:
02:        <h4>Login page</h4>
03:        <div>
04:          <input
05:            type="text"
06:            placeholder="Enter email"
07:          />
08:        </div>
09:        <div>
10:          <input
11:            type="text"
12:            placeholder="Enter password"
13:          />
14:        </div>
15:        <div>
16:          <button
17:            onClick={() => {
18:              Analytics.record({
19:                name: "signInButtonClicked",
20:              });
21:            }}
```

```
22:              >
23:                 Login
24:              </button>
25:          </div>
```

**LINES 1–15:** This is a very simple component, with two input boxes for login id and password.

**LINE 16:** This is our login button where we want to track events.

**LINE 18:** Call the record function whenever the button is clicked, and a unique name is passed in the key name, and this key will be recorded with count and timestamp.

Let's run the React server and see the event recording in action.

Run the frontend server and open the Network tab in the browser before clicking it, this is shown in Figure 7-4.

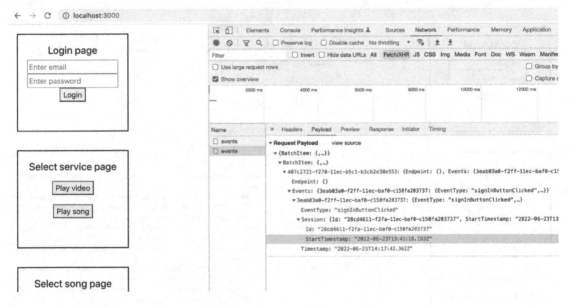

***Figure 7-4.*** *Demo analytics application*

As you click the login button and wait for a couple of seconds, you will notice one API being called with events, and if you expand the payload of the API call, you will notice the eventType with the same name `signInButtonClicked` called, with other metadata like a timestamp and sessions, etc.

# Why Is There a Delay in API Calls After We Click the Button to Record?

I will be very happy to know if you asked this question before reading this question.

If you notice the behavior of how the APIs are being called, they are not real time, so what Amplify by default does is it batches the events to record in a couple of seconds; to explain this in detail, if you click the button ten times continuously, this will batch all the ten event records and call one API, say, in two seconds.

This way, all the records are also published via the API, and Amplify saves on calling ten APIs to record events.

Here is the result if I click the login button five times continuously, shown in Figure 7-5.

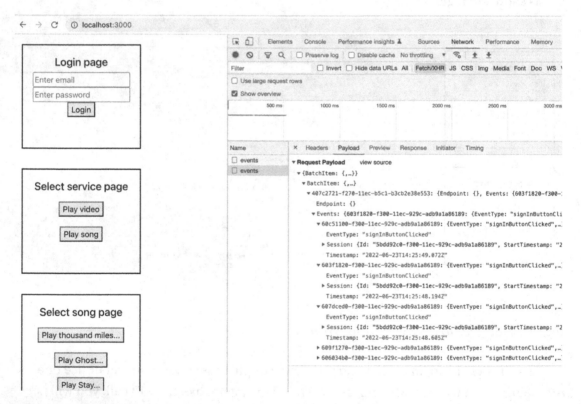

***Figure 7-5.***  *Network calls made with gap to Amplify*

If you notice, there are five items in one API call.

If you don't want to batch these and want to record events immediately, you can configure that as well.

```
1: Analytics.record({
2:     name: signInButtonClicked,
3:     immediate: true
4: });
```

**LINE 3:** In the same record function, pass the boolean flag with key name `immediate`, and set it to true.

Here is the result if I click the login button five times.

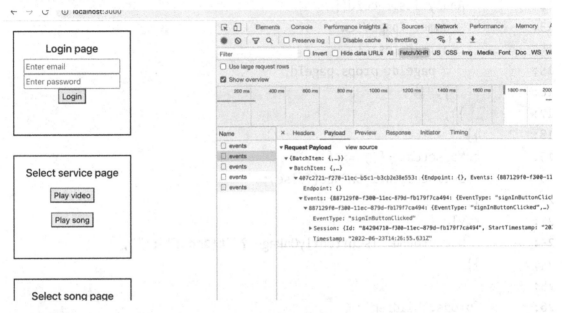

***Figure 7-6.*** *Network calls made immediately to Amplify*

Now there are five API calls that are recorded immediately.

# Tracking Page Views

In our scenario, we have created three smaller components to replicate the pages in less time to understand the crux of analytics. In this case, when the user's mouse hovers over the component, we are considering it a page view; hence, in our scenario, this should also record the page view event in our analytics backend.

Let's see the code snippet to record events on page views:

```
06: const MyPageContainer = (props) => {
07:    const [isCurrentlyOnPage, setIsCurrentlyOnPage] = useState(false);
08:    return (
09:      <div
10:        onMouseEnter={() => {
11:          setIsCurrentlyOnPage(true);
12:          Analytics.record({
13:            name: "pageView",
14:            attributes: {
15:              pageId: props.pageId,
16:            },
17:          });
18:        }}
19:        onMouseLeave={() => {
20:          setIsCurrentlyOnPage(false);
21:        }}
22:        style={{
23:          background: isCurrentlyOnPage ? "#f2edbf" : "",
24:        }}
25:      >
26:        {props.children}
27:      </div>
28:    );
29: };
```

**LINE 6:** This is a common page container, which all the pages in our application will use to create the parent container that wraps some common functionality across any React component and renders the children whatever passed to it. This is a very good example of HOC (higher-order component) which abstracts the logic of registering analytics logic in one place.

---

**Note**    In React, higher-order components (HOCs) are functions that accept a component as an argument and return a new component with enhanced functionality.

---

**LINE 7:** Create the local state to rerender the UI when the mouse enters and leaves.

**LINE 10:** We are listening to when the mouse enters we call a function, which sets the local state to true and records page view event, with the page Id as the attribute so that we can identify each page.

**LINE 19:** Set the local state value back to false when the mouse leaves this component.

**LINE 23:** We are using the local state to decide when to glow the component with background color, which as explained in the previous paragraph depends on when the mouse leaves or enters the components.

**LINE 26:** Given this is a HOC and we want to use this as the component which can wrap around any other component, we are rendering the children as is.

And that's all; if you load your application and hover the mouse in and out, you will see the pageView event getting registered, as shown in Figure 7-7.

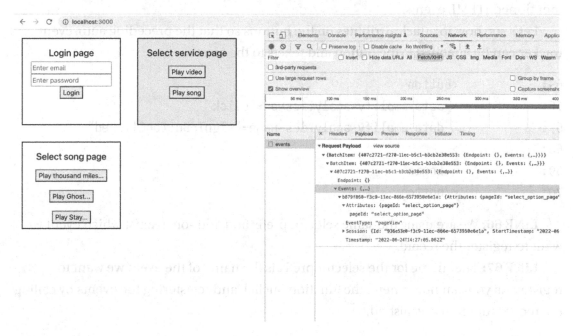

***Figure 7-7.*** *Registers pageView event*

# Automatic Tracking

If you see the pattern of recording events on every button click, everything remains the same code-wise apart from name and attributes, and we have to add in every onclick function, the Amplify has given one more way to add the tracking to the buttons on the various other events.

Let's configure our first auto-event tracker:

```
06: Analytics.autoTrack("event", {
07:    enable: true,
08:    events: ["click"],
09:    selectorPrefix: "data-amplify-analytics-"
10: });
```

**LINE 6:** Call the autoTrack function to configure an auto-event tracker of type event.

**LINE 7:** This flag is required to enable or disable the auto tracker.

**LINE 8:** The list of events we want to track; we are mentioning click here.

**LINE 9:** We need to mention the HTML element selector prefix; we will set this prefix to our buttons, and automatically this configuration will record the events on the mentioned HTML events.

Let's see how to attach attributes on the buttons so that the preceding auto-event tracker can be attached to the button and reacts to the events:

```
65:          <button
66:              data-amplify-analytics-on="click"
67:              data-amplify-analytics-name="signInButtonClicked"
68:          >
69:              Login
70:          </button>
```

**LINE 66:** We are using the same selector prefix and add -on against which event we want to register the record.

**LINE 67:** The -name for the selector prefix is the name of the event we want to register. As you can notice here, the function onclick and registering the events by calling the record function is vanished.

# Events Dashboard on AWS Console

Ideally, when you publish your application to your customers, we want to know how our customers are reacting and which features they are using the most and which pages they are visiting the most.

To see our customer's behavior, log in to your AWS console and open the pinpoint service.

From the left pane, choose Analytics, and click Events, the screenshot in Figure 7-8 shows the same.

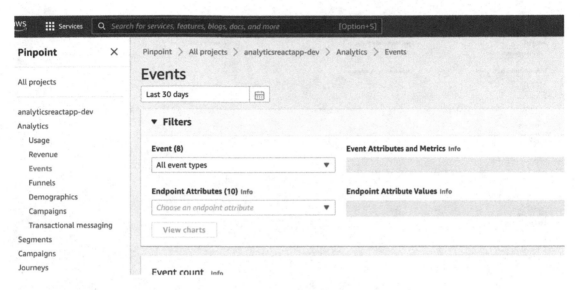

*Figure 7-8.*  *Pinpoint Analytics Events dashboard*

Please refer to Figure 7-8 and open the Filters accordion; in this section, we will be able to see our various events, shown in Figure 7-9.

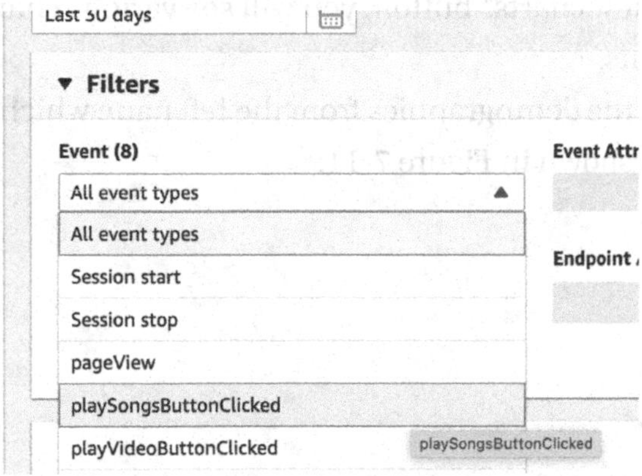

*Figure 7-9.*  *Pinpoint Analytics Events dashboard filter*

Click the events list drop-down.

As you can see, you will see all the events coming from our application.

211

You can select the event which you are interested to know the statistics for,
Figure 7-10 shows a view of the event selected.

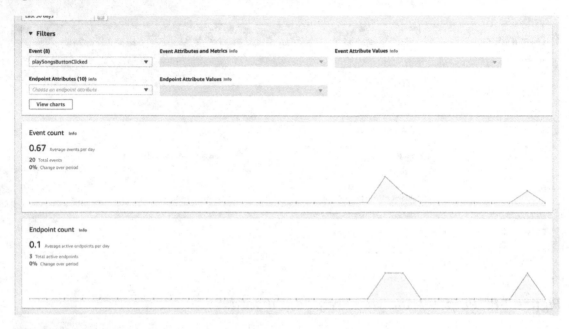

**Figure 7-10.** *Pinpoint Analytics Events dashboard for a event view*

If you click the "View charts" button, you will see various charts against timelines
with the count of events.

You can also click the demographics from the left pane which will tell the users'
demographic data, as shown in Figure 7-11.

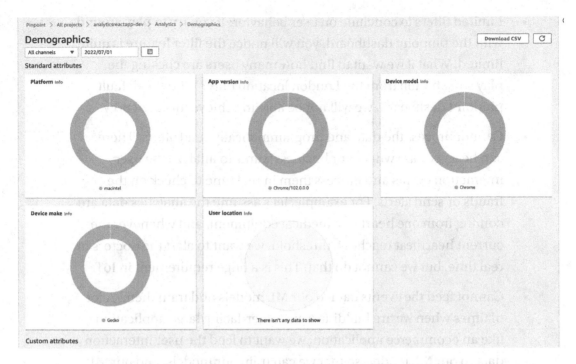

**Figure 7-11.** *Pinpoint Analytics Events dashboard for demographics charts view*

Given that our application is not published on the Internet for the users, and I am running only from my local machine, we cannot see more than one location and more than one device.

# Limitations of AWS Pinpoint Service

In the previous section, using the AWS Pinpoint service, we have seen whenever the analytics events and their metadata are being sent to our analytics backend, the data is collected by the AWS Pinpoint service, and it creates some default dashboards and charts. Pinpoint also provides basic filters where we can roughly analyze how many users are active and how the users are interacting with our application by checking on various events of button clicks and page views. The following are some limitations with Pinpoint:

- Limited charts on the dashboard: The events dashboard in the pinpoint service is limited and will be controlled by Amazon; if we want to read the analytics data and create a custom chart, it is impossible. We will be restricted, and we will have to live with what Amazon provides by default.

213

- Limited filters to conclude on user behavior: If you try to play around with the pinpoint dashboard, you will notice the filter feature is quite limited. What if we want to find how many users are clicking the play song button from the London location only? With the default pinpoint dashboard, we will not be able to achieve this as of now.

- Cannot process the data and programmatically send alerts: There can be a use case where our business wants to analyze the user interaction events and process them in real time to check on the frauds or send alerts. For example, let's assume the analytics data are coming from one heart rate medical equipment, and whenever the current heartbeat reaches a threshold, we want to alert the doctors in real time, but we cannot do that. This is a huge requirement in IoT.

- Cannot feed the events data to our ML models and train them: A lot of times when we are building a customer-facing large application like an ecommerce application, we want to feed the user interaction data to our ML models so that we can train our models, and our ML models can recommend personalized components, for example, if a user buys a washing machine, it can recommend a washing machine cover to that user. For training our ML models, we need these datasets which Pinpoint doesn't provide out of the box.

To mitigate these issues, we need a different approach of recording our event's data, so that we have better control. To mitigate these, we will now learn about the service named AWS Kinesis.

# Introduction to Kinesis

Kinesis is a fully managed, scalable, cost-effective, and flexible service that enables us to collect, process, and do whatever we want to do with the incoming data in real time. This service helps us easily stream the data so that we can store or react instantly instead of waiting for the data to process and draw conclusions later, which might impact the crucial journeys of the application.

Kinesis offers robust capabilities in a cost-effective way, which is scalable and has the flexibility to connect with any tools of our choice to get the maximum output from the data.

Kinesis is not limited to analytics and is a service that we can use to ingest any real-time data like analytics events, application logs, video, audio, or in IoT for various devices' event log data and further use these data to perform any action, send alerts, train ML models, or draw a conclusion.

## Streaming Analytics Data

Now that we understand the capabilities of Kinesis, we will use the Kinesis service to stream our analytics data, and we will discuss how we can plug more tools and processes to consume this stream data and get more output as per our needs. Instead of recording our analytics events to Pinpoint, we will send each event data to Kinesis.

We want to receive the data from users' actions, and we want to write these analytics data in a file with the required metadata and timestamp so that we can do the following:

1.  Translate raw data output into GraphQL APIs, which our web application can use to draw more custom charts.

2.  We can also feed this raw data, massage it in the required format, and feed it to our ML models, and our ML models can draw conclusions or make recommendations for each user.

3.  We can also process the real-time data and check for a few thresholds and send alerts if required.

In the following sections, we will only set up the kinesis backend, stream the analytics data, write the data into the file, and store the file in S3. Let's set up our backend first, and then we will go through the demo.

## Setting Up Kinesis Backend

Let's start by adding kinesis to our project:

```
amplify add analytics
```

This will ask which service we want to use to record our events; this time, we will choose the Kinesis streams, use the arrow key, and press enter:

```
? Select an Analytics provider
  Amazon Pinpoint
> Amazon Kinesis Streams
```

Then it will ask to enter a name; you can name whatever you want. I will choose the default name `reactauthenticationKinesis`.

The next question would be how many shards we want; let's choose one for now.

The configuration is done; let's push the changes to the cloud:

```
amplify push
```

Review and confirm the changes by pressing Y and enter.

Once this is done, roughly we are good at setting up the ingestion stream.

Let's check our AWS console dashboard if the stream is set up.

Log in to your console, and select the kinesis service.

You will see something like Figure 7-12.

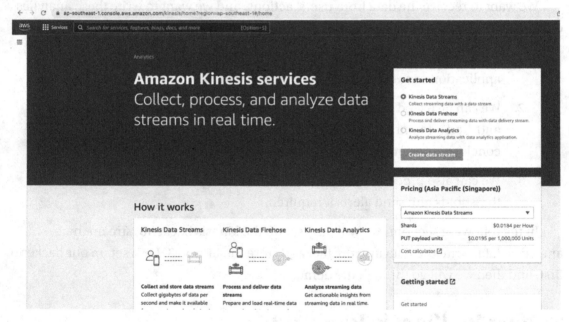

***Figure 7-12.*** *AWS Kinesis services home page*

Click the hamburger menu on the top left, just below the AWS logo.

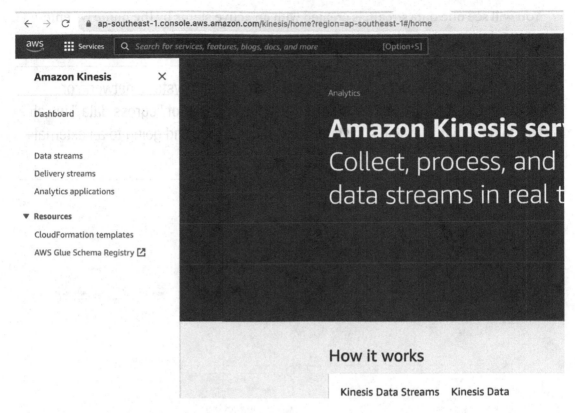

**Figure 7-13.**  *AWS Kinesis services menu*

Click the Data streams.

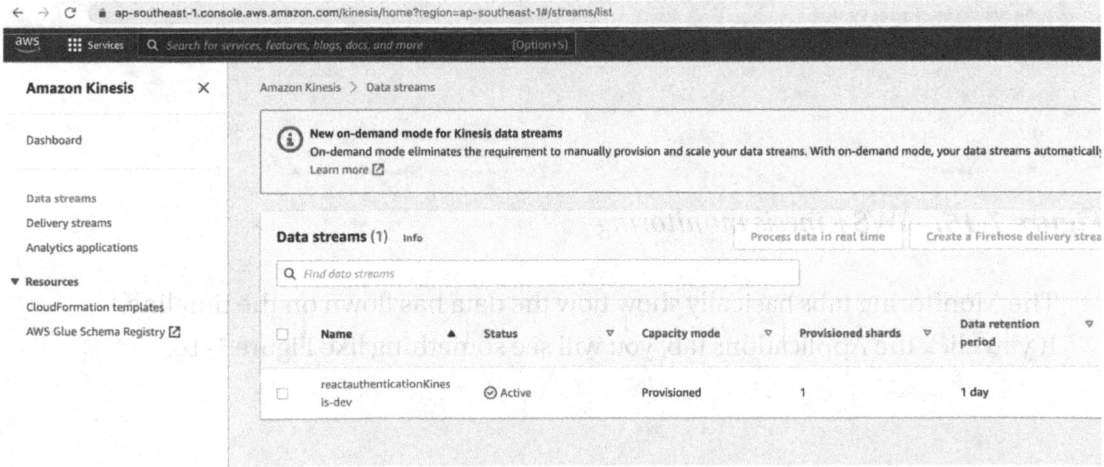

**Figure 7-14.**  *AWS Kinesis data streams*

You will see one data stream is created with an active status by the name we entered in our CLI; yes, this data stream resource is ready to ingress our data.

---

**Note**    "Ingress data" refers to data that is coming into a system, network, or device from an external source or device. It is the opposite of "egress data," which refers to data that is exiting a system, network, or device and going to an external source or device.

---

Click the item and open the page.

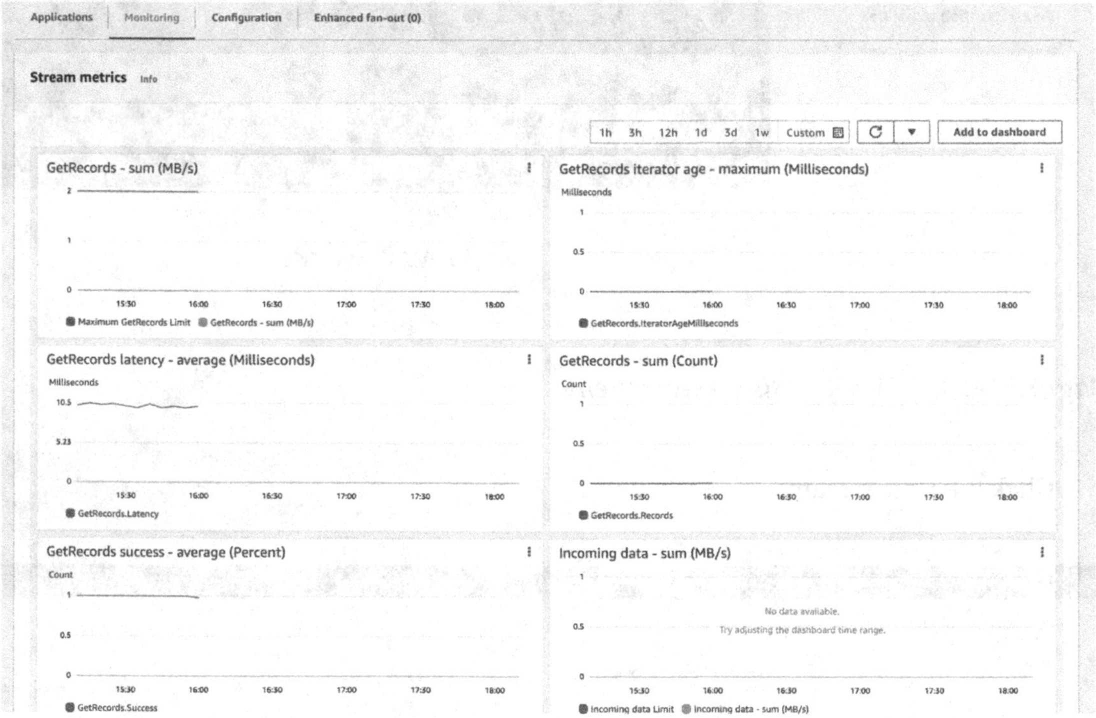

*Figure 7-15.*  *AWS Kinesis monitoring*

The Monitoring tabs basically show how the data has flown on the timeline. If you click the Applications tab, you will see something like Figure 7-16.

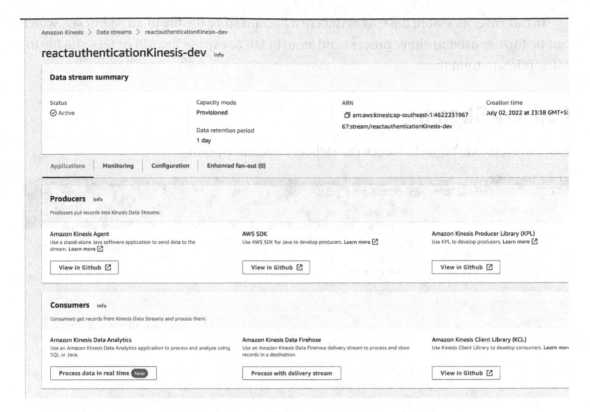

*Figure 7-16.* *AWS Kinesis Applications tab*

The data stream has two important ends:

1.  **Producers**

    This is the initiation end of the stream, the part of the client which produces the data, for example, in our case it is going to be a React.js application, which on user interaction it will send the analytics data. If we were into IoT, the sensors would have been our producers.

2.  **Consumers**

    If the data is produced, then some other tool or program has to listen to it and react as per the requirement; given kinesis is quite flexible, we can do whatever we want to do on the consumer end, either process in real time and call APIs or store as a CSV file in an S3 bucket.

In our case, let's store the events data in a file and store the file in an S3 bucket, which can be further used to either process and store in DB to expose the API or feed the file to ML models to train them.

## Delivery Stream

From the left-side pane, let's click the Delivery streams option.

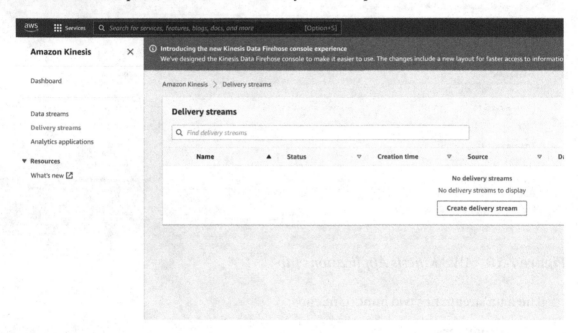

***Figure 7-17.*** *AWS Kinesis delivery streams*

Click Create delivery stream.

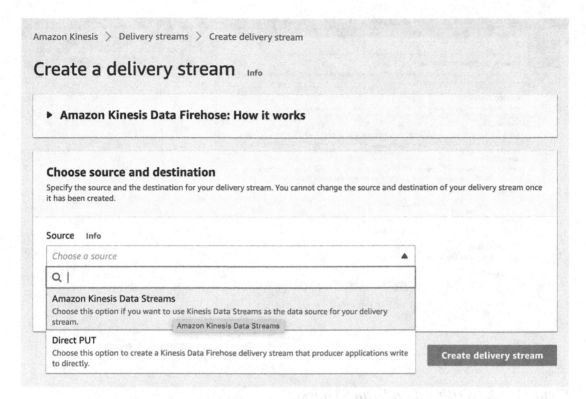

*Figure 7-18.* *AWS Kinesis Data Streams details*

As we want the kinesis data stream, from the source drop-down choose the kinesis data stream option.

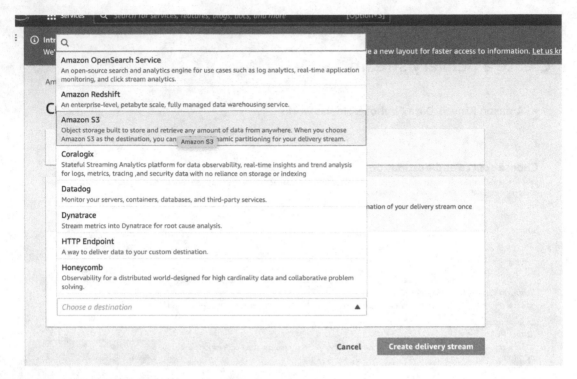

**Figure 7-19.**  *Writing data in an S3 bucket*

# Writing the Data into the File

As we want to write the data in an S3 bucket, let's choose the S3 from the drop-down.

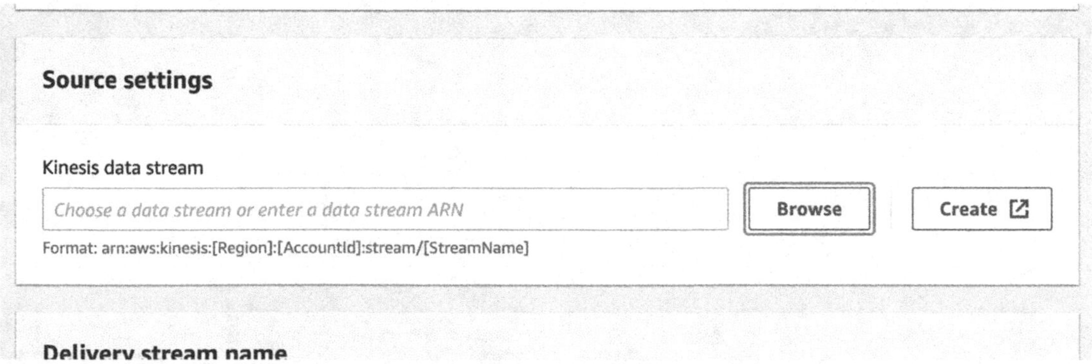

**Source settings**

Kinesis data stream

*Choose a data stream or enter a data stream ARN*     Browse     Create ☑

Format: arn:aws:kinesis:[Region]:[AccountId]:stream/[StreamName]

Delivery stream name

**Figure 7-20.**  *Select source*

We will be asked to choose the source; click Browse.

**Figure 7-21.** *Selecting Kinesis data stream source*

Choose the kinesis data stream we just created.

Enter the delivery stream name; I will go ahead with the default name.

In the destination setting, choose the S3 bucket name where you want to write the file of events.

## Destination settings   Info

Specify the destination settings for your delivery stream.

**S3 bucket**

| Choose a bucket or enter a bucket URI | **Browse** | **Create** ↗ |

Format: s3://bucket

**Dynamic partitioning**   Info

Dynamic partitioning enables you to create targeted data sets by partitioning streaming S3 data based on partitioning keys. You can partition your source data with inline parsing and/or the specified AWS Lambda function. You can enable dynamic partitioning only when you create a new delivery stream. You cannot enable dynamic partitioning for an existing delivery stream. Enabling dynamic partitioning incurs additional costs per GiB of partitioned data. For more information, see Kinesis Data Firehose pricing. ↗

● Disabled

○ Enabled

**S3 bucket prefix - *optional***

By default, Kinesis Data Firehose appends the prefix "YYYY/MM/dd/HH" (in UTC) to the data it delivers to Amazon S3. You can override this default by specifying a custom prefix that includes expressions that are evaluated at runtime.

| Enter a prefix |

***Figure 7-22.*** *Selecting an S3 bucket*

Click Browse and select the S3 bucket from the list.

Click the Create delivery stream button, and on success go back on the delivery stream dashboard.

***Figure 7-23.*** *Delivery stream dashboard*

If you see Figure 7-23 with an active status, congratulations, your delivery stream is ready as well to create a file in the S3 bucket.

Please note in the source column, we have a valid data stream, and in the destination, we have our selected S3 bucket to write the files.

# Streaming the Analytics Data from React App

We will use the same React application and remove the Pinpoint recording registration login from the onClick event function and onMouseEnter event function.

Let's modify our React application code:

```
02: import { Amplify, Analytics, AWSKinesisProvider } from "aws-amplify";
03: import awsconfig from "./aws-exports";
04: Amplify.configure(awsconfig);
05:
06: Analytics.configure({
07:   AWSKinesis: {
08:     region: awsconfig.aws_project_region,
09:   },
10: });
11: Analytics.addPluggable(new AWSKinesisProvider());
```

**LINE 2:** Import the AWSKinesisProvider from the npm package, which will help in streaming the data to Kinesis.

**LINE 6:** Using the analytics, configure the function to configure the kinesis stream.

**LINE 11:** Add the kinesis provider plugin to amplify analytics configurations.

## Recording Event to Kinesis Streams

This is simple, similar to recording in Pinpoint.

Please follow the following in all the buttons or page load events:

```
58:           <button
59:             onClick={() => {
60:               Analytics.record(
61:                 {
62:                   data: {
```

```
63:                    eventType: "buttonClick",
64:                    eventName: "playSongClicked",
65:                    timestamp: new Date(),
66:                 },
67:              streamName: "reactauthenticationKinesis-dev",
68:            },
69:          "AWSKinesis"
70:        );
71:      }}
72:    >
73:      Play song
```

**LINES 59 and 60:** In the event onClick, call the record function to stream the data.

**LINE 62:** Pass the data we want to stream under the key name data.

**LINE 63:** The event type is buttonClick.

**LINE 64:** The name of the event is as required on the event we want to register, in this case, its playSongClicked.

**LINE 65:** We want the current timestamp to process later. Please note, you can add more data if required, like user info, device info, or anything else.

**LINE 67:** As this is a kinesis stream, we need to pass the name of the stream where we want to register.

**LINE 69:** This is a type we need to pass to the analytics provider, in this case, AWS Kinesis.

Once you add the kinesis analytics recording function in all the buttons and page load events, save the changes and load the React server.

Hover on the components, and click various buttons to stream the analytics data on kinesis.

Navigate to the Network tab; you will notice the events data are streamed using kinesis as shown in Figure 7-24. The value in Data key is base64 encoded; you can copy the value and decode the base64 from your terminal or any online tool.

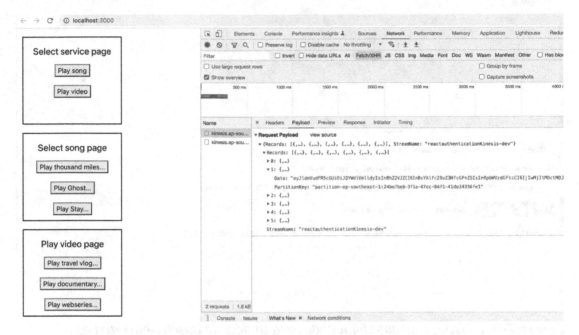

***Figure 7-24.*** *Web application streaming data to Kinesis*

You will see something like Figure 7-25, which is exactly the data that we wanted to record.

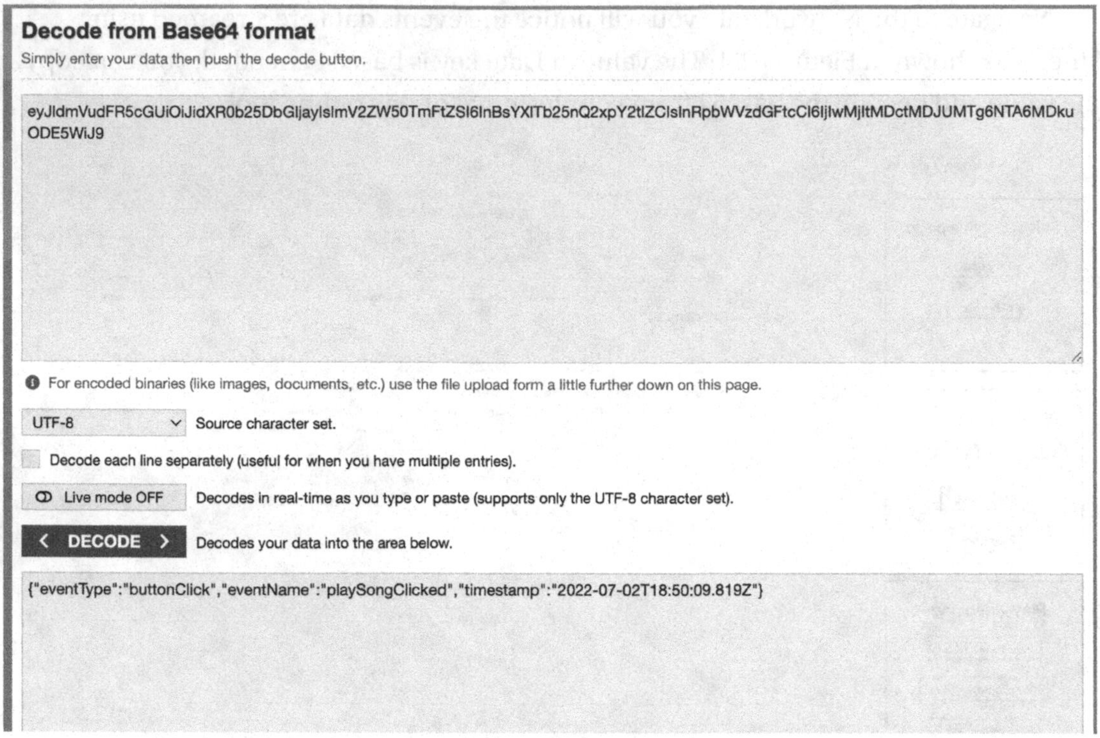

**Decode from Base64 format**

Simply enter your data then push the decode button.

eyJldmVudFR5cGUiOiJidXR0b25DbGljayIsImV2ZW50TmFtZSI6InBsYXlTb25nQ2xpY2tlZCIsInRpbWVzdGFtcCI6IjIwMjItMDctMDJUMTg6NTA6MDku
ODE5WiJ9

ℹ For encoded binaries (like images, documents, etc.) use the file upload form a little further down on this page.

UTF-8 ⌄   Source character set.

☐ Decode each line separately (useful for when you have multiple entries).

⟳ Live mode OFF   Decodes in real-time as you type or paste (supports only the UTF-8 character set).

< DECODE >   Decodes your data into the area below.

{"eventType":"buttonClick","eventName":"playSongClicked","timestamp":"2022-07-02T18:50:09.819Z"}

*Figure 7-25.  Using* www.base64decode.org *to decode base64-encoded data*

Congratulations on integrating from the producers' side of the data stream and successfully streaming our analytics data from the events from the React application.

## Kinesis Data Stream Dashboard

Navigate to the kinesis service on the AWS console on the browser and click the data stream; under the Monitoring tab, you will see something like Figure 7-26.

***Figure 7-26.***  *Amazon Kinesis Monitoring tab*

As you can see, as we interacted on the React application we have streamed the data, and that is reflected on the charts.

## Kinesis Data Delivery Dashboard

Click the data delivery; you will see something like Figure 7-27.

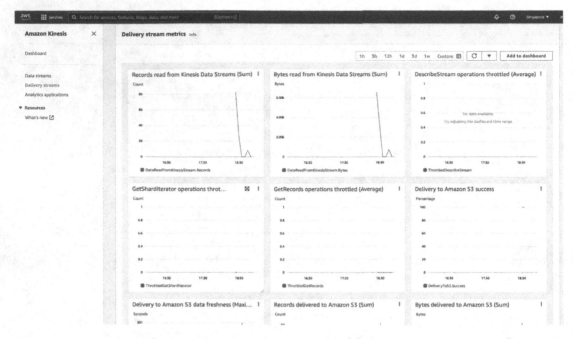

*Figure 7-27.  Amazon Kinesis data delivery dashboard*

# Data in the S3 Bucket

Open the S3 bucket, the one which was selected as the destination in the delivery stream configurations.

You will notice one directory is created, as shown in Figure 7-28.

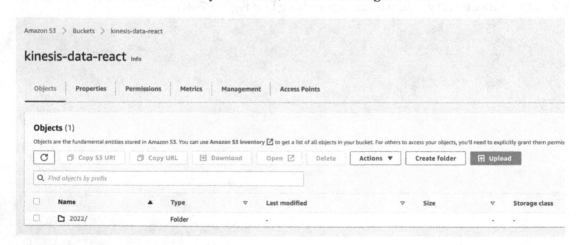

*Figure 7-28.  Amazon S3 bucket*

Open the directories until you reach the files, shown in Figure 7-29.

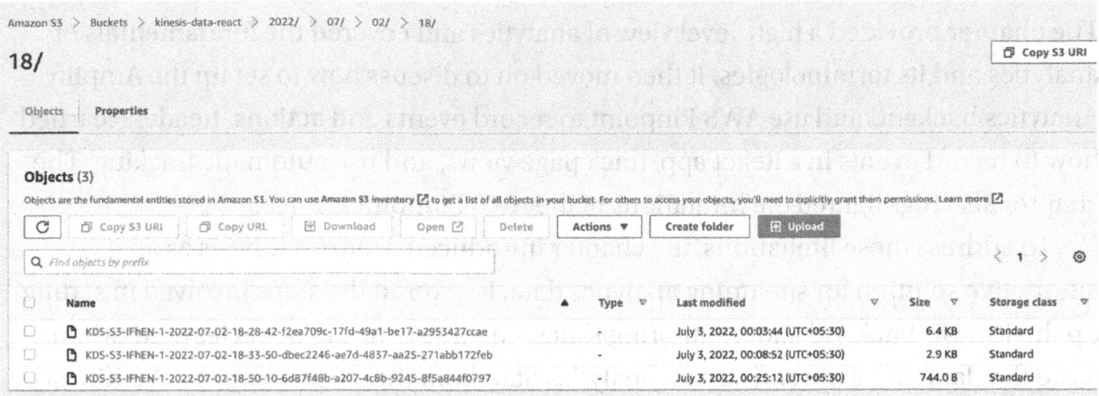


***Figure 7-29.*** *Amazon S3 bucket view data*

In my case, it was 2022/07/02/18. The various directories will follow year/month/date/UTC hour. You will get the directory names and the day and time you receive the stream from your application.

Let's open the file, you will can see the file preview in Figure 7-30.

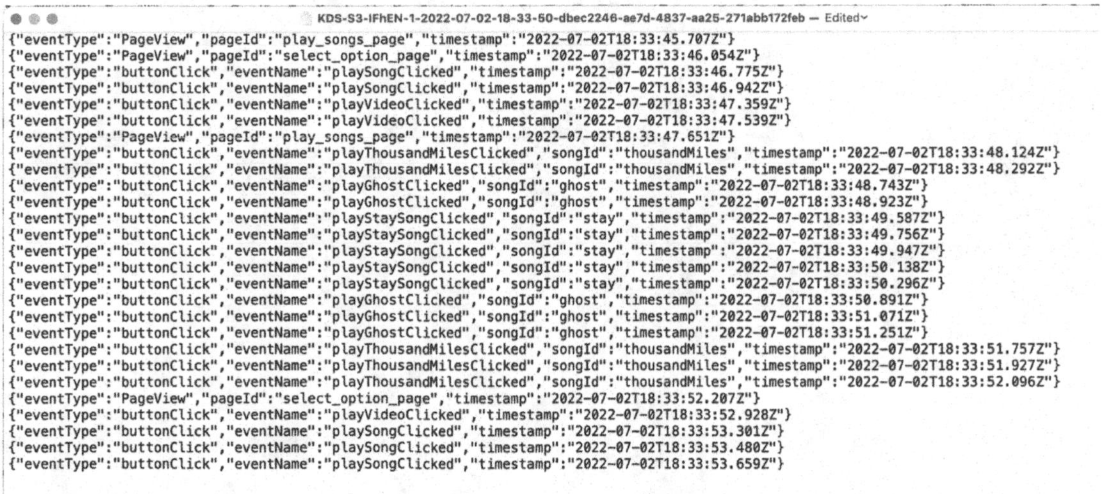
KDS-S3-IFhEN-1-2022-07-02-18-33-50-dbec2246-ae7d-4837-aa25-271abb172feb — Edited


```
{"eventType":"PageView","pageId":"play_songs_page","timestamp":"2022-07-02T18:33:45.707Z"}
{"eventType":"PageView","pageId":"select_option_page","timestamp":"2022-07-02T18:33:46.054Z"}
{"eventType":"buttonClick","eventName":"playSongClicked","timestamp":"2022-07-02T18:33:46.775Z"}
{"eventType":"buttonClick","eventName":"playSongClicked","timestamp":"2022-07-02T18:33:46.942Z"}
{"eventType":"buttonClick","eventName":"playVideoClicked","timestamp":"2022-07-02T18:33:47.359Z"}
{"eventType":"buttonClick","eventName":"playVideoClicked","timestamp":"2022-07-02T18:33:47.539Z"}
{"eventType":"PageView","pageId":"play_songs_page","timestamp":"2022-07-02T18:33:47.651Z"}
{"eventType":"buttonClick","eventName":"playThousandMilesClicked","songId":"thousandMiles","timestamp":"2022-07-02T18:33:48.124Z"}
{"eventType":"buttonClick","eventName":"playThousandMilesClicked","songId":"thousandMiles","timestamp":"2022-07-02T18:33:48.292Z"}
{"eventType":"buttonClick","eventName":"playGhostClicked","songId":"ghost","timestamp":"2022-07-02T18:33:48.743Z"}
{"eventType":"buttonClick","eventName":"playGhostClicked","songId":"ghost","timestamp":"2022-07-02T18:33:48.923Z"}
{"eventType":"buttonClick","eventName":"playStaySongClicked","songId":"stay","timestamp":"2022-07-02T18:33:49.587Z"}
{"eventType":"buttonClick","eventName":"playStaySongClicked","songId":"stay","timestamp":"2022-07-02T18:33:49.756Z"}
{"eventType":"buttonClick","eventName":"playStaySongClicked","songId":"stay","timestamp":"2022-07-02T18:33:49.947Z"}
{"eventType":"buttonClick","eventName":"playStaySongClicked","songId":"stay","timestamp":"2022-07-02T18:33:50.138Z"}
{"eventType":"buttonClick","eventName":"playStaySongClicked","songId":"stay","timestamp":"2022-07-02T18:33:50.296Z"}
{"eventType":"buttonClick","eventName":"playGhostClicked","songId":"ghost","timestamp":"2022-07-02T18:33:50.891Z"}
{"eventType":"buttonClick","eventName":"playGhostClicked","songId":"ghost","timestamp":"2022-07-02T18:33:51.071Z"}
{"eventType":"buttonClick","eventName":"playGhostClicked","songId":"ghost","timestamp":"2022-07-02T18:33:51.251Z"}
{"eventType":"buttonClick","eventName":"playThousandMilesClicked","songId":"thousandMiles","timestamp":"2022-07-02T18:33:51.757Z"}
{"eventType":"buttonClick","eventName":"playThousandMilesClicked","songId":"thousandMiles","timestamp":"2022-07-02T18:33:51.927Z"}
{"eventType":"buttonClick","eventName":"playThousandMilesClicked","songId":"thousandMiles","timestamp":"2022-07-02T18:33:52.096Z"}
{"eventType":"PageView","pageId":"select_option_page","timestamp":"2022-07-02T18:33:52.207Z"}
{"eventType":"buttonClick","eventName":"playVideoClicked","timestamp":"2022-07-02T18:33:52.928Z"}
{"eventType":"buttonClick","eventName":"playSongClicked","timestamp":"2022-07-02T18:33:53.301Z"}
{"eventType":"buttonClick","eventName":"playSongClicked","timestamp":"2022-07-02T18:33:53.480Z"}
{"eventType":"buttonClick","eventName":"playSongClicked","timestamp":"2022-07-02T18:33:53.659Z"}
```


***Figure 7-30.*** *Data file*

As you can read through the file, it contains the various data we streamed from our React application.

# Summary

The chapter provided a high-level view of analytics and covered the fundamentals of analytics and its terminologies. It then moved on to discuss how to set up the Amplify Analytics backend and use AWS Pinpoint to record events and actions. Readers learned how to record events in a React app, track page views, and use automatic tracking. The chapter also highlighted the limitations of the AWS Pinpoint service.

To address these limitations, the chapter introduced Amazon Kinesis as an alternative solution for streaming analytics data. It covered the steps involved in setting up the Kinesis backend and monitoring Kinesis data streams. Readers learned how to write the data into a file and stream analytics data from their React app to AWS Kinesis.

Overall, the chapter provided a comprehensive guide to implement analytics using AWS Pinpoint, React web app, AWS Kinesis, and AWS Amplify. Readers learned how to record and track events, stream data, and monitor Kinesis data streams. The chapter also covered the limitations of the Pinpoint service and how to overcome them by using Kinesis.

# CHAPTER 8

# Continuous Integration and Continuous Delivery/Continuous Deployment

*Continuous integration doesn't get rid of bugs, but it does make them dramatically easier to find and remove.*

—Martin Fowler

## The Goal of This Chapter

1. Understand the CI and CD in detail and their differences

2. Understand Pipeline as Code and its benefits

3. Publish apps in multiple environments

4. Password-protect the development environment using Amplify's access control feature

## Defining CI/CD

Continuous integration/continuous delivery (CI/CD) is a set of practices that an application development team uses to automate and streamline the process of sanitizing, testing, building, and deploying the application quickly and efficiently, as soon as there is any code change.

To deliver high-quality and bug-free code at a high velocity with minimum errors, software development teams rely on fast and reliable CI/CD pipelines. These pipelines enable the team to take an agile approach to deliver the applications.

The guiding principle of CI/CD is the frequent and continuous delivery of software updates, which encompasses a range of activities including integration, testing, building, delivery, and deployment of applications. This end-to-end process is commonly referred to as the CI/CD pipeline, which is composed of multiple phases. Typically, some of these phases depend on previous phases and require the one phase to complete successfully before proceeding further. This process of breaking down the CI/CD pipeline into smaller, more manageable phases gives the team more flexibility and control to deliver high-quality software and helps business by reducing the time to market for new features and updates.

# Difference Between CI and CD

CI and CD have different responsibilities in the pipeline; let's try to understand that.

# Continuous Integration

Continuous integration (CI) emphasizes the need of frequent merging of code changes from the feature branches into the main branch. With typical development teams comprising anywhere from 8 to 10 developers, if all the developers contribute to the repository, there can be a minimum of 10–15 branches. If integration of these branches into the main branch is postponed until the release day, the likelihood of conflicts and delays in the release process significantly increases. To avoid such problems, CI practices require developers to merge their code changes regularly and promptly, enabling them to catch and resolve issues early, leading to a smoother, more efficient release process.

CI enforces continuous integration of code changes into the main branch while validating them through a set of phases.

CI emphasizes a lot on automating the test cases and checking the quality of code to really make sure the application is not breaking by any code change, before merging to the main branch.

# Continuous Delivery

Continuous delivery (CD) is the next phase in the CI/CD pipeline, which involves the automated deployment of code changes to either a test environment or a production environment. After passing through the CI pipeline, which includes phases like testing and linting, the newer version needs to be deployed to the test environment to QAs or in a production environment to the customers. This means after the automated testing and build phase, it's time for the automated deployment of the application, which is as simple as clicking a button of approval whenever the team wants the newer version to appear to the customer.

CD ensures that the delivery process is controlled and planned with a manual button click, allowing teams to maintain greater control over the integration and delivery phases of their application.

# Continuous Deployment

Continuous deployment (CD) significantly steps up the deployment process in the CI/CD pipeline, which emphasizes the automated deployment of code changes to the environments without any manual intervention. With continuous deployment, every approved small change is continuously delivered to customers as soon as possible, automatically.

The CI/CD pipeline recommends frequent and smaller deployments to make it easier to track and identify any issues that may arise. This approach enables businesses to quickly revert small portions of the code, if necessary, rather than having to revert entire features that may impact multiple areas of the business, resulting in a significant amount of time and effort being wasted. By leveraging continuous deployment, teams can significantly reduce the time it takes to deliver code changes to customers, minimize the risk of human error, and ensure the smooth and efficient operation of their software applications.

In Figure 8-1, we can see an overview of the flow of the CI/CD pipeline. When code is merged to the main branch, the CI pipeline is triggered, which consists of multiple jobs. These jobs include testing, code quality checks, and creating a build of the application, either as a zip of files or a Docker image. Once all of the jobs are successfully completed, the CD pipeline is triggered.

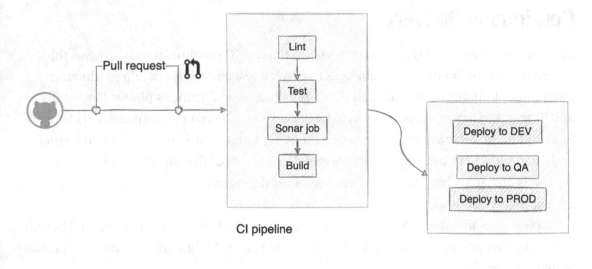

***Figure 8-1.***  *CI and CD pipeline flow*

# The Objective of the CI/CD Pipeline

The primary objective of the CI/CD pipeline is to provide immediate feedback to developers regarding the code modifications they have made. By doing so, it helps ensure that the development team avoids introducing any faulty code into the software automatically and instantaneously. This feedback is a critical component of the development process, as it enables developers to identify and resolve issues quickly, leading to more efficient and effective software delivery. The real-time nature of the feedback allows for the creation of a continuous improvement cycle, where the development team can continually refine their code and delivery processes, leading to better software quality and faster time to market.

# Pipeline As Code

Pipeline as Code is a methodology that entails incorporating the pipeline configuration and definition into the codebase in version control, such as Git, in which it coexists with the application code. If, for example, the team decides to add an integration test phase after the unit test phase, rather than manually adding this phase from some dashboard, a team member must add the configuration to the codebase and raise a pull request against the main branch.

All configurations, such as testing, linting, building the docker image, pushing the image, and deployments, are established by coding, that is part of the repository. With this approach, as long as the pipeline configuration is versioned, it can be tested by adding it to a separate branch, and once the configuration is deemed satisfactory, it can be merged into the main branch.

## Benefits of Pipeline As Code

The Pipeline as Code has effectively addressed various issues that arise from manual configurations of pipelines:

- Version control: Similar to version-controlling business logic code, the team can now create new versions of the pipeline and regulate configurations using code. This enables them to revert to the previous version or create distinct configurations for different branches.

- Audit trails: If we keep our Pipeline as Code, then it is possible to easily track who modified what and when.

- Testing before integrating into the main branch: Pipeline as Code enables the team to carry out the testing of the pipeline prior to integrating it into the main branch. The team can raise a pull request as a feature and test the pipeline in a different branch, which provides assurance before merging it into the main branch.

## Repository and Environments

A team requires multiple environments to cater to different types of users to ensure that one type of user does not interfere with another type of user and breaks the user flow. Typically, there are three types of users for a team:

1. Developers: The developers need a development environment, which they use to integrate basic features and store the most recent changes. However, this environment may have bugs and unstable features.

2.   Testers: The testers require a relatively stable environment to
     test the features that developers have marked ready for QA. Once
     developers are satisfied with their feature, they move it to the test
     environment. This test environment is closer to production and is
     more stable compared to the development environment.

3.   End customers: The end customers use the production
     environment once the feature is thoroughly tested, and only then
     is the feature marked ready for production and deployed to the
     production environment.

It is crucial to maintain control over every environment using specific git branches.
In doing so, the team can follow the agreed git flow to manage the smooth transition of
the features from the development environment to the test environment and finally to
the production environment. It should be noted that the number of environments and
their respective responsibilities are decided by the team members, and the practices and
terminologies may vary from one team to another. As such, there is no universal rule,
and teams work together to create their own set of guidelines.

# Hosting the Application for Development Environment

To commence with the hosting and deployment of an application in the development
environment, the primary step is to create a GitHub repository and push our source
code. We will start with creating a development branch named `develop`, by running the
following git command:

```
git checkout -b develop
```

Should you have any changes that have not been committed, kindly add, commit,
and push the changes to the develop branch. Upon completion, the first step is to
establish a connection between the repository and the branch to our Amplify app.

Access the AWS console and log in to your account. Proceed to the Amplify service,
and click the hosting environment tab. Select your git repository host depending on
where your repository is located. For instance, in our case, as shown in Figure 8-2, we
have pushed to GitHub; thus, we will opt for GitHub.

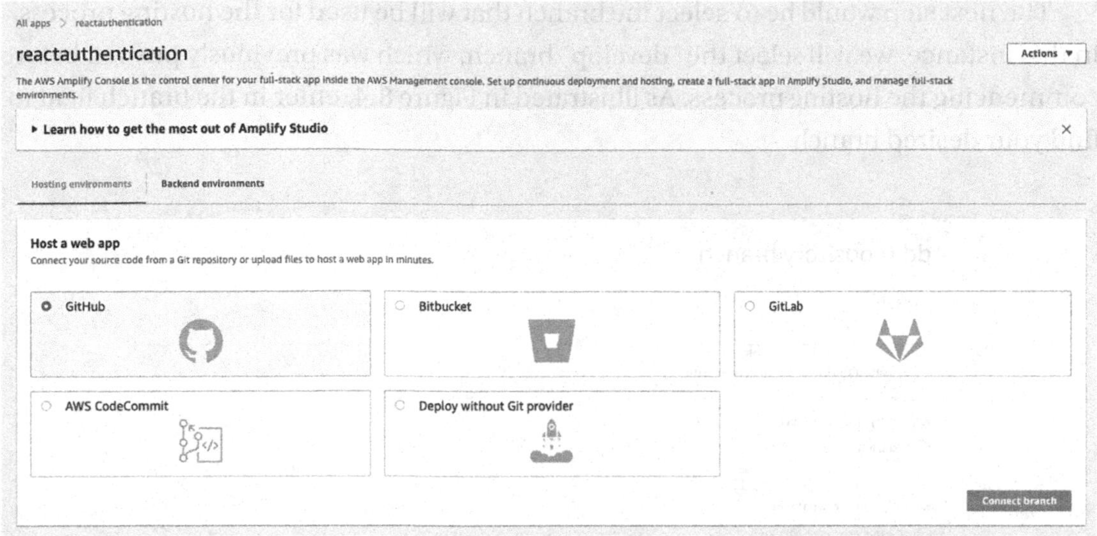

*Figure 8-2.  Connecting the Amplify app with the GitHub repository*

Authorize GitHub by providing your account credentials. You will be directed to a screen. The step is illustrated in Figure 8-3. You will be required to select which repositories you want to grant access to. You can choose to give access to all repositories associated with your account or just one specific repository.

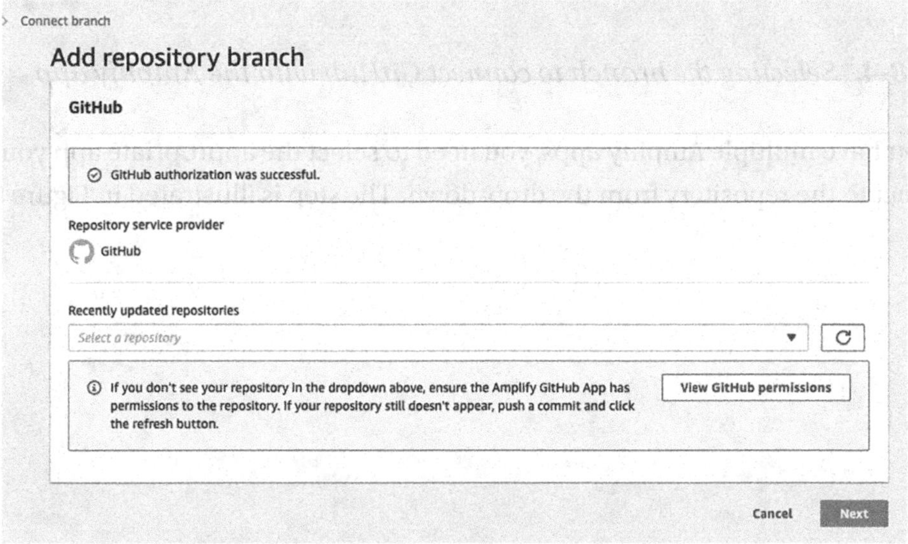

*Figure 8-3.  Prompt after successful account authorization*

The next step would be to select the branch that will be used for the hosting process. In this instance, we will select the `develop` branch, which was previously pushed before commencing the hosting process. As illustrated in Figure 8-4, enter in the branch field to find your desired branch.

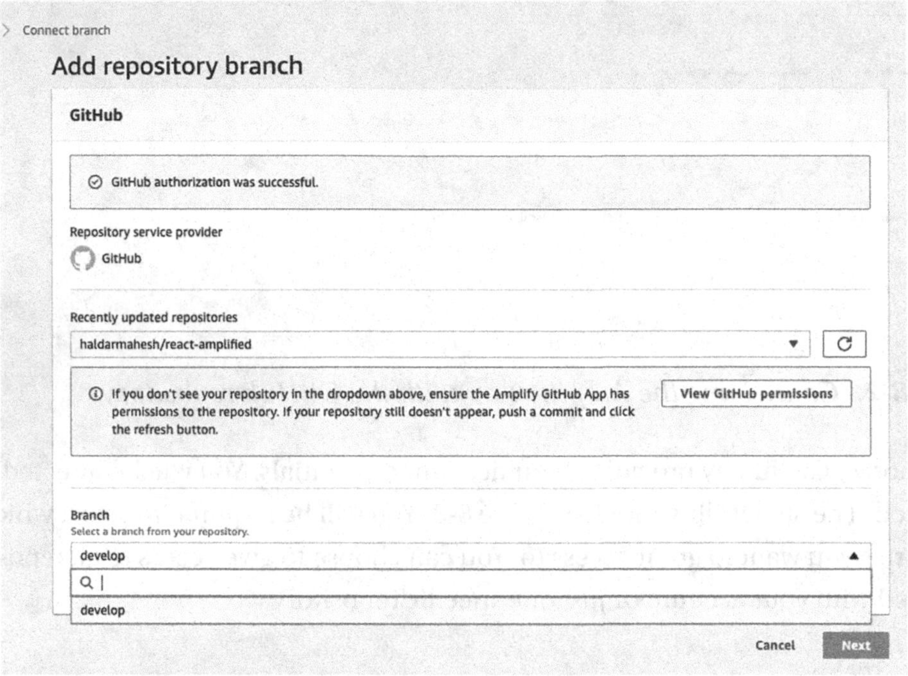

***Figure 8-4.*** *Selecting the branch to connect GitHub with the Amplify app*

If you have multiple Amplify apps, you need to select the appropriate app you want to connect to the repository from the drop-down. The step is illustrated in Figure 8-5.

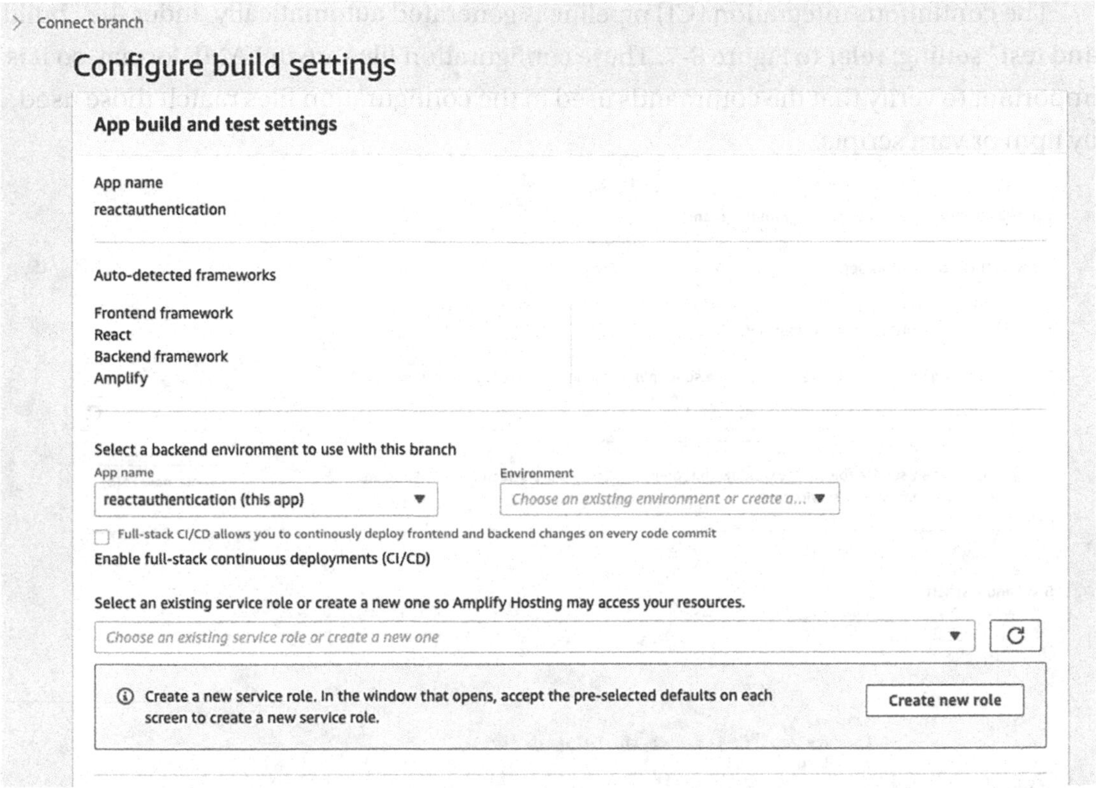

> Connect branch

## Configure build settings

### App build and test settings

App name
reactauthentication

Auto-detected frameworks

Frontend framework
React
Backend framework
Amplify

Select a backend environment to use with this branch

| App name | Environment |
| --- | --- |
| reactauthentication (this app)  ▼ | Choose an existing environment or create a... ▼ |

☐ Full-stack CI/CD allows you to continuously deploy frontend and backend changes on every code commit
Enable full-stack continuous deployments (CI/CD)

Select an existing service role or create a new one so Amplify Hosting may access your resources.

| Choose an existing service role or create a new one | ▼ | C |

ⓘ  Create a new service role. In the window that opens, accept the pre-selected defaults on each     | Create new role |
screen to create a new service role.

*Figure 8-5.*  *Select the Amplify app from the drop-down*

Please select the appropriate environment by navigating to the relevant section in the hosting console. In this case, since we have already created a development environment, we can select it from the list of available environments. Refer to Figure 8-6.

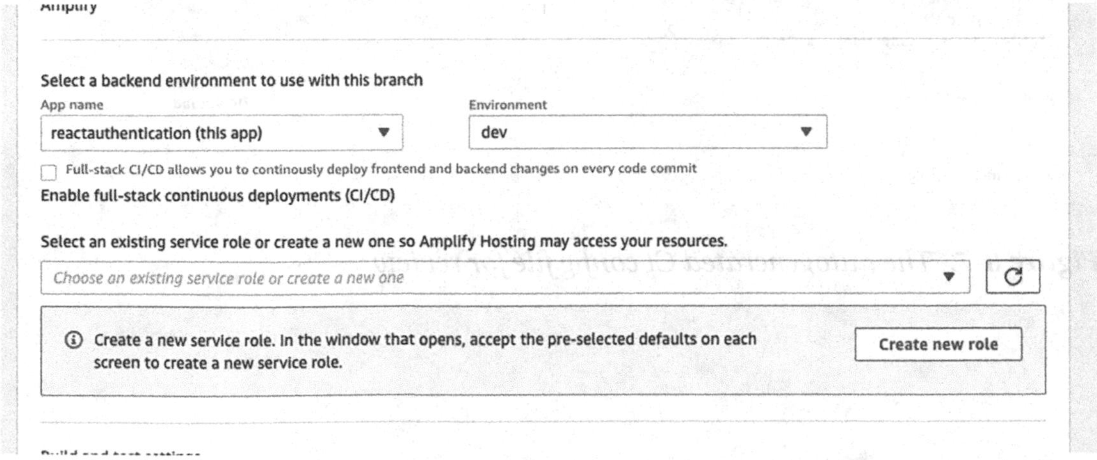

Amplify

Select a backend environment to use with this branch

| App name | Environment |
| --- | --- |
| reactauthentication (this app)  ▼ | dev  ▼ |

☐ Full-stack CI/CD allows you to continuously deploy frontend and backend changes on every code commit
Enable full-stack continuous deployments (CI/CD)

Select an existing service role or create a new one so Amplify Hosting may access your resources.

| Choose an existing service role or create a new one | ▼ | C |

ⓘ  Create a new service role. In the window that opens, accept the pre-selected defaults on each     | Create new role |
screen to create a new service role.

*Figure 8-6.*  *Select the environment*

The continuous integration (CI) pipeline is generated automatically under the "build and test" setting; refer to Figure 8-7. These configuration files are in YAML format, so it is important to verify that the commands used in the configuration files match those used by npm or yarn scripts.

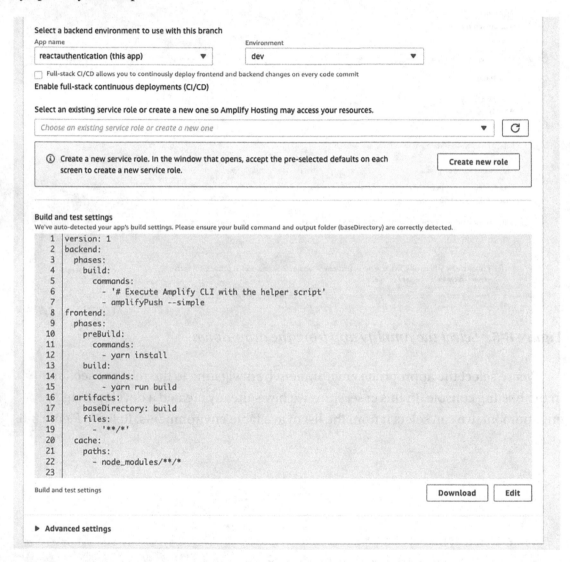

*Figure 8-7.* *The autogenerated CI config file for review*

If an attempt is made to submit it without selecting a role, an error will occur, prompting the selection of a role, as illustrated in Figure 8-8. This role is an AWS role specifically created for the CI/CD pipeline to access AWS resources and deploy the application.

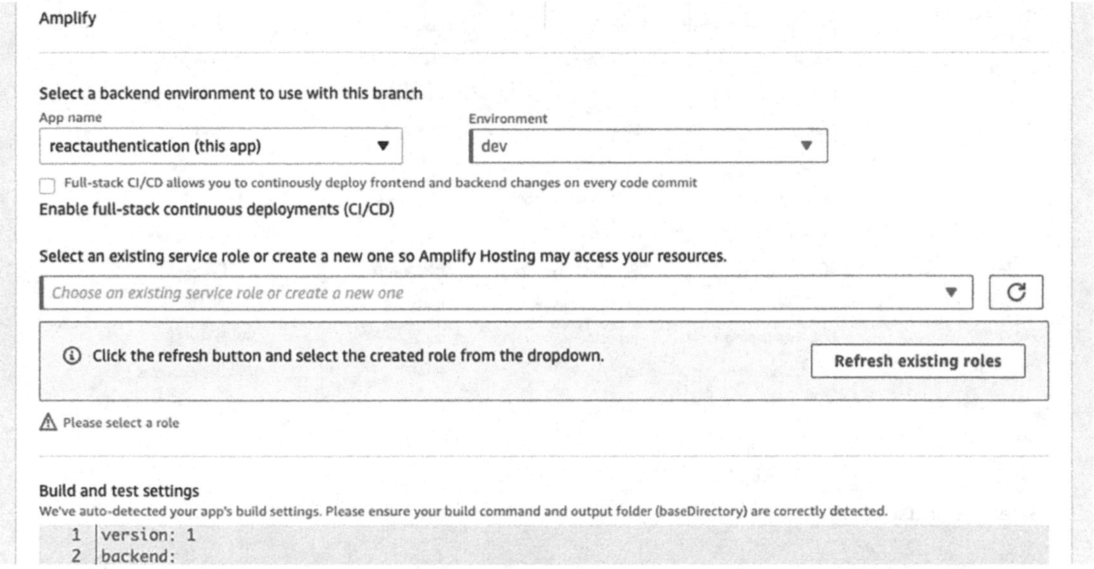

**Figure 8-8.**  *The error state to select the role*

Therefore, it is necessary to create a new role and assign it to the CI/CD pipeline. This role has multiple benefits, including aiding in auditing, access control, and increased application security. In case any access key is leaked, the impact on the application would be minimal. Furthermore, the roles can be disabled at any point in time.

To create a new role, click the "Create a new role" option, which will navigate you to a new tab, as illustrated in Figure 8-9.

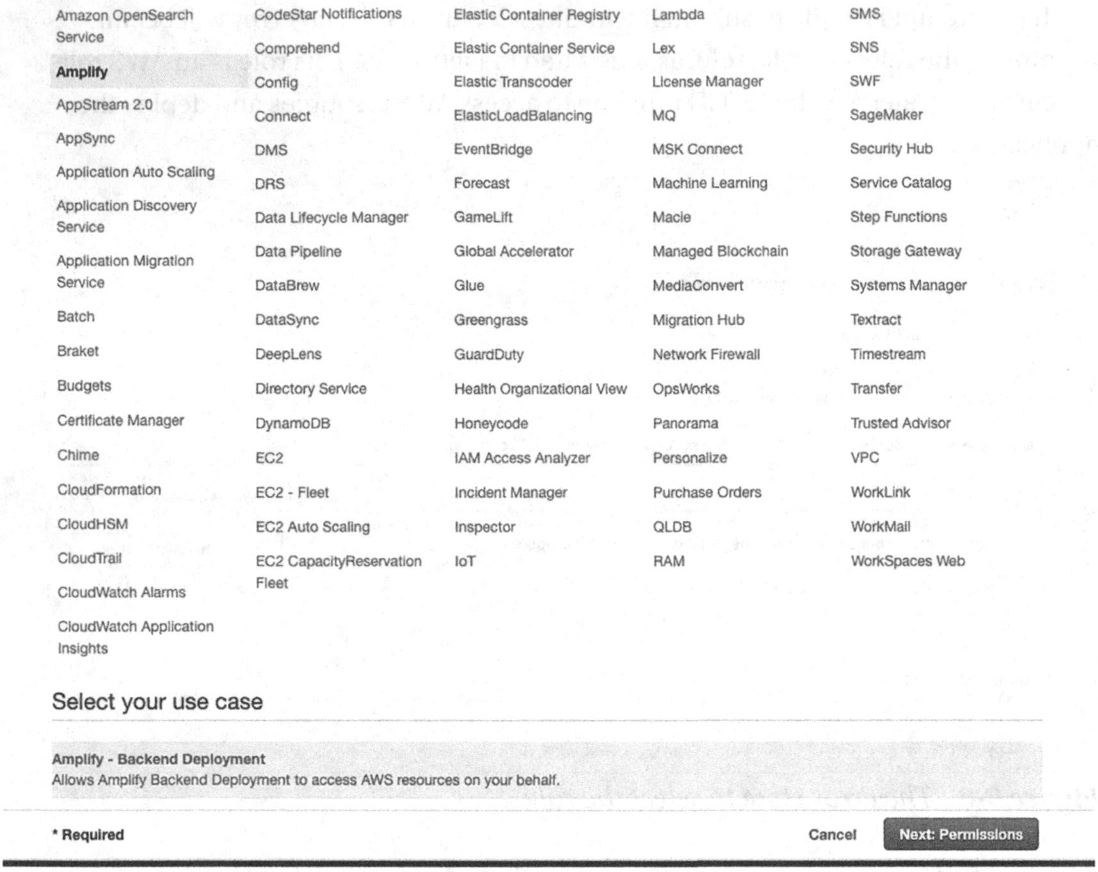

| | | | | |
|---|---|---|---|---|
| Amazon OpenSearch Service | CodeStar Notifications | Elastic Container Registry | Lambda | SMS |
| | Comprehend | Elastic Container Service | Lex | SNS |
| **Amplify** | Config | Elastic Transcoder | License Manager | SWF |
| AppStream 2.0 | Connect | ElasticLoadBalancing | MQ | SageMaker |
| AppSync | DMS | EventBridge | MSK Connect | Security Hub |
| Application Auto Scaling | DRS | Forecast | Machine Learning | Service Catalog |
| Application Discovery Service | Data Lifecycle Manager | GameLift | Macie | Step Functions |
| Application Migration Service | Data Pipeline | Global Accelerator | Managed Blockchain | Storage Gateway |
| Batch | DataBrew | Glue | MediaConvert | Systems Manager |
| Braket | DataSync | Greengrass | Migration Hub | Textract |
| Budgets | DeepLens | GuardDuty | Network Firewall | Timestream |
| Certificate Manager | Directory Service | Health Organizational View | OpsWorks | Transfer |
| Chime | DynamoDB | Honeycode | Panorama | Trusted Advisor |
| CloudFormation | EC2 | IAM Access Analyzer | Personalize | VPC |
| CloudHSM | EC2 - Fleet | Incident Manager | Purchase Orders | WorkLink |
| CloudTrail | EC2 Auto Scaling | Inspector | QLDB | WorkMail |
| CloudWatch Alarms | EC2 CapacityReservation Fleet | IoT | RAM | WorkSpaces Web |
| CloudWatch Application Insights | | | | |

**Select your use case**

**Amplify - Backend Deployment**
Allows Amplify Backend Deployment to access AWS resources on your behalf.

* Required                                                          Cancel   [ Next: Permissions ]

***Figure 8-9.*** *Use case list for creating a new role*

Select the Amplify use case and click Next to add the permissions.

The permission is added automatically to the role, as illustrated in Figure 8-10. As we don't want to add more permissions to this role, we may proceed to the next step by selecting the "Next" option.

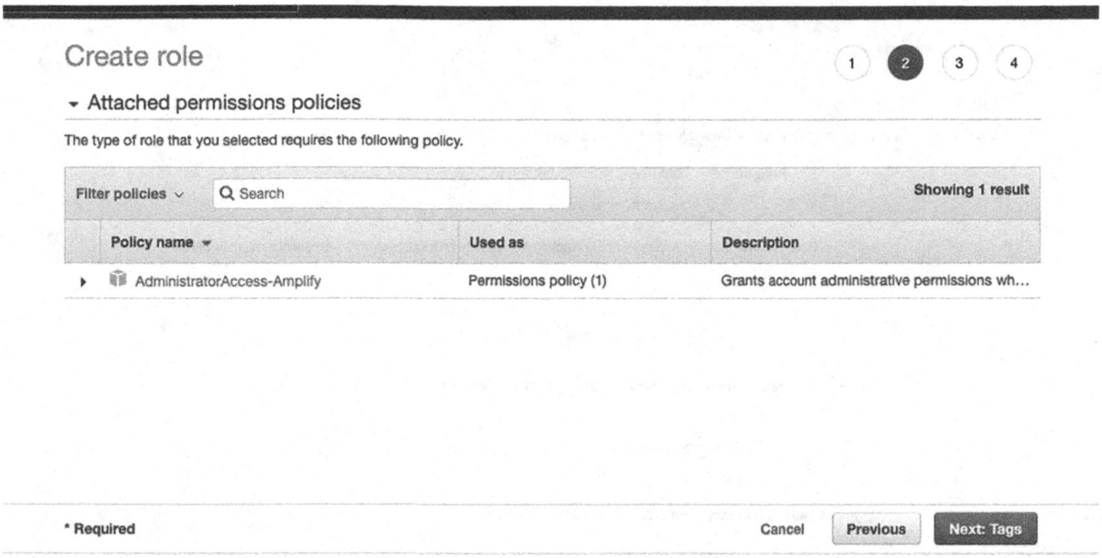

Create role                                              ① ❷ ③ ④

▾ Attached permissions policies

The type of role that you selected requires the following policy.

| Filter policies ∨ | Q Search | | Showing 1 result |
|---|---|---|---|
| **Policy name ▾** | **Used as** | **Description** | |
| ▸ 🗍 AdministratorAccess-Amplify | Permissions policy (1) | Grants account administrative permissions wh… | |

* Required                                      Cancel   **Previous**   **Next: Tags**

***Figure 8-10.*** *The permission policy for the Amplify app*

In the next screen, you will be prompted to add some tags to the role. These tags are used to group roles into desired categories. For now, you can skip this step and proceed by clicking the "Next" button.

In the subsequent screen, you need to specify a name for the role and provide a brief description. The screen is illustrated in Figure 8-11. This will help you identify the purpose of the role when you have multiple roles in the future.

Create role                                    ( 1 )  ( 2 )  ( 3 )  ● 4

Review

Provide the required information below and review this role before you create it.

**Role name***          amplifyconsole-backend-role

Use alphanumeric and '+=,.@-_' characters. Maximum 64 characters.

**Role description**     Allows Amplify Backend Deployment to access AWS resources on your behalf.

Maximum 1000 characters. Use alphanumeric and '+=,.@-_' characters.

**Trusted entities**     AWS service: amplify.amazonaws.com

**Policies**    📦  AdministratorAccess-Amplify 🗗

**Permissions boundary**    Permissions boundary is not set

No tags were added.

*Required                                     Cancel    Previous    Create role

**Figure 8-11.** *Form fields to add the name and description of the role to be created*

After creating the new role, return to the previous tab and refresh it to fetch the newly created role. Once the page is refreshed, the newly created role should appear on the list, as illustrated in Figure 8-12. Select it in order to proceed to the next step.

Select a backend environment to use with this branch

App name                                      Environment

reactauthentication (this app)    ▼          dev                            ▼

☐ Full-stack CI/CD allows you to continously deploy frontend and backend changes on every code commit
Enable full-stack continuous deployments (CI/CD)

Select an existing service role or create a new one so Amplify Hosting may access your resources.

Choose an existing service role or create a new one                          ▲    │  ⟳

Q  Filter service roles

amplifyconsole-backend-role                                                  bles
New role

⚠ Please select a role              amplifyconsole-backend-role

**Figure 8-12.** *Selecting the newly created role from the drop-down*

In conclusion, it is essential to review the entire configuration carefully before proceeding. After reviewing, click the "Save and deploy" button, as illustrated in Figure 8-13, to initiate the deployment process. This step ensures that the application is properly configured and ready to be deployed.

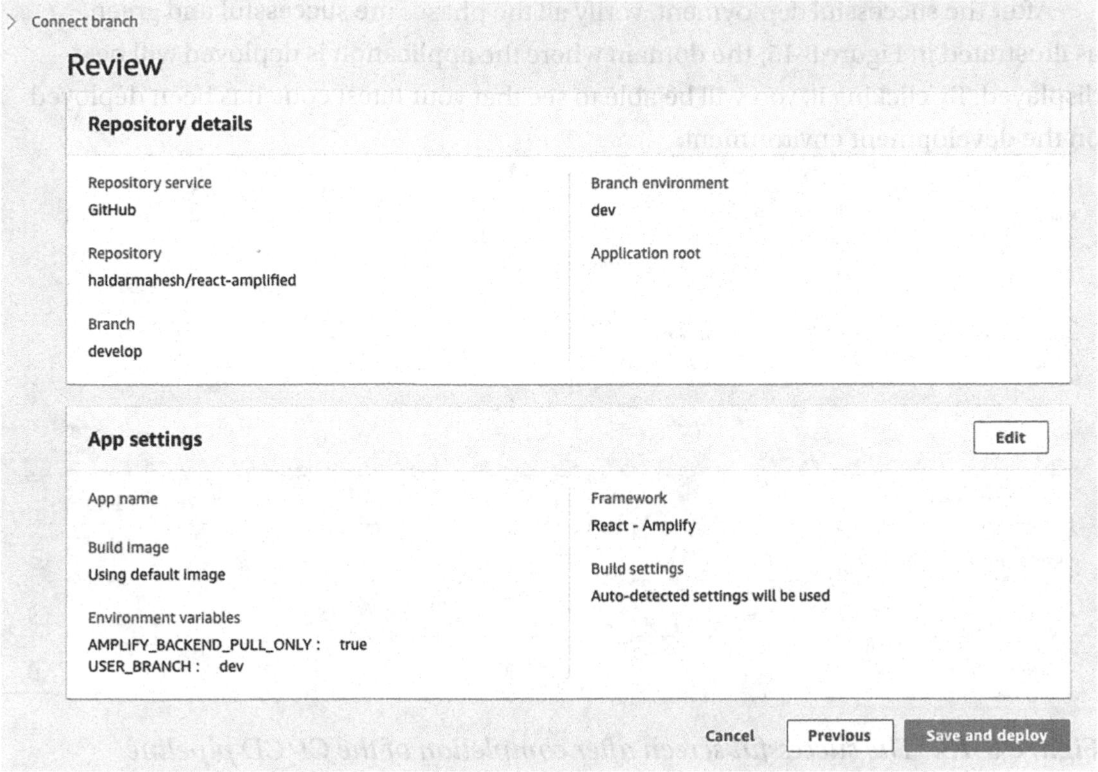

> Connect branch

## Review

### Repository details

| | |
|---|---|
| Repository service | Branch environment |
| GitHub | dev |
| | |
| Repository | Application root |
| haldarmahesh/react-amplified | |
| | |
| Branch | |
| develop | |

### App settings                                                    Edit

| | |
|---|---|
| App name | Framework |
| | React - Amplify |
| Build image | |
| Using default image | Build settings |
| | Auto-detected settings will be used |
| Environment variables | |
| AMPLIFY_BACKEND_PULL_ONLY :   true | |
| USER_BRANCH :   dev | |

Cancel      Previous      Save and deploy

*Figure 8-13.* *The review screen to save and deploy the application*

After completing the aforementioned steps, you can view the CI pipeline in action. The pipeline consists of several phases for CI and CD, which can be viewed in Figure 8-14. To check the logs and details of each job in the pipeline, simply click the respective jobs.

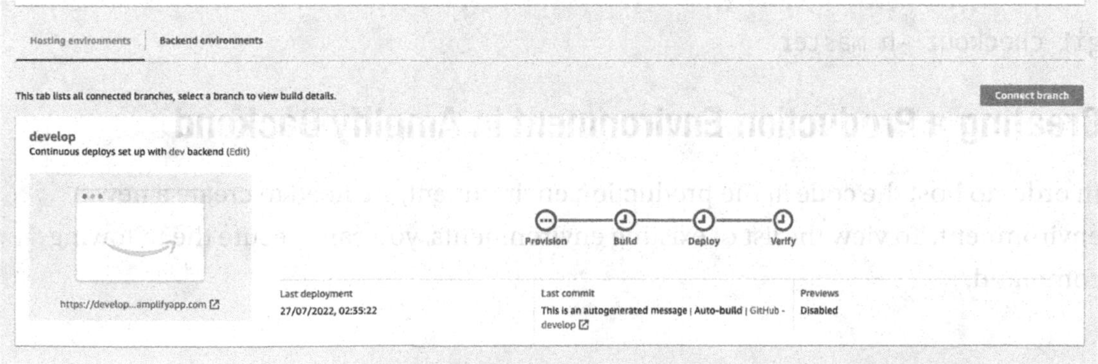

| Hosting environments | Backend environments |
|---|---|

This tab lists all connected branches, select a branch to view build details.        Connect branch

**develop**
Continuous deploys set up with dev backend (Edit)

Provision — Build — Deploy — Verify

| https://develop...amplifyapp.com | Last deployment 27/07/2022, 02:55:22 | Last commit This is an autogenerated message \| Auto-build \| GitHub - develop | Previews Disabled |

*Figure 8-14.* *In progress CI/CD pipeline*

After the successful deployment, verify all the phases are successful and green, as illustrated in Figure 8-15; the domain where the application is deployed will be displayed. By clicking it, you will be able to see that your latest code has been deployed on the development environment.

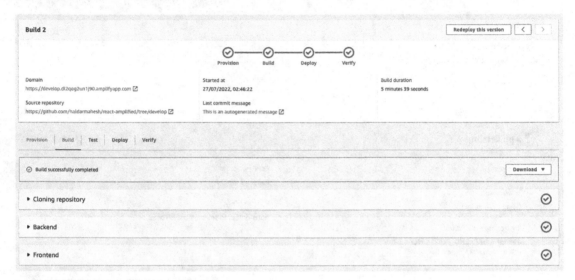

***Figure 8-15.*** *The successful screen after completion of the CI/CD pipeline*

# Creating a New Environment and Hosting It

It is possible to effortlessly create numerous environments for development as desired. Let us proceed to create a production environment.

To create the new environment, it is necessary to create a new branch in git and push it. We shall name the new branch as master and push it to the repository:

```
git checkout -b master
```

## Creating a Production Environment in Amplify Backend

In order to host the code in the production environment, we need to create a new environment. To view the list of existing environments, you can execute the following command:

```
amplify env list

| Environments |
| ------------ |
| *dev         |
```

As we currently have only one environment, which is "dev," the command will display only that environment.

Let's create a new environment.

In the master branch, run

```
amplify add env
```

Enter the name of the new environment; let's name it production:

```
? Enter a name for the environment:  production

? Select the authentication method you want to use: (Use arrow keys)
> Amplify Admin UI
  AWS profile
  AWS access keys
```

Select Amplify Admin UI to authenticate and allow sign-in from the browser.

If you are deploying the same application as created in Chapter 2, the creation of a new environment will require a new Google web client id and client secret to be added. This is because the authentication added in application in Chapter 2, will also be deployed.

Please obtain these values from the Google console app and add them.

```
Enter your Google Web Client ID for your OAuth flow: xx-xx-xx
Enter your Google Web Client Secret for your OAuth flow: xxxxx
```

Once done, you can check the status by entering the following command:

```
amplify status
```

Upon completion of this process, a number of resources will be generated for the production environment. The status is illustrated in Figure 8-16.

```
● → react-amplified git:(master) ✗ amplify status

    Current Environment: production
```

| Category | Resource name | Operation | Provider plugin |
|---|---|---|---|
| Auth | reactauthenticationa10272a0 | Create | awscloudformation |
| Function | todosfunction | Create | awscloudformation |
| Function | todosfunctiongql | Create | awscloudformation |
| Function | S3Triggere0581125 | Create | awscloudformation |
| Api | todosapi | Create | awscloudformation |
| Api | todosgql | Create | awscloudformation |
| Storage | todolist | Create | awscloudformation |
| Storage | amplifythumbnail | Create | awscloudformation |
| Analytics | analyticsreactapp | Create | awscloudformation |
| Analytics | reactauthenticationKinesis | Create | awscloudformation |
| Interactions | reactchatbot | Create | awscloudformation |
| Predictions | speechGeneratordfb39f8c | Create | awscloudformation |

***Figure 8-16.*** *The Amplify status for the new environment*

We can push these by entering the following command:

```
amplify push
```

After confirming the changes, wait for Amplify to finish creating the resources on the cloud.

Let's now set up the CI/CD for the master branch and production environment to provision and host the application.

To do so, navigate to the Amplify application in the Amplify service and click "Connect branch." From there, select the master branch and app name. This step is illustrated in Figure 8-17. Also assign the environment to the branch, as shown in Figure 8-18.

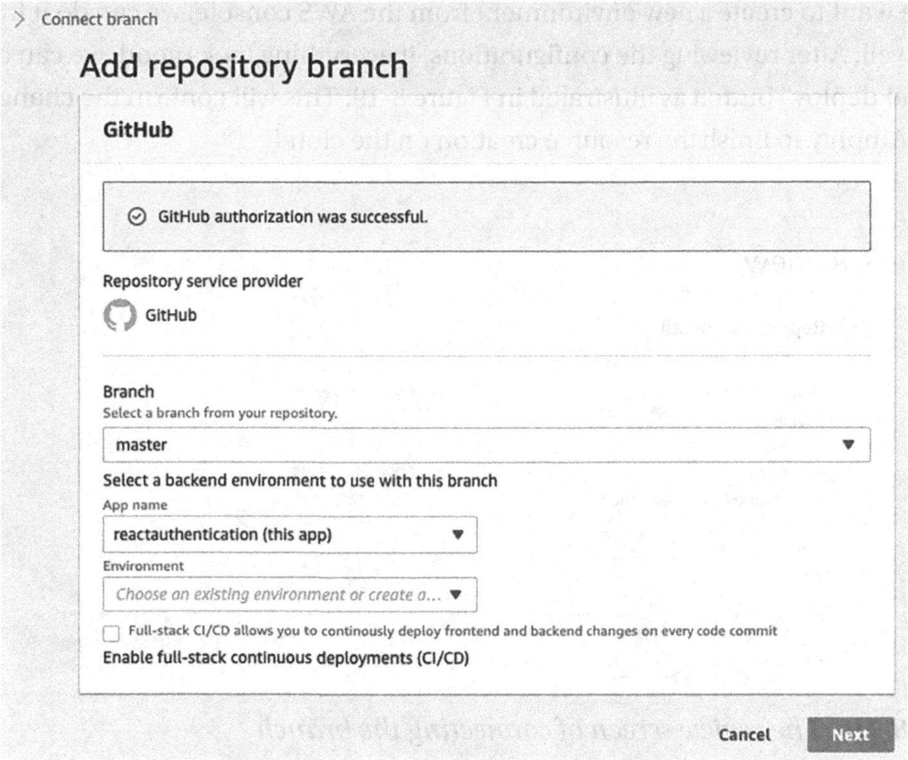

**Figure 8-17.** *Add the branch of GitHub to the Amplify app*

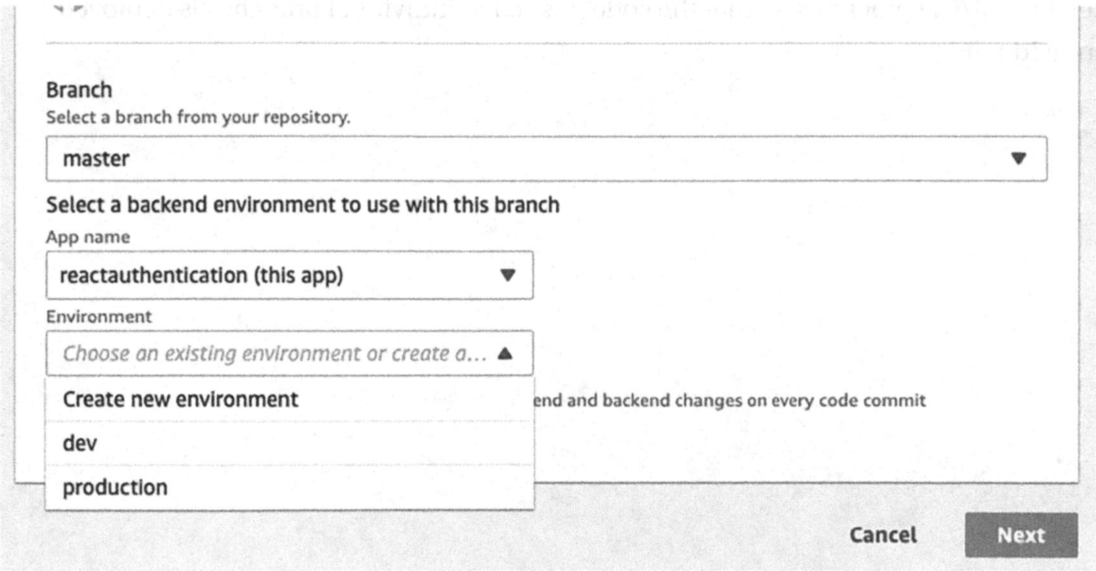

**Figure 8-18.** *Link the branch and environment to our Amplify app*

If we want to create a new environment from the AWS console, we can do it from here as well. After reviewing the configurations, if everything looks good, we can click the "Save and deploy" button as illustrated in Figure 8-19. This will confirm the changes and wait for Amplify to finish the resource creation on the cloud.

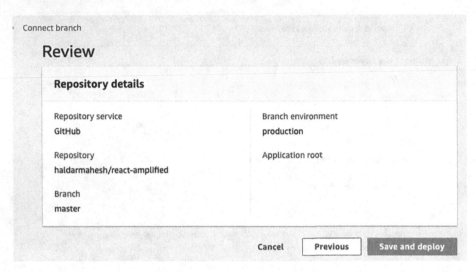

***Figure 8-19.***  *The review screen of connecting the branch*

As shown in Figure 8-20, you will notice the master branch appears which is connected to the newly created environment, production. Furthermore, there are two distinct CI/CD pipelines, so that the code pushed to individual branches is deployed individually.

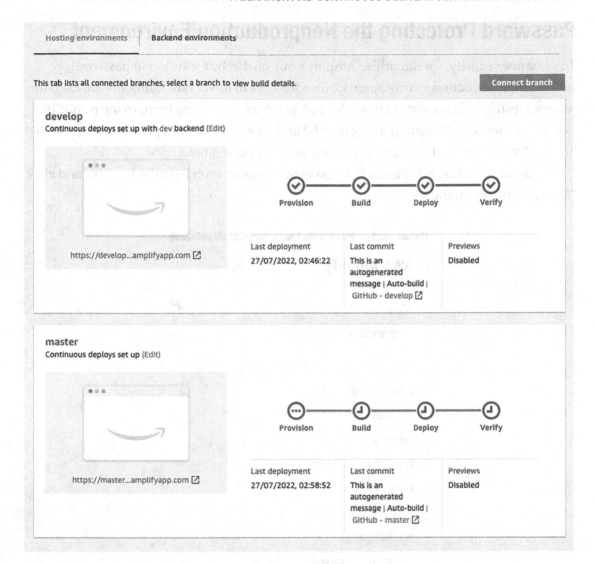

***Figure 8-20.*** *The CI/CD pipeline of both branches*

As soon as the deployment is successful, you can access the application on the production environment. From here on, you can develop a new feature on the develop branch and raise a pull request (PR) to merge it with the master branch. The new feature will be deployed to the production environment.

# Password Protecting the Nonproduction Environment

To enhance security, we can utilize Amplify's out-of-the-box solution to password-protect nonproduction environments. Since features in lower environments are used for internal testing and are not yet ready for public release, exposing them to the public is not recommended. By adding a root user ID and password, we can prevent unauthorized access. By default, all the environments are publicly accessible.

To do this, as shown in Figure 8-21, go to the Amplify screen on the browser and click "Access control" on the left pane.

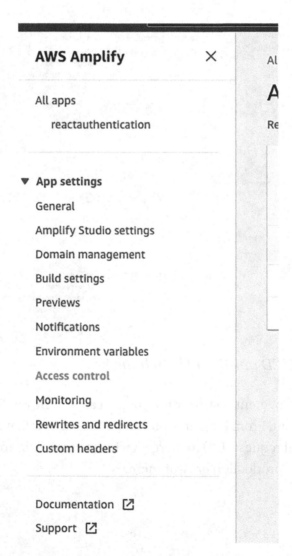

***Figure 8-21.*** *The Amplify options in the AWS console*

As illustrated in Figure 8-22, notice both environments are publicly viewable.

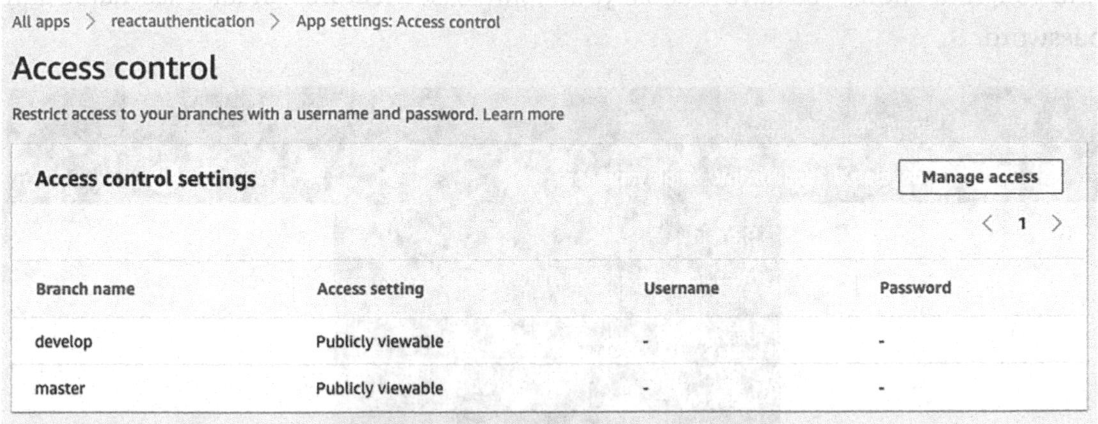

*Figure 8-22.*  *The access control setting of our Amplify app*

Let's password-protect our develop environment; click Manage access on the top right.

Click the "Manage access" button on the top-right corner. Change the access setting to "Restricted" against the develop branch and add a username and password, as shown in Figure 8-23. Finally, click "Save" to apply changes.

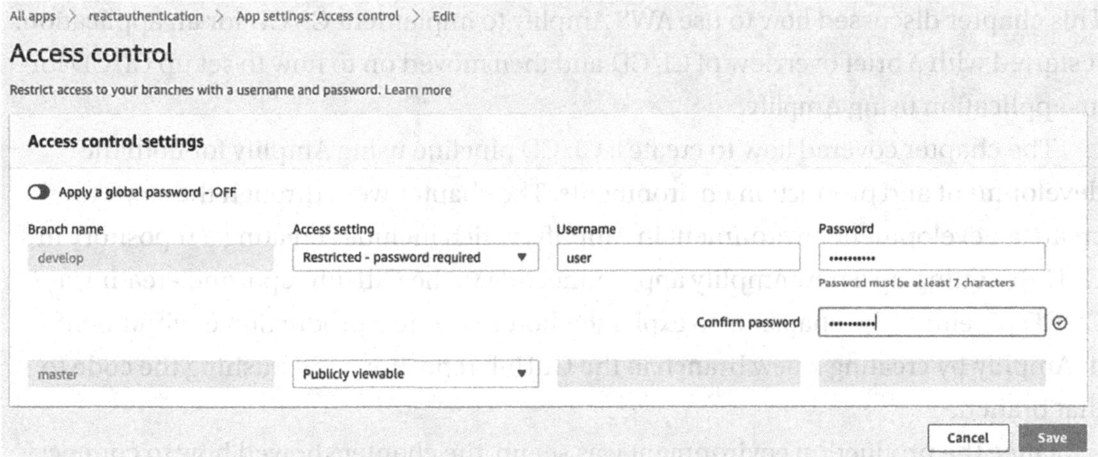

*Figure 8-23.*  *Adding security to our environment for private access*

Now try to open the develop environment.

As illustrated in Figure 8-24, you will be asked to enter your username and password. And congratulations, you have secured your nonreleased features under a username and password.

*Figure 8-24. The credential input dialog to access the private app*

# Summary

This chapter discussed how to use AWS Amplify to implement CI/CD for an application. It started with a brief overview of CI/CD and then moved on to how to set up CI/CD for an application using Amplify.

The chapter covered how to create a CI/CD pipeline using Amplify for both the development and production environments. The chapter went through the steps to create a development environment in Amplify, which includes creating a repository in GitHub, setting up a new Amplify app, connecting to the GitHub repo, and creating a CI/CD pipeline. The chapter also explained how to create a production environment in Amplify by creating a new branch in the GitHub repository and pushing the code to that branch.

Once the production environment was set up, the chapter showed how to connect the production environment to the CI/CD pipeline and how to password-protect the development environment. It also covered how to add new features to the application and deploy them to the production environment using the CI/CD pipeline.

Overall, the chapter provided a comprehensive guide to using AWS Amplify to implement a robust CI/CD pipeline for an application.

# CHAPTER 9

# Amplify Supplements

*The future is not going to be driven by people, but by artificial intelligence.*

—Sundar Pichai, CEO of Google

Amplify is not just limited to these core features which we have discussed in previous chapters – there are also a number of supplementary services and capabilities that can be used to enhance and extend application's functionality. From creating chatbots with AWS Lex service to adding AI/ML capabilities to applications, Amplify provides a wide range of capabilities to enhance the development process. In this chapter, we will explore some of the key features of AWS Amplify, including its support for multiple frameworks, its integration with AI/ML services, and its capabilities for chatbot development. We will also introduce AWS Amplify Studio, a powerful tool for UI development. By the end of this chapter, you will have a solid understanding of the many ways in which AWS Amplify can help you streamline your development process and build powerful, responsive, and scalable applications.

## Building Interactive Bots with AWS Lex Service

A chatbot is a computer program designed to simulate conversation with human users, typically via a messaging interface. AWS Lex helps us to build chatbots that uses natural language processing (NLP) algorithms to understand and interpret the user's queries, and they can provide automated responses to these queries in a conversational way.

AWS Lex is a service that helps us build interactive ML-based chatbots in no time. Lex internally uses deep learning technologies like automatic speech recognition which converts speech to text and natural language processing. Lex is also used to empower Amazon Alexa. Lex will help us to achieve the same output without diving deep into these core technologies.

257

© Akshat Paul, Mahesh Haldar 2023
A. Paul and M. Haldar, *Serverless Web Applications with AWS Amplify*,
https://doi.org/10.1007/978-1-4842-8707-1_9

AWS Lex has also the capability to integrate with other services like AWS Lambda, which can call APIs, write data in the database, or integrate with third-party systems to act on users' requests. In Amplify these capabilities are grouped under interactions; let's now use interactions with Amplify.

Run the following to add interaction using amplify:

```
amplify add interactions
```

This will ask you to give a name to this chatbot; I will name it `reactchatbot`.

```
? Provide a friendly resource name that will be used to label this category
in the project: reactchatbot
```

There are some chatbot configurations; let's choose a sample:

```
? Would you like to start with a sample chatbot or start from scratch?
> Start with a sample
  Start from scratch
```

There are three options; you can choose any of them. For this chapter's scope, let's choose the Order Flowers sample:

```
? Choose a sample chatbot:
  BookTrip
> OrderFlowers
  ScheduleAppointment
```

This will ask if children's privacy policies are applicable; answer accordingly.

```
? Please indicate if your use of this bot is subject to the Children's
Online Privacy Protection Act (COPPA).
Learn more: https://www.ftc.gov/tips-advice/business-center/guidance/
complying-coppa-frequently-asked-questions (y/N)
```

Once this is done, approve and push the changes to the Amazon backend:

```
amplify push
```

Once successful, log in to the AWS console on the browser and open the Lex service from the list (Figure 9-1).

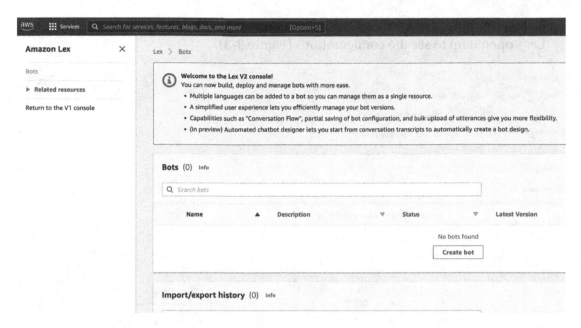

**Figure 9-1.** *Amazon Lex service on AWS Console*

You will probably see no bots created; this is because when we are writing this chapter, Amplify by default creates bots in Lex V1, hence the new Lex V2 console doesn't show up the bots created from the Amplify CLI. Let's hope in near future Amplify will add a support to enable us to choose the version to create chatbots. Let's switch to the V1 console from the left pane, the Lex V1 preview is shown in Figure 9-2.

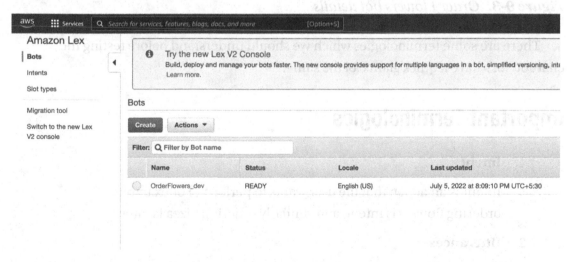

**Figure 9-2.** *Amazon Lex V1 dashboard*

No we can see the Order Flowers bot we created from the Amplify CLI.

Let's open it up to see the configurations (Figure 9-3).

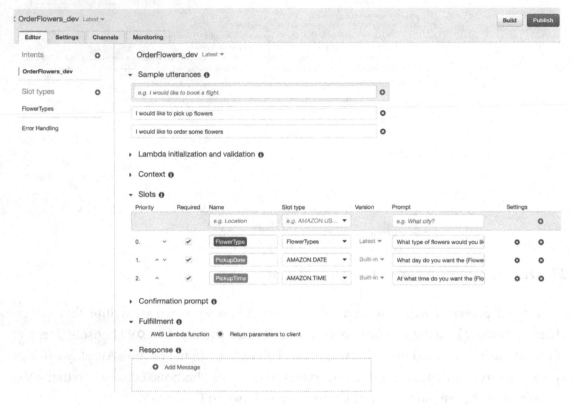

***Figure 9-3.*** *Order Flowers bot details*

There are some terminologies which we should understand before testing the chatbot; let's have a quick glance of the same.

# Important Terminologies

1. **Intent**

   Intent is an action that the user wants to perform. For example, ordering flowers is intent, and similarly ordering pizza is intent.

2. **Utterances**

   Utterances are various ways of conveying the same intent. For example, the following are utterances of the same intent:

  a.  I want to order the flowers.

  b.  Can I order the flowers, please?

  c.  I need help ordering flowers.

3.  **Slots**

    In order to fulfill the intent, the chatbots need some required set
    of parameters without which one intent cannot be fulfilled. For
    example, to order flowers, the required parameters are as follows:

    a.  Flower type

    b.  Pickup time

    c.  Delivery time
    These parameters are called slots.

4.  **Slot types**

    Given slot is a parameter, there will be a type associated with it,
    for example, pickup time would be date-time type, and the flower
    type will be of type Rose, Lilly, or Tulip. The slot types can be built-
    in or custom defined.

5.  **Intent fulfillment**

    Intent fulfillment refers to the set of actions that a chatbot needs
    to perform in order to fulfill a user's intent after it has correctly
    understood their utterance and extracted all the required
    slots. This can be achieved in a couple of ways. One way is by
    integrating a Lambda function that takes the required parameters
    and carries out the intended action, such as creating an order or
    fulfilling a request. Alternatively, the parameters can be passed
    to the client application, which can then handle the fulfillment of
    the intent without relying on a Lambda function. Both approaches
    have their own advantages and disadvantages, and the choice
    between them largely depends on the specific use case and
    requirements of the chatbot.

6. **Lambda function as a code hook**

    The Lex chatbot service also provides a way to attach the Lambda
    function as a hook in various steps, where we can validate the user
    input and show a proper error message to the users. For example,
    let's say if the chatbot asks about the delivery time, and if the
    user enters a past date, the code hook can validate the input and
    respond with a message that the orders cannot be delivered in
    past, please reenter a future date.

# Test the Chatbot

Once you open the chatbot, which is forked from the sample Order Flowers chatbot,
from the AWS console, on the top right there is a test chatbot option, follow Figure 9-4.

***Figure 9-4.*** *Test chatbot*

Click that, and try to add some utterances, as shown in Figure 9-5.

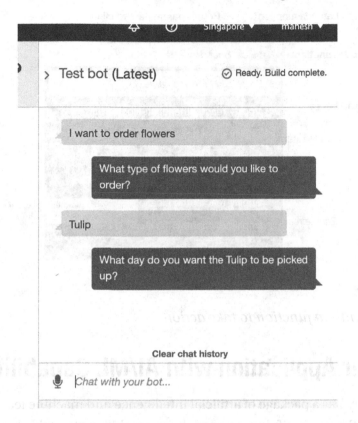

***Figure 9-5.*** *Testing the chatbot with utterances*

Voila, you can further configure more utterances and fulfillment Lambda functions to take action, as shown in Figure 9-6.

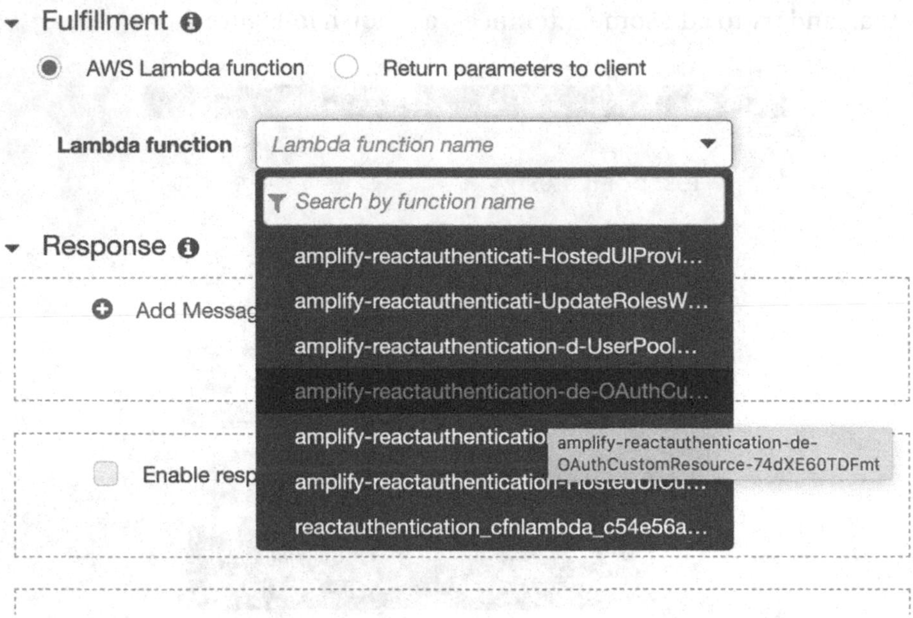

▾ Fulfillment ⓘ

⦿ AWS Lambda function    ○ Return parameters to client

**Lambda function**    *Lambda function name*    ▾

🔽 *Search by function name*

amplify-reactauthenticati-HostedUIProvi…

amplify-reactauthenticati-UpdateRolesW…

amplify-reactauthentication-d-UserPool…

amplify-reactauthentication-de-OAuthCu…

amplify-reactauthenticatio    amplify-reactauthentication-de-
                             OAuthCustomResource-74dXE60TDFmt

amplify-reactauthentication-HostedUICu…

reactauthentication_cfnlambda_c54e56a…

▾ Response ⓘ

⊕ Add Messag

☐ Enable resp

*Figure 9-6. Lambda function to take action*

# Boost Your Application with AI/ML Capability

The AWS Amplify has a package of artificial intelligence and machine learning capabilities. AWS has beautifully packaged those capabilities to make them easy to use instead of diving deep into these technologies. AWS's effort is to let the developers focus more on delivering the business outcome instead of learning the core and reinventing the wheel of AI and ML technologies.

## What Is Artificial Intelligence?

Artificial intelligence (AI) is a field of computer science that focuses on developing machines that can perform tasks that would typically require human intelligence, such as learning, problem-solving, and decision-making. AI technologies rely on mathematical operations and algorithms to analyze input data, identify patterns, and produce output.

AI is being used in various industries to solve real-world problems, such as data analysis, chatbots, and manufacturing. For example, chatbots are computer programs that use natural language processing and machine learning to understand user input and provide helpful responses.

Some specific examples of AI technologies include speech to text, which processes spoken input and converts it to text output, and chatbots, which can simulate human conversation and make decisions based on user input.

# What Is Machine Learning?

Machine learning is a subset of AI that focuses on teaching computers to learn from data and identify patterns in that data. By analyzing vast amounts of data, machine learning algorithms can identify patterns and make predictions about new data that they haven't seen before. For example, if we want a computer to recognize images of dogs, we can train a machine learning algorithm by feeding it thousands of sample images of dogs so that it can learn to identify common features and characteristics of dogs.

AWS provides a range of AI and ML services that can help developers build more powerful and interactive applications. For example, the Predictions category of AWS Amplify includes services such as text to speech, language translation, image recognition, and entity recognition. These services enable developers to add advanced AI capabilities to their applications without having to build these capabilities from scratch.

In addition, AWS offers the SageMaker service, which allows developers to quickly build and train machine learning models using a range of prebuilt algorithms and frameworks. This service can help developers to accelerate the development of machine learning models and bring them to market more quickly.

Predictions is categorized into the following three categories:

1.  Identity: The services in this category will help us in analyzing the input image and finding various things in the provided image. This can identify a particular text, face, entities, chairs, desks, animals, or celebrities from the image provided as input.

2.  Convert: The services in this category will help us in converting the given input from one form to another, for example, translating text from one language to another, converting text to audio speech, or speech to text.

3.  Interpret: The services in this category will help us in listening, reading, or analyzing the input and drawing a conclusion on behalf of a human. For example, it can take the paragraph as input and interpret whether the sentiment is positive, negative, or neutral.

265

# Text to Speech with Amplify

Let's start adding the amplify predictions package:

amplify add predictions

This will ask which category of prediction we want to start integrating with our application:

```
? Please select from one of the categories below
  Identify
> Convert
  Interpret
  Infer
  Learn More
```

You can choose to convert.

Now we have various conversion options, like translation and transcribing text from audio.

Let's choose speech from text:

```
? What would you like to convert?
  Translate text into a different language
> Generate speech audio from text
  Transcribe text from audio
```

Provide a name to this resource and hit enter.

This will ask what the source of the language is:

```
? Provide a friendly name for your resource speechGeneratordfb39f8c
? What is the source language?
  Dutch
  Russian
  South African English
> US English
  German
  Italian
  Chinese Mandarin
```

I will choose US English.

The next option would be the output speaker option:

```
? Select a speaker
  Salli - Female
  Joanna - Female
  Kevin - Male
› Matthew - Male
  Kendra - Female
  Ivy - Female
  Justin - Male
```

If you want to listen to which speaker sounds like what, you can check the AWS Polly service; there will be a sample text, and you can listen to various speakers from the list and choose one, the same is shown in Figure 9-7.

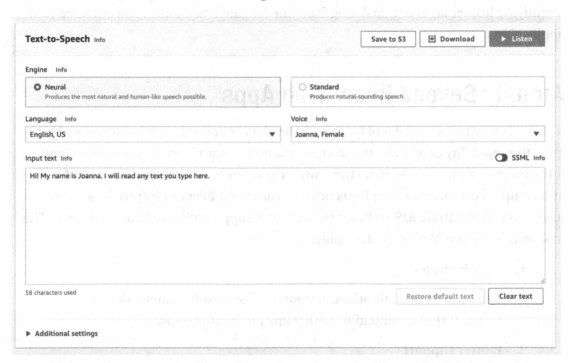

***Figure 9-7.*** *AWS text-to-speech dashboard*

Once done, review and push the changes.

On the client application, if we want to generate an audio buffer from the text, we can call the convert function from Predictions and pass the text as follows:

```
1: Predictions.convert({
2:   textToSpeech: {
3:     source: {
4:       text: textToGenerateSpeech
5:     },
6:   }
7: })
8: .then(result => console.log({ result }))
9: .catch(err => console.log({ err }));
```

Similarly, you can use other AI/ML capabilities from AWS using Amplify like identifying from images or translating from one language to another and enhance your applications.

# Amplify Beyond React Web Apps

Amplify is a super powerful tool for today's developers and software businesses; this gives the capability of building the whole backend system, cloud-based services, and infrastructure with no code, in no time, which is secured, can handle any scale of traffic, and is super cost-efficient. Amplify is not only meant for React web apps, it can also integrate with Android, iOS, or React Native mobile apps similar to React web apps. The following are some highlights of Amplify:

1. **Next.js support**

   The Amplify recently added support for the Next.js framework, which makes it compatible with many production apps.

2. **Flutter support**

   Amplify has also added support for Flutter apps; this makes the whole Flutter community more excited, as Amplify can cater to one more group of developers.

3. **Geo support**

   With Amplify, we can easily create maps, add markers, and search locations just by adding a few lines of code. We can also implement the areas on the map or geo-fencing in the maps.

4. **PubSub**

   Amplify has the capability to send messages in real time from the backend to the client or vice versa. PubSub is available on the MQTT protocol as well, to support IoT devices.

5. **Push notifications**

   The Amplify also can help developers quickly set up push notifications for their mobile applications to quickly receive and send mobile notifications on Android or iOS devices.

6. **AR and VR features**

   Amplify also has the capabilities to implement augmented reality (AR) and virtual reality (VR) content within the applications. This is provided by the component named XR in Amplify.

7. **Internationalization**

   Amplify also helps the client apps to implement and handle the internationalization for the application; we can import the i18n module from Amplify and set the vocabulary of the various languages to load in our applications.

8. **Logger**

   Amplify also has a module named Logger, which helps to log important information and errors on the client side.

9. **Admin UI data explorer**

   Many times, we need to create a user-friendly data explorer UI to manage or modify the data in our system; we cannot give database access to our business owners or content managers. Amplify has this capability; with some configurations, we can get the data explorer UI and invite users to modify and save the data.

10. **Data seeding**

Often in our application, we need to test our application with various edge cases to make it look like a real production application. Amplify has the capability to generate random seed data in our application.

# AWS Amplify Studio

The Amplify team has also recently launched a visual development environment, where developers can also build UI components with minimal code and also can integrate the Amplify powerful backend configurations from this UI-based development studio.

Developers can now create UI components, set up the Amplify backend, and connect the two from this powerful tool. This tool can also create React components right from the Figma (tool used by designers and developers) designs to accelerate further the whole development cycle so that developers and the business team can launch their applications as soon as possible.

To enable the Amplify Studio, open the Amplify project and click Set up Amplify Studio, as shown in Figure 9-8.

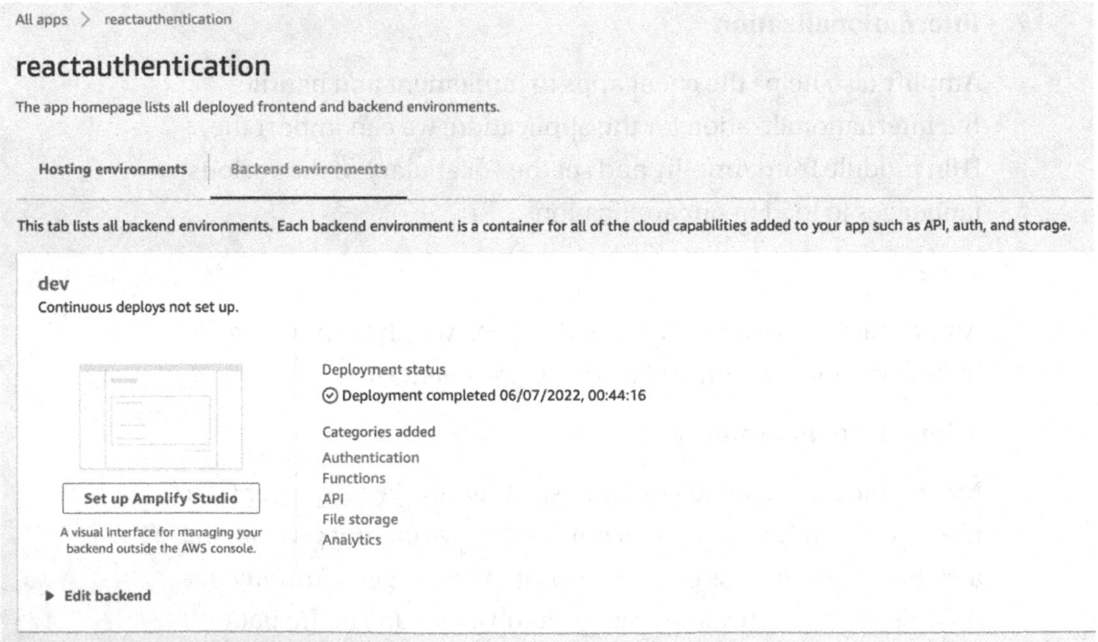

*Figure 9-8.* Setting up Amplify Studio

Once approved and done, wait for some time and click Launch studio to open Amplify Studio.

As you can see, in Figure 9-9, we have almost all the Amplify components and UI library to start creating UI and create or configure the Amplify backend components and bind both of them, including the authentication, storage, REST API, analytics, etc. Go ahead and explore the Amplify Studio. Since this tool is out of scope, we will skip getting into details.

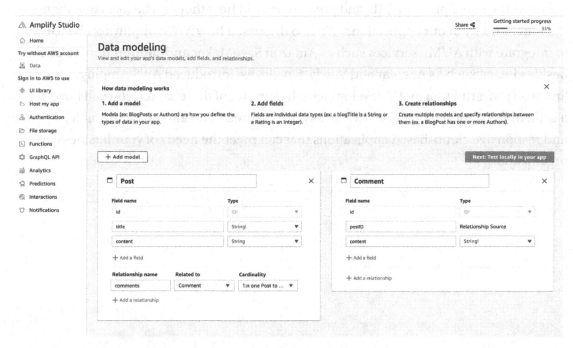

*Figure 9-9. Amplify Studio for UI development*

# Summary

In this chapter, we explored the many ways in which AWS Amplify can help developers build powerful, cloud-based applications quickly and easily. We started by discussing how AWS Lex service can be used to create chatbots and examined the important terminologies associated with building chatbots. We then looked at how AWS Amplify can be used to create chatbots and add AI/ML capabilities to our applications. We explored the concepts of AI, ML, and predictions and how they can be used to enhance the functionality of our applications. We also discussed how AWS Amplify can be used to integrate with AI/ML services such as Amazon SageMaker and support frameworks besides React, such as Angular and Vue.js. Finally, we introduced AWS Amplify Studio, a powerful tool for UI development. By the end of this chapter, you will have a solid understanding of how AWS Amplify can be used to create robust, scalable, and responsive cloud-based applications that can meet the needs of your business or organization.

# Index

## A

© Akshat Paul, Mahesh Haldar 2023
A. Paul and M. Haldar, *Serverless Web Applications with AWS Amplify*,
https://doi.org/10.1007/978-1-4842-8707-1

Printed in the United States
by Baker & Taylor Publisher Services

Printed in the United States
by Baker & Taylor Publisher Services